THE CHILD IN THE WORLD

D1474592

LANDSCAPES OF CHILDHOOD

General Editor

Elizabeth N. Goodenough, Residential College,
University of Michigan

Editorial Board

Louise Chawla, University of Colorado
Robert Coles, Harvard University
Donald Haase, Wayne State University
Roger Hart, City University of New York
Gareth Matthews, University of Massachusetts
Robin Moore, North Carolina State University
Michael Nettles, Educational Testing Service
Zibby Oneal, author of children's books
Valerie Polakow, Eastern Michigan University
Pamela F. Reynolds, Johns Hopkins University
John Stilgoe, Harvard University
Marcelo Suarez-Orozco, Harvard University
Jack Zipes, University of Minnesota

A complete listing of the books in this series can be found online at wsupress.wayne.edu

THE CHILD IN THE WORLD

*Embodiment, Time, and Language
in Early Childhood*

EVA M. SIMMS

Wayne State University Press
Detroit

© 2008 by Wayne State University Press, Detroit, Michigan 48201. All rights reserved. No part of this book may be reproduced without formal permission. Manufactured in the United States of America.

12 11 10 09   5 4 3 2

Library of Congress Cataloging-in-Publication Data

Simms, Eva M.
   The child in the world : embodiment, time, and language in early childhood / Eva M. Simms.
         p.   cm. — (Landscapes of childhood)
   Includes bibliographical references and index.
   ISBN-13: 978-0-8143-3375-4 (pbk. : alk. paper)
   ISBN-10: 0-8143-3375-3 (pbk. : alk. paper)
   1. Child psychology.   I. Title.
   BF721.S53528 2008
   155.42′3—dc22

                                                            2007035344

∞ The paper used in this publication meets the minimum requirements of the American National Standard for Information Sciences—Permanence of Paper for Printed Library Materials, ANSI Z39.48-1984.

Some parts of chapters 1, 3, 4, and 5 were published in the following journals or edited volumes but have been significantly expanded and revised:

1999. "The countryside of childhood: Reflections on a hermeneutic-phenomenological approach to developmental psychology." *Humanistic Psychologist* 27 (3): 301–27.

2001. "Milk and flesh: A phenomenological reflection on infancy and co-existence." *Journal of Phenomenological Psychology* 32 (1): 22–40.

2002. "The child in the world of things." In *The phenomenology of childhood*, ed. D. Smith. Pittsburgh: Simon Silverman Phenomenology Center.

2003. "Play and the transformation of feeling—A clinical case study." In *All work and no play . . . How educational reforms are harming our preschoolers*, ed. S. Olfman. New York: Geenwood/Praeger.

Designed and typeset by The Composing Room of Michigan, Inc.

Composed in Janson and Tiepolo

For Michael,
with respect and admiration

And how awed is the womb-born creature
who must fly. As if startled by itself
it rips through the air, just like the crack
going through a cup. So the tracery
of the bat rends the porcelain of evening.

Rainer Maria Rilke, *Eighth Duino Elegy*

CONTENTS

ACKNOWLEDGMENTS

A book is a long time in the making, and there are many friends who assisted in the creation of this one. I want to thank Michael Simms, my husband, for his unfailing encouragement of my writing and his willingness to read and edit every page many times; my children, Nick and Lea, for making me a mother, showing me their world, and putting up with my rambling talks about philosophy; Russ Walsh, Tony Barton, Dick Knowles, and Bill Fischer at Duquesne University for support and conversation; the late Ivan Illich for hospitality and inspiration; Robert Romanyshyn for rearranging my mental furniture when I was a graduate student; Wilfried Lippitz for introducing me to the continental tradition in child studies (and the lovely once-a-year evening suppers in my hometown in Germany); David Abram for being a fellow traveler through the chiasm; Bep Mook, Jim Morley, and Anne Johnson for hatching the first schemes for a phenomenological child psychology; Fred Wertz for generous editing; Max van Manen, Bas Levering, and Stephen Smith for the Perugia conference on childhood; the Merleau-Ponty circle and Beata Stavarska for welcoming my ideas; my friends at the Waldorf School of Pittsburgh, especially Anne Clair Goodman, Melissa Becker, and Taye Ormsby, for showing me that it is possible to educate children with care for their bodies, minds, and hearts; and last, but not least, my graduate students at Duquesne University, who are the perfect audience: passionate, smart, and willing to make a difference in the world.

Introduction

This book was conceived when my children were small. I vowed to be "a thinking mother," which meant to me that the phenomena of our lives as parents and children were worthy of philosophical reflection. On the one hand, I hoped that thinking about childhood could inform my scholarly concepts and help articulate a philosophy and psychology that includes childhood as part of the whole picture of who the human being is; on the other hand, I hoped that exploring childhood through philosophical concepts could deepen my understanding of my own children's lives. This double intention of the writer as both scholar and parent guides the following chapters. Some sections might be of more interest to the parent, others to the scholar, but I have tried to keep both in mind most of the time. The language of this book tries to avoid academic jargon, and when philosophical concepts are used (particularly from the continental tradition), I explain them in plain language and illustrate them with real-life situations.

One of my most exciting discoveries in thinking and writing about childhood phenomena relates to the process of thinking itself: the closer attention I paid to a phenomenon and the more faithfully I described it, the more thoughts about it were generated. When I wrote about breast-feeding, for example, I noticed that the making of milk was not an internal, maternal physiological event but a shared reality between mother and infant. This required reconceptualizing how I thought about the body and where it ended. The phenomenologist's call "to the things themselves" (here the very act of breast-feeding) is an appeal not to literalism but to the generative power that is freed when the human mind listens to what things have to say. Attention and description anchor thinking in the world of experience and keep it from slipping into abstractions. The activity of thinking, on the other hand, illuminates the multifaceted significances of even such a humble phenomenon as giving milk.

In the next few pages, I want to address the general reader, the parent reader, and the scholar reader in three different sections; each reader may consider her- or himself addressed in all sections or choose to skip a part.

TO THE GENERAL READER

Once upon a time we all were children. Now that we are parents or researchers or clinicians or teachers or philosophers, we have forgotten what childhood was like. We came from a womb, learned to take our first steps, needed our special blanket or teddy bear for comfort. But because so much of early childhood experience precedes articulation, we have only a vague impression of that time. The daily fullness of early life escapes us.

This book is an attempt to articulate some of the key experiences of early childhood. It assumes that the child's experience of the world is different from that of the adult in one essential feature: child consciousness is profoundly *nondualistic*. This means that young children know little of the distinction between mind and body, self and other, inner and outer world (Piaget 1929/1951). They are not self-reflective and are mostly unaware of the difference between reality and thought: words are bound up with things, which gives language a particular power; external things are less material and have their own intentionality and will; self and other are inextricably bound up with each other. In the young child's experience there is no *inner* world. There is also no *outer* world.

The second assumption of this book is that for children and adults alike, mind is not an internal, human phenomenon but a field of significances in which each of us finds him- or herself constantly engaged. Mind is not in us, but we are in it. This paradigm shift has been one of the key insights of *existential phenomenology*, articulated first in Heidegger's notion of "being-in-the-world" (which replaces talk about "the self") and radicalized through Merleau-Ponty's concept of the "chiasm" (which articulates the entwining of mind and world).

In order to focus and articulate our thinking about the experienced worlds of children, we will examine some of the fundamental structures of human existence as they have been articulated by continental philosophy and psychology. We will look at the experience of *embodiment*, our bodies initially a gift from another human being. Our early consciousness is woven into *relationships with others* and the social worlds of customs and ideas they bring with them. We are placed into a matrix of *spatial relations* in the world that surrounds us, where we encounter a host of *things* that significantly influence our feeling life. We experience *time* in the anticipation of things to come or in the trauma of past events. *Language* introduces us into the symbolic dimension of our culture and shapes the way we think. Every child is a *historical being*, born into a culture and time with a particular view of childhood that results in particular cultural practices. *Embodiment, coexistentiality, spatiality, things, temporality, language*, and *historicity:* the architecture of this book is built on these fundamental existential themes (Boss 1979; Heidegger 1962; Merleau-Ponty 1962), taking them up from the perspective of child psychology. Following these themes allows us to speak of the dimensions of childhood that go beyond cognition and to illuminate the latent or subconscious influences of the lived world on the child's mind.

We begin chapter 1 with an examination of coexistentiality and the body through the phenomenon of breast milk, which, even though it is a biological phenomenon, constitutes the body and the human subject as intersubjective and relational. Here, and throughout the rest of this book, the research findings on infancy and early childhood from the field of developmental psychology are integrated and reinterpreted from a nondualistic existential perspective.

Chapter 2 examines the experience of spatial forms and their contribution to the developing structures of child consciousness. From the boundedness of intrauterine space, we move with the infant through an ever-widening circle of spatial experience: arms and lap, cradle and floor, house and neighborhood, night space and secret space.

Chapter 3 investigates the nature of participatory consciousness through children's art and bodily expression and provides guidelines for a respectful and productive encounter with drawing and play.

Chapter 4 enters the circle of things and shows how the gestures of things are woven into our psychological lives from the beginning. We will revisit "cross modal perception" (Meltzoff and Borton 1979), "object permanence" (Piaget 1954), and "transitional objects" (Winnicott 1971), meditating on them "from the inside"—that is, through a reconstruction of children's particular experiences of pacifiers, celluloid storks, and fuzzy blankets.

Chapter 5 follows a particular child through her play therapy and shows the powerful transformation that can happen through preverbal play. While play therapy is play at the edge of pain, it nevertheless illuminates some of the essential features of more ordinary play that are essential to healthy child development.

Chapter 6 contrasts lived time and clock time and explores how present, future, and past are experienced by children. Embodiment, other people, spaces, things, language, and even play return here under the aspect of temporality because there is actually never a clear separation between them in the fullness of everyday human experience.

Chapter 7 traces the preverbal and presymbolic elements of language acquisition by bringing together research from the field of psycholinguistics with a radical existential understanding of language. The musical dimension of speech, the protosymbolic activity of infant pointing, and the sedimentation of first words are explored through careful description and interpretation to show language as an embodied, intersubjective phenomenon. The second part of this chapter develops the notion of a "lived grammar," in distinction from the formalized grammar of linguistics.

"Childhood" is not a static concept, and chapter 8 researches how the Western understanding of the child has undergone some radical historical transformations. We will travel with the twelfth-century children's crusade, encounter mumbling monks and insane merchants, and look into printing presses, confessionals, and schoolrooms. We will find that the child is a child only in relation to adult existence, and that the changes that have marked adulthood since the Renaissance (individuality, interiority, literacy) are reflected in the philosophies and practices that identify and shape childhood today.

A note about the style of writing the reader will encounter: my attempt is to describe well some of the significant phenomena of childhood existence. Because I want to be faithful to children's experiences and articulate a nondualistic, world-oriented psychology, the following descriptions of childhood phenomena and their interpretations try to chart a course largely independent of cognitive/rational and psychoanalytic theories and languages (which are fundamentally dualistic and Cartesian). I am convinced that good description teaches the writer and the reader to see a fuller spectrum of reality, and that it gives birth to new concepts. I invite the reader to follow me through the multiple forms of discourse that link everyday childhood experiences to philosophical and psychological concepts. We cannot grasp the importance of milk, peekaboo, or the first pointing finger until we push our language into poetry—and from there language drops our thinking into the yet-uncharted dimensions of our children's everyday lives.

TO THE PARENT READER

As a parent, what you do or don't do with and for your children matters directly. There is nothing theoretical about comforting a crying child or making a decision about what kindergarten to send your child to. You see the effects: sometimes immediately, sometimes over months and years. We carry the fate of our children in our hands, especially in the first few years, and often we do not have guidance from the previous generation or other parents who have been through some of the same struggles. We live in a time and culture saturated with advice books for parents, ranging from medical manuals to advice on attachment to Christian fundamentalist guides about disciplining your child. This book is not an advice book. Rather, it tries to support your basic insights as a parent who observes and thinks about her or his child and aims to give you a better understanding of what the world might look like from the child's perspective. I hope that, even though it is philosophical, you will also find it very practical—and maybe empowering.

My own experience has been that caring for our children's well-being has brought my family into conflict with the values of the society we live in. Instead of finding ourselves smoothly nestled into the cultural flow, issues of breast-feeding, cosleeping, media exposure, medical treatment, schooling, and literacy became major stumbling blocks and traumatic events in our family life. The patterns of child rearing offered by the conventional educational, medical, and cultural institutions were hurting our children, and we continually bumped into roadblocks that forced us to make unconventional choices on their behalf. During our son's birth we explicitly asked for natural childbirth methods, but the doctor insisted on an internal fetal monitor, which kept me laboring on my back for a very long time. When he removed the sensor—which, incidentally, is pushed into the scalp of the baby—a clump of my child's black hair was attached to the end! For our daughter's birth we chose a midwife center and had a much more peaceful and intimate birth experience.

Breast-feeding my son in the hospital after birth was difficult because the staff fed him sugar water in the nursery, and I was told that the colostrum, which is the first clear liquid the breast produces, was not good nutrition. (Today we know that colostrum contains high doses of carbohydrates, protein, and antibodies that help clean out the waste products from the birth process and protect an infant's mucus membranes in throat, lungs, and intestines.) Nursing my daughter in the room at the midwife center was encouraged, and she never left my side. Over the following years we had to argue with our pediatrician—who, by the way, is a very good man—over antibiotics and steroidal asthma medicine.

We thought that schooling would be easy; we even moved down the street from an elementary school. In first grade the light seemed to go out of my son, who had always been a bright and inquisitive child. The teacher recommended "testing" since he had trouble reading and seemed kind of dull. One day as we walked past the school building, he said to me: "Mom, do you know why they give us recess? So that they can take it away from us!" Scrambling around to find another school in midterm, we moved him to the local Waldorf School—where after two months his asthma cleared up, he learned to read, and he flourished. It also gave our family a community of other parents who felt that their children deserved an environment of care and respect for the whole child. Now that our son is in public high school, we struggle, once again, with the absence of an adult community: we do not know the parents of his friends and have no circle of adults who together keep an eye on our young men and women as they navigate the pervasive culture of sex, violence, and drugs. Throughout all this we learned that we could not be complacent as American parents but had to be critical, active, and think outside the box. It also meant that we had to rethink our home environment, our neighborhood choice, and the *absent* "village" community that it takes to raise a child.

This book is a product of the struggle to be a socially aware parent and not take for granted the ideology of childhood implicit in our public institutions and the academic discourses that support it. It is also a product of the struggle to find a better way of thinking and a better language for understanding more deeply how children experience the world—and to do something about it. Raffi Cavoukian, the children's troubadour, calls this socially engaged, conscious commitment to care for children "child honoring," and he sees it as the "next *ecological* paradigm" (Cavoukian and Olfman 2006, xxi) because the future of our children and the future of our planet are intimately entwined. The womb, after all, is the first human ecosystem, and it exists in a precarious balance with the air, the food, and the water of the family's larger ecosystem (Steingraber 2001). Within these entwining ecosystems our concern for our children's well-being issues a direct call to our adult conscience. Care for our children and care for the earth are an ethical mandate.

TO THE SCHOLAR READER

This book is an attempt to describe the primal situations that all human beings—adult and child—share, irrespective of historical or cultural background. All human beings are embodied, live in places, engage with things, and experience time. On the other hand, each era or culture takes up embodiment, spatiality, or temporality and shapes or inscribes them in particular ways. The main focus of the following chapters is on the structural, universal elements of human development. The last chapter, though still phenomenological in method, investigates the cultural/historical construction of Western childhood through adult practices of elaborating selfhood and instituting literacy.

In the critical discourse in the contemporary field of childhood studies, great care goes into understanding the power structures that permeate the educational or psychological institutions that deal with childhood (Burman 1994; James, Jenks, and Prout 1998; Popkewitz and Brennan 1997). However, within these critical writings, terms like *body* or *space* have generally been constructed along Cartesian lines—that is, as self-enclosed anatomical or geometrical objects open to manipulation by the powers that be (Canella 1997). Child "bodies" have come to mean abstracted collective units that are inscribed by the power structures of a particular culture, and space "is an essential element necessary to technologies because of the focus on the presence and absence of ordered bodies within ordered space" (Canella 1999, 40). This kind of discourse, while illuminating the political dimension of child existence, obscures at the same time the multiplicity of embodiment and spatiality and their entwining, and erases dimensions of human experience that cannot be adequately captured through an analysis of power relations. Before a critical deconstruction of children's educational "space" or their place vis-á-vis adults can be undertaken, a careful and situated investigation of the *experience* of embodiment (along with the entwined experiences of spatiality and temporality) needs to be done. Necessarily, an investigation of the situated body is always bound to a particular place and time and is permeated with cultural practices: my own writing is no exception, since I am a German American, educated, female parent.

Nevertheless, description and interpretation of particular and situated experiences of embodiment open up a more detailed sense of what it means to be embodied in general. While, for example, breast-feeding is "inscribed" by all sorts of cultural taboos and customs, it still is always situated in the relationship between a woman and an infant, who exchange bodily contact and communication through gesture, sound, and sight. Bottle-feeding is a variation of this pattern, which can range from fathers holding their babies in their arms and feeding formula from a bottle to guinea-pig-style feeding bottles tied to the stiles of cribs, as has been observed in the Romanian orphanages of the 1980s. Each essential change of the pattern brings with it psychological changes in the relationship between adults and children. Thinking about the situated aspect of an infant's embodiment allows for greater sophistication when we see the social construction of infant lives: the outlawing of cosleeping by American pediatricians (AAP 2006) is not merely the enforcement of separation and individualization of a child from others (parents and siblings) but also the enforcement of feeding techniques and the creation of separate sleeping quarters. When children sleep apart from their parents, a whole host of soothing practices becomes necessary to make the transition from waking to sleeping and from daylight to dark bearable for the young child: night-lights, soothing toys, bedtime stories, carrying or even driving the baby around till it falls asleep. Parents are agonizing over whether they should let an infant cry him- or herself to sleep, and they consult the parenting books written for just this occasion. Sleeping arrangements are not surface phenomena, and a change in their practice ripples through many aspects of a family's life. Paying attention to the chiasmic web of body-space-time in all human experience lays bare the great fullness of the phenomenal realm and can reveal how deeply cultural practices penetrate the structures of children's lives. This is an insight that phenomenological psychology can contribute to the discourse on childhood in the human sciences.

This book on the phenomenology of childhood experience stands squarely in the postmodern and post-Cartesian hermeneutic tradition. Within that tradition there are, as Paul Ricoeur (1970, 1981) identified, two streams, or "fundamental philosophical gestures." One stream comes through Nietzsche, Marx, Freud, and Habermas and is continued in Foucault and Derrida. It is defined by a "hermeneutics of suspicion," which in its critical stance "is a tearing off of masks, an interpretation that reduces disguises," a "reduction of the illusions and lies of consciousness" (Ricoeur 1970, 30, 32). It takes as its perpetual task the critique of ideology. The other postmodern stream comes through Husserl, Heidegger, Merleau-Ponty, Levinas, and Gadamer. Its proponents believe that the field of meaning, which has been obscured by the modern/Cartesian philosophy of being, can be reclaimed through careful attention "to the things themselves": "it seeks, through interpretation, a second naïveté. Phenomenology is its instrument of hearing, of recollection, of restoration of meaning" (28). Its primary attitude is care or concern for the object of study and the wish, through explication, to submit oneself to the movement of meaning that emerges in the process of engagement. This stream can be called, to borrow an idea from Gadamer (1984), a "hermeneutics of participation." Ricoeur suggests that these two streams should not battle and erase each other but play a complementary role: participatory hermeneutics needs the critical distance and understanding of cultural power dynamics that critical theory and deconstruction provide in order to reawaken its political sensibility and self-awareness; critical hermeneutics needs phenomenology in order to remain relevant to the lives of children and adults and avoid falling into the trap of a sterile and closed academic discourse structure that has no ethical connection with the people or situations it describes. Ricoeur advocates a creative, critical hermeneutics that holds the tension between suspicion and recollection of meaning: it combines multiple methods and approaches and is sensitized to and makes room for opposing perspectives (Ricoeur 1981).

Through personal preference, my work leans toward a hermeneutics of participation. I like to write in prose that ties the philosophical to the given, and I ask the reader to walk with me *through* the landscapes of childhood before, in the last chapter, we step out on the hill and overlook the geography of the whole cultural field. I write and teach in an academic environment that is struggling with the question of ethics: how do you connect and act on behalf of children or the natural world after you have analyzed the cultural discourse practices that threaten their health or their very existence? I am convinced that attempting to give voice to the depth structure of the *situated and local* in children's lives and to let *it* shape our thinking complements a critical analysis and keeps it grounded. Someone, after all, has to speak for blankies and teddy bears.

ONE

Milk and Flesh

Infancy and Coexistence

MILK

The day after our daughter, Lea, was born, I watched her sleep next to me on the big bed. Even before she stirred I could feel the milk come down into my breasts. Lea whimpered, opened her eyes, and I picked her up. Greedily she nuzzled around for the target, locked on, and began sucking.

The need of a mother for her baby to consume the milk she produces is a very strange phenomenon. My body was ruled by her need; her need called forth from it an immediate and uncontrollable response. Never in my life have I felt so much given over to and identified with my body than when my children were infants. Never have I been in such close contact with another being's skin, arms, and mouth than during those early weeks of continuous holding and feeding. I made milk, smelled like milk, was sticky with this stuff that was me, but not me, which produced in me the need to give it away. Keeping it myself was painful, impossible. After the first few wobbly days, Lea and I developed a simple rhythm of giving and taking, waking and sleeping. The miracle was that she and my body were one, that she, more than I myself, controlled what my body made in milk. When she consumed less because she was ill, it took my body a few days to adjust to the new rhythm and make less milk. Disturbances in rhythm meant that I became uncomfortable with the need to give the milk away. It leaked all over the place; unexpressed, it made my breasts tender and painful to the touch. We call the one who feeds us, who cradles us close to her body, our whole length pressed into her, *Mama*, all identified with the Latin *mamma*, the breast. We "live from" her and she is the first nourishment, the first experience of enjoyment and happiness (Levinas 1969).

Nursing a baby is such a primal event. It is the miracle of becoming food for another being, of sustaining life out of oneself. We share this with all other mammals—wolves, dolphins, cats—but above all, I felt connected to cows. The stillness and earthiness of the cow spoke to me most during those early days on the bed with my new baby. Milk, milk, everything was milk. And I felt heavy and complacent, bovine and earthy, content to empty myself out in an infinite stream. The days and nights passed in their quiet circle. I was all body and almost soil again, my own mother taking care of me and standing sentinel against the world adumbrating my primal, undifferentiated, and indifferent being.

Babies do not stay infants for very long. The making of milk fades away, often not even a memory. Its traces of pleasure and pain, its resonance of milky perfume and sticky skin remain written into the folds of the female body: illegible, dark traces of a mystery that perhaps one day my hands will share with my daughter as they ward off the world encroaching on her lying-in.

I was her house, but more than that I was the field that nourished her, the rain that quenched her thirst, the sun that warmed her skin. And it is such a miracle to have seen that small, red, wrinkled creature take in my milk and grow: smooth skin, stretching limbs, and no longer little whimpers but a loud and demanding voice. I often looked at her and marveled that even though she had left my body, she still grew through it. Milk was the line that tied us together, the very special stuff that gave her life, growth, and contentment. Milk is the glory of our animal being, the need to give of ourselves and pour out our care and love because our body says, "Thou shalt." And the wonder is that for a brief time we are one with the world.

BEING IS ROUND

In his meditation on the house Gaston Bachelard suggests, almost in passing, a radical revisioning of existential ontology: "Before [the human being] is 'cast into the world,' as claimed by certain hasty metaphysics, he is laid in the cradle of the house" (1994, 7).[1] Before experiencing the existential fear of being thrown into a cold, hostile, and unpredictable world, human beings experience the "well-being" of being warm and encircled in maternal waters. Bachelard calls us to think of being not in terms of being-toward-death, which marks a Heideggerian ontology (Heidegger 1962), but to grasp it as essentially woven into and supported by life-giving presences. We are housed before we are cast into the world, we are cared for before we care for ourselves. Prior to "being thrown," prior to facing the world from a distance, prior to the struggle with finitude, fear, and isolation, the human being is housed in the circle of a maternal space. The primary metaphysics Bachelard evokes is one of roundness, wholeness, and well-being.

The poet Rilke expresses the same sentiment in the *Eighth Duino Elegy* (1999, 127) when he writes:

> O bliss of the tiny creature who
> remains forever in the womb that bore it:
> O happiness of the gnat, who still leaps *within*,
> even on its wedding day: for womb is all.

This image of an animal consciousness inhabiting the world without distance contrasts sharply with Rilke's description of the adult human being, who is marked by an attitude of "forever taking . . . leave":

> And we: spectators, always, everywhere,
> turned toward all this and never beyond it.
> It overfills us. We arrange it. It falls apart.
> We arrange it again, and fall apart ourselves.

Bachelard would argue that even Rilke's wanderer who, from the hill, wistfully looks back at his valley as he is "forever taking leave," can leave only because he is grounded in the more primal experience of housedness.

Bachelard is not suggesting that we do away with the "secondary metaphysics" of being as conscious being that stands reflectively before the world. But he calls us to the work of exploring human existence as it is woven into primary spatial and intersubjective holding structures that we experience in our early childhood: they form the background music of our lives. We begin, arise out of, and are supported by a primal housedness and well-being. Only because, deep in our bones, we know the bliss of the tiny creature do we also know the tragedy of the one who is forever taking leave.

In the following pages we will take up Bachelard's understanding of primal well-being and look at the phenomenon of milk as the visible manifestation of original hospitality. Through Merleau-Ponty's notion of the flesh we will articulate the ontological status of milk: it belongs neither to the mother nor to the infant but to an "in-between" space that transcends bodily and biological separation and psychological dualism. Milk is a *coexistential*, interpersonal phenomenon.

MILK: COEXISTENTIAL FORMS

The mother's body is the first house of being, a shadowy and round abode for the unborn. A great paradox rules pregnancy: are there two bodies or one? Two beings or one? After birth it seems clear: two bodies, breathing separately, one tiny and vulnerable, the other large but vulnerable, too. But the separateness is an illusion. Infants are born with involuntary, responsive capacities ("reflexes") that already constitute the maternal form. Infant reflexive responses illustrate that "reflexes" are not internal biological mechanisms: they constitute and are constituted by a particular human world (Merleau-Ponty 1962). The mouth that opens when its side is touched ("rooting reflex") orients to and already outlines the shape of the mother's nipple. The newborn's body molds itself into the mother's arms, fitting along the groove between her arm and abdomen. Newborn eyes can see the perfect distance of twelve inches: the bull's-eye of the breast's aureole and the maternal face. Infants love to gaze at their mothers, a gaze that is one with the rhythm of breathing, sucking, and swallowing, which are reflexive responses as well. Babies are perfectly made for taking in their mother's milk, calling it forth with a gesture or a cry. The skin as the boundary line between two bodies is breached again and again in the evocation and gift of milk.

Milk reveals to us that the body, even in its organic dimension, is not enclosed in itself but is engaged in a meaningful web of relations: the infant other is part of the structure that determines what milk is. Perhaps more than any other substance milk is the visible sign of the invisible, the in-between body, the chiasm, the flesh of mother and infant. Its fluidity refuses to belong to one or the other and it eludes the "thou art that" of any definite identification (Irigaray 1985).

The shape and size of the infant's mouth and the rooting and sucking responses present an organic openness that already presupposes and is ready to receive the nuclear properties of milk—rather than those of bits of grain or predigested meat that we find in other species. The infant going after the milk strives for that convergence of milk and body that makes sense of the reflexive actions of the mouth. The primary experience of the human infant is the experience of moving toward a world of things and others *that is already prefigured in one's own body*. We cannot *not* move toward the (m)other with our mouth and gaze. The maternal milieu extends an invitation, yet the structure of the neonate's embodiment determines the nature of that invitation by necessitating the shape of the nipple and the texture of milk. Milk is made only when the dance of giving and receiving extends over time, and when infants learns their own steps and exercise them in synchrony with the (m)other. Merleau-Ponty would designate the nursing dyad as a *form:* it "is a visible or sonorous configuration (or even a configuration which is prior to the distinction of the senses) in which the sensory value of each element is determined by its function in the whole and varies with it" (1963/1983, 168). *We begin life not as separate monads but as entwined presences, as aspects of significant wholes where the newborn's action finds its complement and completion in the actions of the (m)other.*

The phenomenon of milk is one of the most powerful illustrations of Levinas's description of "living from" (and it explains the mythic proportion that the image of the mother assumes for the human psyche): "Life's relation with the very conditions of its life becomes the nourishment and content of that life. Life is *love of life*, a relation with the contents that are not my being but more dear than my being: thinking, eating, sleeping, reading, working, warming oneself in the sun. Distinct from my substance but constituting it, these contents make up the worth [*prix*] of my life" (1969, 112). The encounter with the mother's milk is the primary matrix of nourishment and enjoyment, the original contour of happiness. To despair of life, Levinas says, "makes sense only because originally life is happiness. Suffering is a failing of happiness" (115). Like Bachelard's "roundness" and "well-being," Levinas's "living from" precedes and permeates all intentional acts of consciousness. Our being is nourished and sustained by the elements of the world. Because we are housed, we can be well; because we are nourished, we can be happy. Suffering and despair are a "failing of happiness" because they are possible only against the background of the primary and harmonious insertion of the human body into the structures of a world that provides for it.

Like the current of vision that makes sense of the eye organ, milk is the current of nourishment that makes sense of many newborn responsive actions for which the embryo has been prepared during gestation. Merleau-Ponty's insight about vision applies also to the other structures of the neonate's body: "In spite of all our substantialist ideas, the seer is being premeditated in counterpoint in embryonic development: through labor upon itself the visible body provides for the hollow whence a vision will come, inaugurates the long maturation at whose term it suddenly will see" (1968, 147). Milk will flow when rooting, breathing, and sucking come together with the prepared maternal breast. The flesh is the possibility of this current, the meeting ground of the perceiver and the perceived. Milk, like vision, is its sensuous manifestation.

Implicit in the first cry, the first turning of the head toward the (m)other's voice, the first search for the breast is an intentionality, a directedness that presupposes that there is something to turn to. The gesture of *turning to* is supported by healthy infants' immediate cradling of their bodies along the corporeal lines of mother or father. They fit their bodies to the arms that hold them, closing the gap of distance that is also always there after birth. The maternal milieu (much of which fathers also can constitute) is perfectly designed to respond to and evoke the baby's intentionality.

Roundness and well-being presuppose that ideally the fit between infant intentionality and milieu is perfect, so that the world's response to infant desire is complete and immediate. But life is not like that. Even Winnicot's "good enough" mother (2002) cannot erase the colic pains of the three-week-old baby or the bump on the head of the fallen toddler. Parents sometimes fail to respond, and this rift of asynchrony, the missed steps of the disturbed dance, bring frustration and pain to the infant. The child's intentionality reaches for completion of its roundness but in asynchrony is thrown back upon itself, is missing the world as the other side of its flesh. The form is broken, the gap appears, the infant's wail transverses the abyss and appeals to the primal empathy of the adult to come and make the form whole again. Early infant action appears in this rift and attempts to restore the harmonious synchrony between body and world.

The ability to bear the rift to a certain degree is also given to human infants. Erikson (1950/1963) characterized this as the infant's capacity to bear some amount of frustration and mistrust due to parental inconsistency. Coming to terms with a little bit of frustration does not destroy the baby's essential trust in others and might actually strengthen trust in his or her own sense of agency. But when infants are neglected and not responded to over prolonged periods of time, they sense that their own intentionality cannot find a complement in the world. Ultimately they will give up trying to bring about change. We call this "learned helplessness," and Seligman (1991) found it in animals as well as people.

The circle of need and response is structured differently in different cultures but still takes account of some fundamental existential parameters. Woodson and da Costa's (1989) research on infant social interactions of three different ethnic groups in Malaysia found that Chinese, Tamil, and Malay infants were in physical contact with someone for over half of the observed time. Chinese and Tamil infants had more extra adults present besides the mother, and there were more older children around for the Chinese infants. These other familiar people are part of what I want to call the infant's "attachment ensemble," that is, the group of adults and children who are responsive to infants and hold, feed, clean, and comfort them. A culture can structure the attachment ensemble by restricting it to the mother or by widening the circle to include others. The limits of this structure, however, are determined by the infant's and the caretaker's ability to respond to each other and to find the "fit" between infant need and adult capacity to provide what is needed. Beyond the limit lie neglect and abuse.

The infant's cry is an attempt to reestablish comfort, enjoyment, and well-being. And it works, most of the time: infant cries evoke stress and anxiety in adults, no matter if they have children or not (Bleichfeld and Moely 1984). Hearing an infant cry leads to bodily responses that raise the level of tension and call for action. Here again, we witness the dance between adult and infant bodies that constitutes the active dyad, the web of *operative intentionalities* (Merleau-Ponty 1962) that lies beneath the *intentionality of act* that we usually associate with human volition and judgment. Operative intentionality implies the natural and prethematic unity of the world and our lives. It appears most directly in our desires and in our immediate grasp and evaluation of situations. Operative intentionality is the intentionality of the flesh, the pathic and immediate direction that the bodies of (m)other and infant assume in their mutual gestures toward each other. In milk we find the expression of this prethematic unity between a new life and the one who has been its home.

Infant intentionality is driven by the passage of time. Bodily processes lead to hunger, sleepiness, wetness, discomfort. Time, as it is inscribed in the rhythms of the body, calls for periods of being awake and active to address growing needs. Newborns cannot maintain comfort and well-being by themselves. The passage of time, if not mediated by an adult, destroys the infant. Infants "fail to thrive" (Karen 1994) if not given physical and emotional nurturing over time. Child therapist Eliana Gil (in James 1994), in a case vignette, describes a four-year-old girl, Niki, who showed the typical symptoms of severe neglect of the abandoned or minimally cared-for child. Niki suffered from malnutrition and untreated rashes and infections. At four years of age, when her

age-mates climb the monkey bars in the playground and play out involved story scripts that they invent themselves, she could not walk,
could barely talk, and was not toilet trained. She also *did not cry* even
when soiled or hungry and stayed mostly in one spot in her crib, clutching her blanket. Not only did she have severe impairments of her senses
and motor ability, she was also deeply restricted in her ability to apprehend the scope of the world. She had learned to be helpless and not
reach out to an unpredictable, unresponsive world. In Erikson's sense,
she had failed to develop trust in others, which then also stunted her
trust in herself and led to mistrust of the world at large (Erikson 1950/
1963).

The abandoned, uncared-for child gives up her cries because she does
not expect a response from her world anymore. Like Niki, babies as
young as five months of age do not cry anymore—even in response to
the infliction of pain—if they have unresponsive caregivers. The operative intentionality of the infant's cry has been severed from its responsive counterpart in the adult's care, and the child does not anticipate a
future gesture from the (m)other. Niki has given up on enjoyment and
happiness, restricting the pleasure of life to the narrow confines of her
crib and the rigid, passive sensory engagement with her blanket. Without well-being and enjoyment, the horizon of a child's world is severely
limited.

Infants who are not cared for show signs of severe sensory and intellectual impairment after only one year (Ayers 1979; Dennis 1973). Research in the relatively new field of sensory integration has shown that
the development of our senses unfolds in interaction with the world
made inviting by caring adults. Children who are kept in nonstimulat-
ing, sterile, and isolated environments have difficulty with hearing, seeing, touching, and tasting. Their sense of balance, depth perception, and
motor coordination are so disturbed that they will bump into cars when
walking in a parking lot or fall when climbing stairs (Ayers 1979). The
infants' senses, if not engaged by caring adults, will limit their engagement with the world to familiar structures: the minute shadings of the
white crib, a distance that spans a few feet, the touch of others that restricts itself to the feeling of a spoon on one's lips or maybe the grasp of
hands under one's arms when placed on a potty chair. After their release
from isolation, these children will show autisticlike symptoms, and
without intense therapeutic sensory work their chances for succeeding
in an ordinary family and school situation are not very good (Greenspan
and Benderly 1997). In chapter 5 we will follow Niki's struggle to es-

tablish a relationship with her therapist as she comes to terms with the great betrayal of her early years: the world had no nourishment for her, or, as she finally articulates it: "Titty, no milk. No milk for the baby" (James 1994, 143).

Simply feeding a child, however, does not mean that the child is truly nourished. Even Niki received food from her mother once in a while. Harlow's research with primates demonstrated clearly that even in animal species closely related to humans babies do not love those who feed them: they are attached to whoever holds and soothes them (Blum 2002; Harlow and Harlow 1986). Nourishment goes beyond food. Happiness comes from the gestures surrounding the giving and receiving of milk. Milk, the original nourishment, is not merely a food for the stomach. It feeds the child's senses: the perfume of the (m)other's skin, the gaze of her eyes, the rhythms of the soothing voice all invite the infant to enter a world that is new but safe. Enjoyment and happiness open the horizon of perception, while abandonment and despair foreclose it.

Bachelard understands that the experience of milk—the "maternal water," as he calls it—is the "root metaphor" for all later forms of love, and "that the one who nourishes us with her milk, with her own substance, puts her indelible mark on very diverse, distant and external images" (1983, 116). The gift of milk becomes the matrix, the "material presence" for later "passionate liaisons" with other people and with natural things that give themselves to us in their splendid fullness. The nourishing image governs all other images, and well-being is the fountain of the creative imagination. Milk provides the first boundless happiness that we can also feel when nature gives herself to us in a sweeping landscape or in our first encounter with the sea after a long absence. "Has milk not overwhelmed us, submerged us in a boundless happiness? In the spectacle of a heavy, warm, productive summer rain one might find the living image of a downpour of milk" (123).

THE FLESH BEYOND THE SKIN

The infant's body, from the beginning, transcends the matter it is made of by having an intentionality that ties it to the body of the (m)other. Flesh here means the intentional *chiasm*, or entwining, between dyadic bodies, the invisible form of the other that is inscribed in each. Merleau-Ponty writes: "Once again the flesh we are speaking of is not matter. It is the coiling over of the visible upon the seeing body, of the tangible upon the touching body which is attested in particular when the body sees itself, touches itself seeing and touching the things, such that, simultaneously, *as* tangible it descends among them, *as* touching it dominates them all and draws this relationship and even this double relationship from itself, by dehiscence or fission of its own mass" (1968, 146).

In touching, infant bodies are complemented by the tangibility of the mother's body. The skin as the boundary between bodies becomes the coiling place of the flesh, the locus where touching complements the touched and the tangible issues its invitation. The mouth transgresses the skin's demarcation, it opens and takes in, and the body of the (m)other gives itself in liquid form. Rhythmic nursing alters between breathing, sucking, and swallowing, a rhythm that is reciprocated in the touched breast by the pulsating appearance of milk. The dehiscence of the flesh, the fission of its own mass that Merleau-Ponty speaks of, is a phenomenon that develops over time and already belongs into the domain of separation and the kind of consciousness that is marked, as Bachelard said, by being "cast into the world" (1994, 7). It does not yet mark *infant* consciousness. Infant consciousness is submerged in the flesh and immersed in the coiling over of the sensible world. It is "wild Being" (Merleau-Ponty 1968, 203), which can be accessed only by a leap of the reflective imagination. The dialectics of tangible/touched, visible/seen, and the attitude that allows for their distinction mark the end of infancy and arise only gradually. The demarcation of the body as a closed system, the identification of one's own possessions, the naming of oneself as "I" are later phenomena, but they all have their origin in the submergence of consciousness in the flesh. In the language of psychoanalysis, milk marks the *chora*, the archaic, preverbal, instinctual, semiotic dimension that always remains the foundation and background of later symbolic activities and identifications of the ego (Kristeva 1984). It is through understanding our fundamental housedness in the flesh and the dance we are engaged in with the (m)other that we can see human consciousness and selfhood arising out of its bodily, coexistential substratum.

The world that touches the infant's senses stimulates and directs the newborn's active intentionality. Eye and ear, nose and mouth, skin and hand are engaged and nourished by their encounter with the things of the world. Newborn babies follow the red ball with their eyes, gaze into their (m)other's faces after they are satiated, orient to the voice that is familiar, recognize and turn to the perfume of their mother's milk after a few days (Cole, Cole, and Lightfoot 2005). Merleau-Ponty speaks of the "magical relation" between the contours of things and the path traversed by the eyes:

> This pact between them and me according to which I lend them my body in order that they inscribe upon it and give me their resemblance, this fold, this central cavity of the visible which is my vision, these two mirror arrangements of the seeing and the visible, the touching and the touched, form a close-bound system that I count on, define a vision in general and a constant style of visibility from which I cannot detach myself. . . . The flesh (of the world or my own) is not contingency, chaos, but a texture that returns to itself and conforms to itself. (1968, 146)

The eyes and the skin and all the other sense organs are part of the visible, touchable world. The sensory world inscribes itself into the senses, and the senses lend themselves to be shaped by what is seen and touched. Newborns, for example, imitate facial expressions and stick out their tongues when others model it for them (Bower 1977; Maratos 1998; Meltzoff and Moore 1998). Piaget insisted that this was impossible because newborns had not yet acquired the proper body schema to compare what they see with what they know (1962). In Piaget's cognitivist assumption, neonates construct an intellectual schema by comparing the visual schema they have of the (m)other's face with the introceptive schema of their own tongues in their mouths. Merleau-Ponty (1964a) critiqued this model of imitation in his lectures at the Sorbonne, pointing out that framing the infant's activity in this reductionistic way assumes a level of mental activity and body awareness from the infant that is much too advanced and complex for this period of development. The problem of infant imitation "can come close to being solved only on condition that certain classical prejudices are renounced" (116): we begin to see the psyche not as a closed-off entity that contains mere "representations" of the world but as a dynamic force that is woven into the fabric of the world.

Merleau-Ponty's later work on the flesh (1968) suggests a framework that elaborates this earlier answer and allows us to interpret the newborn's action in a comprehensive, context-sensitive way. Early on, the human gaze follows the contours of what is seen. For the newborn the presence of thing-qualities is marked by a preference for contrast and movement, but this soon becomes more differentiated. The contours of the experienced world invite the four-month-old infant to reach and grasp and the toddler to walk among things. The fineness of the grasp, the overreaching of the goal, the faltering of the step are modified in the encounter with things. *The world teaches our senses how to be explored.* If the fabric of the world is radically narrowed and if the children are denied the expansive horizon of sensory exploration, as we saw in Niki's case, their perceptual abilities will atrophy (Bower 1977).

Within the horizon of their sensory capacities, newborns follow the contours of the (m)other's body through vision, touch, and gesture. Just as the limbs are conformed to fit into an adult's arms, so the face mirrors the world side of the flesh, conforms to the contours of the visible. We accept, generally without question, that infants can coordinate sucking, breathing, and swallowing fairly quickly, adjusting to the pulsating flow of milk in their mouths. But it is quite a feat. Learning at this basic level means that newborns adapt to the contours of the flesh of the world, fit into the fabric of possibilities that is woven around them and of which they are a part. This "fit into the fabric of possibilities" applies also to the facial interactions of infants with their parents, which seem so prematurely developed. Newborns stick out their tongues not merely because they see but because through their immersion in the flesh *they become what they see:* seeing is action, perception is participation. Without the distance of a reflective subjectivity, the human being is not merely *in* the world but *is* the world and delivered over to *its intentionality.* The newborn lives the prereflective and unmediated "wild Being" of the flesh, which adults experience consciously only in moments of great ecstasy or breakdown of the cogito and conscious self-concepts, but which, nevertheless, remains the continual substratum of adult experience (Merleau-Ponty 1962).

The urge to imitate the (m)other, the call of her face to the gaze of the infant, and perhaps even the global nature of the young baby's gaze, which remains focused on the *contours* of the face and the areas of *movement* and greatest *contrast* (Bronson 1997), guide the eyes of the infant in continual and predictable ways. Light and shadow are always present and the movement of the mother's head is always defined by a specific outline. To the infant's hearing, the maternal voice has always the same timbre, calls to the ear with its particular style. Within all the variations of human expression, *there are still some constants that never change because the (m)other is also a body and she expresses herself through the range of human gestures.* Her human embodiment defines the infant's vision and provides the sense that the world is not chaotic but fundamentally ordered because of the coherence and inherence of things. The (m)other is the anchor of the flesh, the place where "the flesh . . . is not contingency, chaos, but a texture that returns to itself and conforms to itself" (Merleau-Ponty 1968, 146). Perception is possible because the texture of things evokes the same or at least a similar response from the perceiver over time. The newborn can return again and again to the play of light and shadow along the (m)other's hairline. "*There is a true vision, a ray of generality and light*" (147) at the point of contact between the flesh of the world and my own.

The (m)other, on the other hand, fits her perceptions into the folds of the visible of the infant's body: she scans the contours of the baby's face, catches his or her eyes, gets a feel for how to position and hold the always-changing body. The child's desires are intimated from small gestures and facial expressions. "Their landscapes interweave, their actions and their passions fit together exactly" (Merleau-Ponty 1968, 142). The *dyad* is actually a *triad*: the flesh of the world, the third, transcends the two. Both mother and infant are turned to and tuned into the sensory properties of a shared world, and express the assumption that this world is the same for both of them. This fundamental sensory certainty, this "true vision," has its origin in what Merleau-Ponty calls "intercorporeal being." "There is here no problem of the *alter ego* because it is not *I* who see, not *he* who sees, because an anonymous visibility inhabits both of us, a vision in general, in virtue of that primordial property that belongs to the flesh, being here and now, of radiating everywhere and forever, being an individual, of being also a dimension and a universal."

In the beginning the maternal world and thing-world are the same. The "true vision" of the constancy of the (m)other's smell, features, voice, and touch finds the "ray of generality" also in the blanket whose fuzzy texture predictably caresses the cheek in the same way, or the railings of the crib that progress always with the same rhythm from one bright bar to the next. When, however, the maternal world narrows and does not issue an invitation to explore the thing-world, the thing-world atrophies. The well-being of a "housed," happy infant-(m)other relationship radiates out to include the things that are waiting to be explored. The world of the "unhoused" infant loses its radiance and invitation. Ainsworth et al. (1978) found that one-year-old-babies who have experienced neglectful or unpredictable parenting are anxious and do not feel comfortable exploring new things when they are in a strange room with their mothers. They lack a "secure base" from which to engage unfamiliar situations.

The well-being of the maternal world opens new horizons, so that growing human beings encounter a widening world of things. In order to feel safe without the mother's presence, young children adopt a blanket or a teddy bear or another soft and comfortable thing that is fiercely loved and possessed. Winnicot (1971) calls it a *transitional object*. This loved thing is an extension of the maternal space (as we will see in chapter 4) and is pervaded by the primal well-being of the maternal world and reconstitutes it in times of change or stress. Well-cared-for infants use their transitional things to face the dark, to be comforted during illness, or to make the transition into a new situation. Then they can let it go. Niki, on the other hand, cannot let it go. For her, the clutched blanket remains all that is left of a safe world.

IDENTITY AND THE CHIASMIC BODY

My own body, as Langeveld says, "is always the foundation of my sense of identity, and the unity of the experienced world relates to the unity of my body, which always moves 'as I myself' through spaces and around things to the far or near limits of my walking, seeing, or reaching" (1968, 125). Identity and difference are rooted in the body. But Langeveld also observes that the sense of unity with the world—the immersion in the flesh—is much less dissolvable in the child, and that the differentiation between body and self is only very rarely achieved in young children. The development of the self is intimately tied to the development of the body as it is experienced as the locale of action and address by others.[2]

Infant bodies are entwined with the bodies of their mothers. Human bodies are openings toward other people and things and perish when these openings are closed. On the most basic level, we must be open to take air and water into our bodies. Immersed in the flesh, identity and selfhood are fluid and do not end with the boundary of the skin. If we speak of selfhood at all, it must be deliteralized. The relative coherence of human identity has its foundation not in the outline of the skin but in the coherence of a lived body as it is chiasmically woven into the places, people, and things of its world. Selfhood is a field of being, a particular matrix of interpersonal and spatial relationships with the body at its center. It is a *style* of being in the world. If you diminish and restrict the quality of the other side of the flesh, its world-weaving, both body and psyche will atrophy. In the following chapters we will trace the development of identity and self-awareness as chiasmic phenomena. We will examine how people, spaces, things, time, and language are part of the evolving fabric of a child's embodied self.

Milk, the visible bond between maternal and infant bodies, does not last forever. The end of breast-feeding, the cessation of the downpour of milk, is inevitable. The process of weaning, either induced by the mother at a specific time or happening by degree, marks the infant's entry into a more independent relationship with the parent. Psychologically, the term *weaning* does not designate merely the literal cessation of breastfeeding; it refers to the crossing of a threshold out of the natural realm that is shared by human and nonhuman creatures. "To enter the human world the child must sacrifice a relationship of absolute and natural intimacy with the mother and accept living at a culturally elaborated distance from her" (Jager 1999, 76). The cultural elaboration of the distance happens, however, against the background of well-being, and weaning is possible only as a consequence of being nourished. Milk prepares the body to incorporate the world: as the first food made by the bodies of our mothers, it precedes the foods made by plants and animals, and it even precedes water. From the first intimate sphere of maternal nourishment babies expand their horizons *until they eat and incorporate the world.*

The pleasure of eating and all the imaginative, cultural variations of food and hospitality recall the "maternal water" that a member of the human community served to us once without asking for anything but that we take it in. If in our later journeys through the world we encounter the largesse of true hospitality, it originates in our hosts' generous attitude: they nourish us as if we were their own children. For a brief period we are allowed to delight in the kind of nourishment, once again, that *we did not have to work for.*

TWO

The World's Skin Ever Expanding

*Spatiality and the Structures
of Child Consciousness*

SUNLIGHT

Spatiality is inscribed into our bodies and souls. The toddler, called by curiosity and desire, steps into the spatial web and moves along its threads. The sunlight falls onto the bare floorboards and beckons. It lights up the hand that moves into the sunbeam out of shadow. Small flecks dance in the light, which smells of warmth and dust and feels good on the skin. The child curls up on the floor to fit the toes into the patch of light. The world recedes. Hands hold still. Attention wanders. The body is enfolded by light. Time for a nap.

IN THE BEGINNING: BEING SITUATED

In *Phenomenology of Perception* (1962), Merleau-Ponty identifies space not as the quantitative, logical setting in which things are arranged and placed by their geometrical coordinates but as "the means whereby the positing of things becomes possible" and as "the universal power enabling them to be connected" (243). From the "spatialized" space of the logician, we move to the "spatializing space" (244) of human experience, which forms the matrix of placement and relationship for all beings in the world. Direction, depth, and movement, beyond their measurable quantities, are preobjective and prethematic qualities of a person's hold on his or her world. Merleau-Ponty leads us back to this "pre-logical" and "phenomenal layer" (274), where "being is synonymous with being situated" (252). Child experience, as Merleau-Ponty argued in his lectures at the Sorbonne (1964a, 1994), allows us to come closer to this prelogical and phenomenal layer of human experience. Following Merleau-Ponty, Benswanger (1979) defines the goal for phenomenological research on children's experience of spatiality as the task "to rediscover the layer of living experience through which spaces and places are first given to us. Implicit in this endeavor is the conviction that an understanding of the phenomena as they emerge in childhood will lead to an enlightened understanding of the psychological implications of spatial experience at all stages of human life" (115).

The experience of spatiality comes to us through the senses in various ways. Touch gives us the contours of things at arm's reach, their texture, their coolness, their weight. The eye sees the sweep of space from the closeness of my hand to the expansion of the distant horizon and locates things within this extension: near and far, here and there. The ear pinpoints coming and going and, especially in the dark, is attuned to the particular sounds that announce a comforting or threatening presence in space. The nose provides us with the traces of things that have happened or will happen in this particular space, and the memories it leaves with us are the deepest and least reflected. Taste bridges the boundary of the body and creates the immediate link between the world at hand and body itself; together with the rise and fall of breathing, it opens up the possibility of an interior space in all its metaphorical ramifications.

We can think of the eyes, ears, nose, and mouth as variations of the sense of touch: all the major sense organs are openings in the skin, are folds of vulnerability where the sense of touch intensifies because the boundary between the inside and outside of the body is breached.

In the following pages we will examine the establishment and function of primary boundaries and their expanding horizons in the infant's development. We will watch how spatial forms are inscribed into the structures of perception and consciousness by following the toddler *into* the world of the upright posture (Straus 1966/1980)—and feral children *out* of it. Continuing the developmental trajectory, we will trace the three-year-old child's new sense of "lived distance" (Minkowski 1970) and the four-year-old's terrifying experience of night space. The chapter ends with a topo-analysis (Bachelard 1994) of the older child's secret spaces.

INSIDE AND OUTSIDE: OUR FIRST HOME

Intrauterine space is marked by a caressing, liquid darkness, which over time touches the fetal body ever closer and tighter. In a powerful description of deep-sea diving, Lingis (1983) compares the experience of going into the deep with the desire to return to the womb. His description can give us an approximation of the experience of fetal spatiality: "Denuded of one's postural schema, of one's own motility, swept away and scattered by the surge, one does nothing in the deep. One takes nothing, apprehends nothing, comprehends nothing. One is only a brief visitor, an eye that no longer pilots or estimates, that moves, or rather is moved, with nothing in view" (11).

The upright posture is relinquished, moving and being moved are indistinct, the boundary of the skin becomes permeable in the caress of the waters. There is nothing to take by the hand, apprehend through the senses, or comprehend by the mind. The I has nothing to bump against, nothing to do, nothing to want. In the liquid deep the diver's parameters of existence change. What once was taken for granted as the world is now fluid. World, as we experience it when we are standing on solid ground, is "a cosmos, is the order, the ordinance, extending according to axes of close and far, intimate and alien, upward and downward, lofty and base, right and left, auspicious and inauspicious, within which things can have their places, show their aspects and stake out paths" (Lingis 1983, 3).

Intrauterine space, like the deep-sea space, is a world with a different order, a cosmos not determined by the axes of the upright posture and the depth perception of eye and ear. Things do not invite the reach and grasp of hand and mouth, nor do they lure the step further away into newness. And yet, the growing fetus in the womb is not without a world. Its depth is not measured by distances but by the profound darkness, closeness, and mystery of spatial being.

The darkness of the womb's space is not the absence of light but the tangibility and materiality of spatial being that is "penetrating to the very depths of our being" (Minkowski 1970, 405). This primal darkness has a depth that transcends our usual biopic perception, and it returns in young children's fear of monsters in the closet and the adult's love-hate relationship with the night: "Contrary to light space, it will have no 'besides' or distance, no surface or extension, properly speaking; but there will nonetheless be something spatial about it; it will have depth—not the depth which is added to length and height, but a single and unique dimension which immediately asserts itself as *depth*. It is like an opaque and unlimited sphere wherein all the radii are the same, all having the same character of depth. And this depth remains black and mysterious" (430). Cataldi (1993) points out that depth is not the third dimension, added to height and length, but the primary spatial dimension that penetrates all living forms, a spatiality that precedes the differentiation of the senses and permeates their development.

Unlike the deep-sea diver, the fetus has never known the sun-filled world above the waters. The deep space of the womb is *the first place in which the senses awaken*. And also unlike the diver, the fetus is not merely a visitor to the fluid world of the womb: the womb is its habitat, which feeds and sustains it. Even though it is said that the womb is a warm, dark, quiet place, fetuses develop eyes, ears, noses, mouths, and skin in the first weeks of gestation. Out of the umbra of deep space the body's sense organs begin to differentiate. The liquid darkness of the uterus is not the place that dissolves the body but the alembic that allows the organism to anticipate and grow toward seeing, hearing, smelling, tasting, and touching.

Videos of fetal development show how the fertilized zygote (morula), already engaged in cell division, finds its place on the uterine wall and immediately begins to form an outside and an inside layer of cells (blastocyst). The new uterine environment interacts with the morula and leads to change: the outside layers form a protective but permeable barrier that later will be formed into the fetal membranes, which hold the amniotic fluid and make the placental transfer of nutrients possible; the inner cell mass, clustered along one side of the cavity created by the outer cells, will develop into the fetus (Cole, Cole, and Lightfoot 2005). During implantation, before differentiation into the basic organs of the human body, the developing organism creates a space out of itself, forms a *limes*, a boundary line between itself and the environment that determines the location where its life will unfold.

The act of drawing a line and delineating a location is one of the primary, archetypal forms of inhabiting space. A fragment from the Greek poet Acusialus from the seventh century BC speaks of creation as "first Gap the unknown, then Erebos, he bounded, Night, she boundless; their children: Aither, Eros, Metis; their children's children: the other gods" (Doria and Lenowitz 1976, 165). The bounded and the unbounded arise together and in their interaction begin creation. Rome, the story goes, was laid out by Romulus with the help of a plow. His twin, Remus, defiantly stepped over the demarcation and was killed in the ensuing melee. In the history of human cultures, the founding of a place lies in its differentiation from the undifferentiated "chaos" around it, which thus establishes a point of orientation and an ordered world of here and there. The bounded place becomes the *imago mundi*, the center of the world, from where commerce with other places or beings becomes possible (Eliade 1959).

In human development, claiming a location is the act that makes development possible by settling in a particular environment and exposing oneself to its influence. The embryo, embedded in the uterine wall, is changed by its new habitat; development becomes possible through the interaction with the uterine environment, and without this relationship the fertilized ovum dies. Implantation anchors a world that already anticipates a future. For Eliade, the claiming of a place establishes the order of the cosmos, the here from which the there of time and space can unfold. For all human beings the *umbilicus mundi*, the navel of the world, lies, quite literally, below the navel of their mothers.

Once it has established its location within the uterus and the fetal membranes, the embryo develops brain, spinal cord, heart, and blood vessels by the third week after conception. Limbs, eyes, ears, nose, bronchial buds, muscles, and nerves follow in rapid succession. By three months the fetus can turn its head and flex its legs. By five months most of the neurons it will ever have as an adult are all there. The fetus now senses changes in the mother's posture and adjusts its position as it floats in the amniotic fluid (Cole, Cole, and Lightfoot 2005). If the adult world-order is structured by *our* upright posture, the fetus's cosmos orients itself in relation to the shifting axis of the *mother's* body. The fetus perceives the pull of gravity in the inner ear and follows its demand: heavier body parts go down, lighter limbs stay up. The horizontal and vertical axes of the human world have been established in the heaviness or lightness of the limbs in relation to the pull of the earth, and intersect already in the floating liquid bubble. As soon as there is a body, it lives spatially: up and down. The body subject, prior to reflection and cognition, adheres in space, constitutes it and is constituted by it. A spatial world exists for it before we are aware of our "here" and take it up intentionally.[1] Merleau-Ponty (1962) argues that the body's "blind adherence to the world," this "prejudice in favor of being" (254), is given to us by a prepersonal, prehistorical tradition: we are born with it. "Space and perception generally represent, at the core of the subject . . . a communication with the world more ancient than thought. That is why they saturate consciousness and are impenetrable to reflection."

Spatiality is not an epistemological phenomenon spread out before contemplating thought; it is one of the irreducible, primary structures (what Heidegger [1962] called "facticities") that make being possible. Irrevocably and prereflectively we adhere to it, and it is by means of space that being exists.

The boundary that surrounds the fetus is permeable: nourishment, oxygen, light, sound, and movement animate the solitude and darkness within. Its skin has opened itself to let in light, sound, smell, fluid, and eventually air. *The function of the boundary is not to keep out but to create a location from which to encounter the other in a particular and individual style.* It is the location of the "coiling of the flesh" (Merleau-Ponty 1968), where the seer and the seen work on each other. Its function is to open itself, but not all the way, and to close itself, but not all the way. The eyes and ears begin to respond to light and sound: in the fifth month the fetus can hear sounds, which can make its heart rate go up, and at six months it moves in response to light (Cole, Cole, and Lightfoot 2005). In the weeks before birth fetuses recognize and remember sound patterns (DeCasper and Spence 1986), are very sensitive to small differences in musical notes, and prefer the sounds of the language that is spoken around them (Lecanuet et al. 2000). In the coiling of the flesh the world of the perceived calls forth an organ that can perceive it. In the coiling of the flesh the fetal body prepares itself to meet the call of air, light, fluid, sound, and warmth. Fetal growth anticipates breathing, seeing, eating, hearing, and touching, and is open to the world that will require them.

The coiling of the flesh has also a dark side: the infant's uterine ecosystem is embedded within the larger field of the mother's bodily environment. Contaminants in the mother's air, food, and water pass the placental barrier: mercury, lead, PCBs, pesticides, and other toxic chemicals lead to birth defects, premature birth, or long-term impairments of the physical and psychological functioning of the child. The fearful list of environmental pollutants and their impact on fetal development is extensive (Steingraber 2001). The fetus's health and the well-being of future generations is intimately entwined with the health of our planet. The infant is the missing ecological link between human beings and the natural world: the damage to our environment is not just "out there"— it goes as deep as our human bones.

NEW BIRTHS: THE WORLD'S SKIN EVER EXPANDING

Birth brings with it a radical transition between two worlds. The by now cramped and completely filled space of the uterus narrows even more, drains its liquid buffer, and the baby is squeezed and pushed through the birth canal. From the perspective of the senses, this experience is the most intense touch a human being will ever experience: the walls of the birth canal close up around the baby and mold skull and limbs into the shape of the passage, as if giant hands would reshape the form the fetus had received. This must be the first time that the human being experiences the encroachment of the world, the push of forces against the boundary of the skin that was there but heretofore never felt. And then, after the crowning, the infant emerges into the coolness, brightness, clearness, and expansiveness of extrauterine space where, in contrast to the narrow passage, nothing holds its body-form together. The first breath draws inward, and the voice emerges in a cry.

Touch, after this, is particular: no longer all-over pressure but a squeezing of the newborn skin as hands encircle its chest, the coolness of a hard surface on the back, the warmth of the mother's skin along its sides as she holds the baby for feeding. Though it covers the body, the skin rarely comes to awareness as a whole but appears, like the continents on a world map, as regions of sensation here and there: wherever the world touches us.[2] The primal space of the dark and its all-over touch recedes into the background of experience—until it returns to the four-year-old in nightmare and fear of the dark.

Within the regions of sensation, however, newborns are biased perceivers. In the first days after birth they have definite preferences for particular perceptions: the mother's voice, the language that the mother speaks, the smell of their mother's breast milk, the patterns of sounds in poetry and music that they have heard during pregnancy. We know this because newborns turn their eyes and ears toward the mother when she speaks and turn away from a stranger. They change their rate of sucking when they hear a familiar poem read and ignore the unfamiliar one. In the new space babies orient toward what is *familiar* and reconnect with aspects of the new world that are connected with the intrauterine world from before. Space is not an indifferent expanse of sensation; from the beginning it is structured by the desire for reconnecting with what the infant already knows.

Past perceptions that were allowed to sediment over time—like the poetry from *The Cat in the Hat* that DeCasper and Spence (1986) read to fetuses in the last six weeks of pregnancy—become the gateway for selecting the part of the perceived world that is worthy of attention. Familiar events—but also very unfamiliar ones, like loud noises, sharp visual contrasts, or other impressions that overpower the perceptual field—demand attention and elicit orienting behavior in the newborn.

Much of the infant's preferences target the mother. She is the magnet for infant perception, the vortex that pulls hearing, seeing, smelling, tasting, and touching into its center. Her voice bridges the two worlds of deep space and the directional space after birth: her heartbeat still beats the same rhythm, her arms encircle the newborn as an echo of the uterine embrace, her milk makes two bodies one for a while. In the safety of the other's arms the newborn finds an anchor that structures and orients the cool, bright, horizontal world. As Bowlby (1969) recognized, the mother is the *safe base* around which early spatial experience is organized and the anchor for the baby's exploration of its environment. *From the beginning, perception is never neutral but shot through with memory and desire: memory of past perceptions and desire for connecting the present with the past.*

The early anchorage in maternal space remains a keystone in the depth of our spatial experience in general. From here on, no matter how far we roam, we claim a place around which we organize our world. For most of us city dwellers, our home becomes the anchor around which the order of our activities unfolds. For nomads, the gathering of tents, although they change location frequently, still remains the umbilicus mundi, the focal point around which the horizon of daily life expands. And all of us travelers find a hotel, a tent, or even a train station where we leave our things in order to explore the range of the new city. Our human need for sleep, which renders us as vulnerable as a baby, leads us to claim the umbilicus mundi for most nights of our lives, and from there our existence achieves its dimensions of familiarity and strangeness. The "here" is familiar; the "there," in its radiating expansion, becomes stranger and stranger. The "here" we can know very well, but the "there" is infinite and we know it only in bits and pieces.

The homogenous expansion of the space measured by geometry is not space as it is experienced. Like the newborn's experience of skin, lived space in its there-ness comes to us in bits and pieces, in small islands of consistency: I know my house, my street, my neighborhood in Mount Washington within a certain range, but even the alleys a mile away are strange and unknown to me; I know a particular area in the Pennsylvania game lands because I have ridden my horse there many times, but the farms and forests between there and my home are un-known to me; I know a particular hill in Perugia and the lovely sweep of its landscape extending to Assisi, but most of Italy is familiar only as pearls along the string of highways leading to that bench on the hill.

In a beautiful passage from *An American Childhood*, Annie Dillard (1987) describes a child's attempt to push the boundaries of her known world further out day by day and connect the small remembered islands of consistency into a coherent map of her world. As a six-year-old she leaves home every day to find a new street some distance away. Then she has to find her way back home from there. The infinity of "there-ness," its indeterminacy, can be terrifying, and its expanse overwhelms the person's sense of presence. To find one's way back to the anchor is a matter of survival, a "dead reckoning." For the child there is the tension between the safety of home and the pull of the patches of world that are already familiar but promise that more can be known and understood if one follows the call of the "there." At night before sleep she rehearses the path traversed and figures out how it fits into her already familiar neighborhood. She finds joy in having braved and conquered an un-known world and found her way home. "What is a house but a bigger skin, and a neighborhood map but the world's skin ever expanding?" (44).

The "there," as Bowlby (1969) noted, pulls the young child's curios-ity out into ever-wider circles of exploration. To venture into the un-known means at first to be tethered by an immediate parental anchor that makes the world safe. But then, like Annie, the child begins to let go of the parent and explores her neighborhood on her own, but she is still anchored by the family home, still anxious that she might lose the way back there. Later, the adolescent becomes her own world-center, remodeling her childhood room and going from there to places that the parents know nothing of. "Here" is now where her body is, and perhaps the adolescent's coming ever more fully into her body also means that her umbilicus mundi is less in the family home and more where she chooses to rest her body.[3]

The gestures of maternal anchorage, like swaddling, cradling, hold-ing, embracing, are repeated in forms that adults experience. In the dark we return to our homes and make sure that the doors and windows form a locked protective circle around our vulnerable, sleeping bodies; we give up the upright posture and fall into the embrace of soft pillows and blankets and swaddle ourselves under the mound of down covers to stay warm. When we sleep, we choose to arrange our worlds so that they

echo the womb. In human life the house brings continuity and cen-
teredness. "Without it, man would be a dispersed being. It maintains
him though the storms of heaven and through those of life. It is body
and soul. It is the human being's first world" (Bachelard 1994, 7).

INFANT AND TODDLER: THE UPRIGHT POSTURE

Becoming upright is one of the profound transition points in human
infancy. From the primarily horizontal position, which brings with it
reverie, sleep, and dependency, one-year-old infants lift themselves up
and move through the world in a newly attentive, active, determined
way. In the weeks before walking, mobility increases through crawling
and the eyes achieve their full depth perception. Cultures structure children's exploration and "floor time" in different ways. As soon as children become mobile, Malay, Tamil, and Chinese families supervise their
children more frequently. Malay children, however, have fewer adults
in their attachment ensemble and are focused more strongly on their
mothers. In traditional Malay homes, crawling babies have more floor
freedom because the living space is furnished in a way more conducive
to crawling infants: there are soft rattan mats on the floor (rather than
bare cement floors, as in the homes of the other ethnic groups), and the
spaces are sparsely furnished (Woodson and da Costa 1989). Infants
who are mobile learn about the qualities of their environment and come
to be apprehensive of heights (Campos et al. 2000). The child's experience of space alters depending on the range of the senses and the hands:
at first the world is close at hand, and things on the other side of the
room exist in a blur; crawling, the baby is still close to the ground, but
depth and distance come into clearer focus; but when the child walks,
space becomes a matrix for desire. The ball down the hallway beckons,
the cookies are just out of reach in the jar on the counter, the cozy cubbyhole between the cabinets invites the toddler to squeeze in. The experience of distance is determined by the relation between the beckoning thing and my power of grasping it (Merleau-Ponty 1962). When the
child walks, space acquires depth and distance and truly becomes "*action
space*"—that is, an arena for the "I can do" body (Straus 1966/1980).

The upright posture, as Erwin Straus has shown, creates a particular
environment for the human being, different from that of other species.
It "pre-establishes a definite attitude toward the world; it is a specific
mode of being-in-the-world" (1966/1980, 139). As such, the transition
from infant horizontality to toddler verticality restructures the child's
environment and what calls for *attention* and *activity*. Attention and ac-

tivity are two key elements of waking consciousness that are markedly increased when a baby becomes mobile.

ATTENTION AND KALEIDOSCOPIC CONSCIOUSNESS

Uprightness requires resistance against gravity and the constant work of opposing its pull. Human walking is arrested falling: a carefully balanced play between letting oneself fall forward and arresting the fall through the movement into the next step. It requires the courage to let go of the father's hand or the table's edge and risk hitting the floor. It is truly amazing to watch an infant fall and pick him- or herself up over and over again in order to be upright. And how exciting it must be for a toddler to cruise though the living room, initiating movement forward but then be carried along by its velocity! Without motility, the upright posture is hard to maintain. We cannot stand still for hours on end, and every night sleep forces us to give into gravity and recline: "in sleep we no longer oppose gravity; in our weightless dreams, or in our lofty fantasies, experience becomes kaleidoscopic and finally amorphous" (Straus 1966/1980, 142). *The posture of the body determines the quality and range of attention and activity.* Letting go of uprightness restructures the experienced world, as every bed-bound hospital patient knows. We become dependent on others, unable to care for ourselves, and we easily fall into reverie and sleep. The horizon of the world closes in around the bed, and the beckoning "action space" is lost in the fog of amorphous and fragmented events. With activity restricted, attention tends to wander and lose its focus: it becomes kaleidoscopic.

ACTION AND THE STABILITY OF THINGS

Before an infant can crawl and walk, the world has the same kaleidoscopic quality: events and people come and go, but there is little spatiotemporal coherence in their coming and going. Infants' lack of object permanence is not so much their incapacity to remember and grasp that things exist but the lack of a spatiotemporal connection between objects. Once infants experience the world as their own action space, things assume their place in the web of spatial connections: here and there, within or out of reach, near and far. As they actively and attentively visit the objects in their living room or kitchen, toddlers inhabit their space as "the means whereby the positing of things becomes possible" (Merleau-Ponty 1962, 243), and in return objects are found to be more or less permanent in relation to each other. Object permanence is not the abstract acquisition of internal object categories but an extension of the infant's ability to act upon the world and a result of a changed "I can do" body.

"Places stay put" (Tuan 1977, 29), and the exploration of their stable matrix allows for the relationship among things to appear. The cubby can be visited again and again, the Tonka truck parked under the coffee table waits patiently, the front door opens the same way every day (though the toddler has to stretch hard to reach the handle) and opens up to the porch, the front yard, the sidewalk, the car. All can be moved toward or away from, all can be touched, all can be anticipated in relation to each other.

Things are intimately tied into spatiality: space is the web of their interrelation and of their action upon each other. In the sphere of experience, *the identity of the spatial matrix becomes the ground upon which the possibility of a person's identity is established.* Bachelard's (1994) call for acknowledging the original housedness of human beings is a call to appreciate that we are cradled among places that stay put, and that one of the primary dimensions of spatiality is its identity: under us the earth does not move, and above us the sky changes in predictable patterns of night and day, summer and winter. Spatiality is inscribed into our bodies and souls. The toddler, called by curiosity and desire, steps into the spatial web and moves along its threads. But there are times when the world is too much. Attention has to be relinquished, action has to be restrained, the upright posture given up: time for a nap.

FERAL CHILDREN AND HUMAN SPACES

Citing Wertheimer, Merleau-Ponty writes: "We remain physically upright not through the mechanism of the skeleton or even through the nervous regulation of muscular tone, but because we are caught up in a world" (1962, 254n). The call of the world, the desire for the web of things, beckons the human infant to arise on two feet and take up the human environment. Because we are caught up in a human world that our family inhabits as a human action space, we become upright. Feral children, raised in solitude or by other mammals, do not walk upright. They take up the posture and assume the lived space of those who raised them: Kamala, a child raised in a wolf den before she was, at the age of eight, taken to a missionary orphanage in India in 1920, walked on all fours and could not stand upright; bit and scratched when approached; had incredibly developed night vision, sense of smell, and hearing; and could not bear the touch of clothes on the skin. Her arms, hands, and nails had adjusted to a four-legged existence, and her senses were attuned to a wolf environment: once she located the entrails of a fowl outside the compound, eighty yards from the dormitory, where she was caught "red-handed" eating them (Candland 1995, 61). Kamala, caught up in the world of wolves, selected things important to wolves as worthy of her attention and action. Her action space was that of a wolf cub, her body had adjusted to a wolf's needs. Her identity was shaped by the places of wolfhood. In the human world of the orphanage she mostly slept or sat apart from the other children with her face to the wall and an absolutely blank expression. Unable to get caught up in a human world, unable to desire what her caretakers offered beyond food and shelter, Kamala retreated behind a wall of solitude and silence.

TIME'S RED CARPET

In infancy, body, space, and others appear together as an indissoluble unit. They are part of the existential ensemble of elements that make up the deep structure of the human world. The intimate connection between the gestures of the body, the spatial organization of things, and the call of the world as a human and coexistential endeavor make the discussion of infant spatial experience a very complex task. To make it even more difficult, the experience of time as the fourth existential theme is also woven into spatial experience. As the infant begins to walk, the temporal dimension of existence undergoes a transformation as well. Walking is a rhythmical movement, a sequence of steps that cover ground. Time is what it takes to get from here to there, the effort a body makes to relocate in space. Young children, as Piaget (1970) has shown, see time as identical with motion: the further a snail travels, the longer it must have taken (the child disregards differences in speed). Time clings to space, adheres in its unfolding, like the red carpet that clings to the floor as it is unrolled. Time is situated for the young child in this particular spatial setting and among these things, unlike the clock time of the adult, in which an abstract, numerical system is true and valid for all and rules all things. Lived time comes to young children through the rhythmic unfolding of activity around them. Snack time means the specific event of eating, in the specific place of the kitchen, with specific things like plates and spoons, with the specific people who provide the food. Nap time calls for a different spatial organization and a different structure of things and people. When children enter the nap room and their sleeping mats are on the floor, they know that it is now time to lie down. Time is measured by events: it is *time to do something in this place.* Like a thread, time unfolds through the changing uses of space, and the child grasps: *now* it is time to eat, and *after that* it is time to nap. The rhythmic sequences of inhabiting space give time its predictability and order. If adults disturb the order—for example, by having nap time before snack time—children become upset and apprehensive and "act out" because the transparency of the future has been occluded and they do not know what to expect anymore. The red carpet of time has lost touch with the ground and lies bunched up at the child's feet.

THE HAND AND THE TRANSCENDENCE OF THE WORLD

We honor walking infants by bestowing a new name on them: they are now "toddlers"—that is, human beings who walk—but are not yet very secure on their feet. We saw how the rhythmic activity of stepping forward moves consciousness out of its kaleidoscopic state into a more focused, attentive, and directed activity, in which space and time acquire the rudimentary coherence of here and there, now and then. The ability to walk is preceded and accompanied by the infant's ability, at around nine months, to follow a pointing finger's line into the distance. The younger infant gets stuck at the "here" of the pointing hand, and does not understand it as a sign that points beyond itself. The nine-month-old, however, grasps the transcendence of the "here" (the immediate sensory perception on the hand) and its connection to the "there" (the distant thing intended by the pointer), and soon after is able to follow it with her or his own pointing finger and locomotion (Butterworth 1997). Nine-month-old Talton would sit on the floor and propel one of his toys forward into the room ahead; then he would crawl after the toy, pick it up, and throw it again. The somewhat haphazard "there" of the toy in the room ahead is like a magnet pulling his own movement forward. Talton is experimenting with the openness of space: his intentionality is still bound to the movement of things, but he is at the cusp of freely moving into the space ahead. Like the pointing finger, the orientation of the toddler's gaze forward structures the "there" and singles out one of its regions for attention. The kaleidoscopic experience of distance is restructured when a location is singled out. The toddler has a specific goal now, a place to move toward because something there stands out and beckons.

As parents, when we "childproof" our homes we understand the toddler's voracious desire to pick up and touch and handle things within reach. Erwin Straus has shown how the upright posture frees the hand, which "becomes an organ of active gnostic touching—the epicritic, discriminative instrument par excellence" (Straus 1966/1980, 150), and which works as a sense organ only when it is actively moved. As a new sense organ, which the year-old infant can use with much delicacy, the moving hand is animated by the child's intentions. Toddlers feel the coldness of the glass table, the furriness of the toy rabbit, the crumbliness of the cookie, and the delicacy of the cookie crumbs under the table. The hand brings the *qualitative dimension* of space into focus. The spatial, sculptural dimensions of things—their hollows and ridges, their in-turnings and out-thrusts, their height or their emptiness—come into being under the touching hand. Piaget discovered that in children's understanding of geometrical forms the topological quality precedes the identification of abstract Euclidean shapes by many years: two- to seven-year-olds grasp and understand proximity (near/far), openness and closure (in/out), intertwined and separate long before they identify and represent the difference between a circle, a triangle, and a square (Piaget and Inhelder 1956). Active, spatial experience furnishes the qualitative topological matrix by which shapes are known before they are abstracted into conceptual figures.

The toddler seems obsessed with touching everything from chair legs to stereo buttons, from leaves to dirt—and to move it from the hand to the mouth as if to intensify the qualitative dimension by bringing things close to eye, ear, nose, and tongue. The walking, grasping baby extends the reach and immediacy of sense perception: the receptive eye, ear, and nose are complemented by the active hand. In the action space of the toddler, the body carries the senses into the world. Walking follows the reach of the outstretched hand, which in turn follows the desire of the eye. Perception is continually transformed by movement. The upright posture changes the eye and the mind: they are flexible now and can change location, which repeatedly shifts the experiential horizon; and they are given the versatile hand, which picks up and rearranges the world. Space has become truly an "action space" when the infant walks, a space filled with possibilities for doing and initiating changes. Child-proofing is the parent's response to the toddler's constant and unconventional attempts to rearrange the world.

BOUNDARIES BEYOND THE SKIN

Erwin Straus sees the origin of all possessive relationships in the experience of control of one's own body: it is mine. From a developmental perspective, however, a different picture emerges. In our early childhood the experience of the body in itself is overshadowed by the things in its action space: that is where attention, desire, and awareness go. The hand disappears in its reach for the cookie, the foot vanishes in its hurry toward the door. Before I possess my body, I am possessed by things. Infants, even before they walk, attach themselves to their first possession, the transitional object of blankie or teddy bear, which achieves its greatest importance and emotional value at times when the baby is horizontal and inactive during illness or right before sleep. Even the concept of the body as a self-enclosed entity remains vague for a long time. Children, like adults, encounter the body's limits in pain: falling down hurts, touching the hot stove burns. Pain recoils the body upon itself for a while and reduces the action space. But we know from preschoolers that even pain is not so much located in the body as in the thing that causes it. There are many stories of children crying when someone else is hurt: one's own body is confused with that of the other. Or a toddler might slap the door after bumping into it (and I know adults who, enraged, kick a closet door when it sticks, resenting its resistance!). *The body as mine is given to me not in itself and through the recognition of the boundedness of its skin but as an element in the equation of action space.* Space clings to bodies because bodies have an action history. The body becomes predictable in encounters with the things and people of its action space, and particular gestures and experiences repeat and sediment in the flesh. The carpet is furry under my bare feet, but its edges can trip me up and hurt me. The hot cement on the front porch makes me pull up my feet and jump back onto the doormat. *The boundaries of my lived body lie at the limits of my action space.* My action history has left tracks in the world, and "I" end where the tracks run out. Development is a continual extension of action space.[4]

In a phenomenological observational study of three toddlers, Benswanger (1979) found that in every observed situation the children began to "recognize, to recall, to depend on, to discover and anticipate the responses evoked by [their] own presence" (119), which over time leads to an awareness of themselves as distinct and separate from other persons and places while they remain related to them. The "self" is reflected back to the infant through the density of lived space, and the body is discovered when it bumps against the contours of things and people. As lived space sediments into the sense of "home" through repeated, active experience, the "I can body" achieves the fluid grace and competence of the walker, who is a toddler no more. The walker's sense of self is marked by a repertoire of situated scripts that are memorized and understood, and by a lived body that is, in the familiar environment, in synchrony with its surroundings. Benswanger refers to this as the element of "presence," that is, the horizon of familiarity in which the "I can body" is fairly competent.

TRANSCENDENCE AND DISSONANCE

The toddler's competence, however, is challenged by changes in the world and in the body. The young child continually bumps into a world that does not conform to desire. In one of my graduate students' observational studies, we saw a thirteen-month-old boy who loved to walk and play under the kitchen table. By the time he was sixteen months old, he kept bumping his forehead on the edge of the table. Soon he figured out that he had to duck to get into the familiar space, but it took him a while to understand that he also had to bend when he got up to get out of his hidey-hole! This "transcendence" and otherness of the world "implies an inherent dissonance between the subject and his surroundings. The spatial milieu of the child includes aspects that are alien, indifferent, hidden or hostile as well as those that are familiar, comfortable, and accessible" (Benswanger 1979, 120). Young children encounter elements of the world that resist their intentions, and just when they figure out how to smoothly occupy the space under the table, the world puts obstacles in their way and hurts them. A door refuses to open, a beloved toy breaks, Mom puts the blankie in the washing machine and destroys all its delicious scents. And because of constant changes in the developing body and mind, the child's world is never static, which intensifies the tension between presence and transcendence that marks all human existence. The equilibrium between the "I can do body" and the experienced world must constantly be readjusted, and the sense of the child's identity is continually challenged.

ANCHORAGE AND TRACE

How can we understand the relationship between spatial experience and the genesis of self-awareness? As we saw above, the child's repeated experience of being the center of a constantly shifting horizon creates a visceral, prereflective sense of identity. The experience of *anchorage* in the here is fundamental to the child's growing sense of identity. The body remains relatively constant in a changing world, which changes because I move in it. The "I can do body" in its activity relocates the child's horizon: literally by moving about but semantically by inducing changes. I am anchored in the center of my roving horizon.

The *I* learns that when I do "this," the effect will be "that." The particular child's style, his or her unique way of being in the world, is always in interchange with the world through a continual temporal feedback loop. The *I* discovers itself in the changes it makes in the world, in the *traces* it leaves in the faces of others, in the toys broken by curious exploration, in the particular book it desires to be read each night before sleep. Like *anchorage*, the *trace* is a key aspect of our contingency, which expresses itself in "the uncaused and tireless impulse which drives us to seek an anchorage and to surmount ourselves in things" (Merleau-Ponty 1962, 283). The trace is visible evidence of the child's desire to surmount him- or herself in things. Anchorage and trace are two early experiences that allow for an existential, but not necessarily reflective or cognitive, sense of personal identity.

LANGUAGE AND ACTION SPACE

Much of parental verbal interaction with young children centers on *what they do*, that is, the visible, spatial aspects of their intentionality. "Please" and "thank you" evaluate the act of giving, "yes" and "no" encourage or prohibit an action, praise affirms that the child did something well. It is surprising to notice that so much of early language experience centers on comments on what the baby *does*. In the third year, the time of the "terrible twos," the toddler's intentionality is on a collision course with the structures of her or his familiar, habitual world. Desire reaches beyond the toddler's grasp, is frustrated by the limitations of a two-year-old body or the restrictions of adults: no, you may not have that shiny pack of cigarettes at the grocery checkout. The I is appealed to as the "you" that is not allowed to do something. Through the speech of others, the "I can do body" becomes the "you cannot do body." The space the child inhabits and desires is large enough now that it interferes with others' intentions. Besides the carefully structured, childproofed home that the parents have arranged to be without danger to the toddler, children now find themselves on a crowded bus, or the busy playground, or the nursery school, environments that bring different dangers and have new rules. At home you can go to every place you can reach, but on the bus you are restrained to your mother's lap, and on the playground you get whacked when you take someone else's shiny toy. "You cannot do that": the I achieves its contours by being delineated as the "you" for others, before it assumes the "I" of its own self-appellation. The delineation of the "you" by the other is a restriction, redirection, and reshaping of the child's action space.

THIS PASSIONATE LIAISON OF OUR BODIES

So far we have explored the bodily, sensorimotor dimension of lived space, but spatial experience is also a deeply affective process. In her observations of toddlers, Benswanger found that their places have a particular atmosphere that is colored by a mood or feeling tone. She calls this the theme of "attuned space": "The child's sense of comfort, familiarity and security invariably affects his perception of a place and his behavior there. . . . The door where father was expected to appear, the familiar properties of the bathtub, the comforting rhythm of the rocking chair, the alien atmosphere of the neighbor's backyard—these places were already imbued with the meanings of attuned space" (1979, 117).

Early spatial experience is suffused with feeling, and the toddler is attuned to the mood of a particular place. Young children are particularly sensitive to the moodedness of a place, its quality of openness or secrecy, danger or coziness, excitement or tranquility. But is the feeling dimension merely a projection of an internal, subjective feeling onto the canvas of spatial expansion? In order to understand the world of young children, I think it is essential to find a way of articulating a nondualistic, radically post-Cartesian approach to spatial experience that gives feeling a place prior to and beyond projection.

Gaston Bachelard offers a way of deepening our understanding of the feeling dimension of space, to go beyond the reflections on the upright posture that are still human centered, and to radically imagine spatial experience from the perspective of space itself. This can be done only by means of an exact poetic imagination, a "topoanalysis," as he calls it, "the systematic psychological study of the sites of our intimate lives" (1994, 8). Bachelard imagines and describes the psychology of the cellar, the hut, the nest, the box, the miniature, the shell, the corner. He pays deep attention to the varieties of spatial forms and their impact on human consciousness. His topoanalysis is particularly appropriate when we study child consciousness, which is, as we saw, less self-reflective and more turned toward the world. For toddlers their home becomes an "organic habit" (14), as Bachelard calls it, a web of gestures that stabilizes over time and becomes inscribed in the body: "We are the diagram of the function of inhabiting that particular house, and all the other houses are but variations on a fundamental theme. The word habit is too worn a phrase to express this passionate liaison of our bodies, which do not forget, with an unforgettable house" (15). The house that shelters our infant sleep and encourages the direction of our first steps, where we are fed and warmed and embraced and talked to, becomes the touchstone for all later experiences of well-being; it is the dream of a "material paradise" (7) and the archetypal image of interiority and intimacy.

The house is a "psychic state" (Bachelard 1994, 72), and children's drawings of their own houses reveal its deep emotional form: well-being and protection. I have seen a drawing by a young Puerto Rican boy that, like almost all children's drawings of their houses, had a big chimney with lots of smoke coming out of it: "When the house is happy, soft smoke rises in gay rings above the roof" (72). The boy's actual house, located in a tropical climate, had no central heating and no chimney, but to him his happy home did have a chimney, which completed the house's gesture of overflowing warmth and well-being. Chawla (2003) reports that many drawings from children in a Johannesburg squatter camp had trees and flowers surrounding their homes. When the researchers went there and checked, there was no green anywhere near the shacks. What the South African and Puerto Rican children showed in their drawings was their home's physiognomy, its gestural presence, which to the children is more real than the literal structure of the house. Unhappy houses, or houses that fail to nourish and protect, have also particular features in children's drawings. Bachelard describes an exhibit of drawings by Polish and Jewish children who had suffered the cruelties of Nazi occupation. Their houses had been invaded and destroyed, and their drawings showed rigid and motionless houses that were closed off and not welcoming.

How does one become a psychologist of houses? Bachelard asks. By paying attention to the fine details of spatial forms and the images and feelings they evoke. If consciousness is always consciousness of something, as Husserl said, then the more differentiated and attuned the "of something" is, the greater the content and range of consciousness will be: "Wardrobes with their shelves, desks with their drawers, and chests with their false bottoms are veritable organs of the secret psychological life. Indeed without these 'objects' and a few others equally high in favor, our intimate life would lack a model of intimacy. They are hybrid objects, subject objects. Like us, through us and for us, they have the quality of intimacy" (Bachelard 1994, 78).

It is not surprising that wardrobes, desks, and chests play an important part in children's literature and are often gateways to a secret, concealed dimension of existence. The inside of the cubbyhole, the jack-in-the-box, the toilet bowl under its lid, the small hinged box that has to have something in it: they are all variations on the themes of inside/outside, visibility/concealment, expansion/constriction and provide a model for intimacy. They hold something inside, conceal it from others. There is joy in rattling a metal box that contains a couple of buttons, a mysterious pleasure in digging a tunnel through the bottom of the sand castle, a delicate excitement when we look into the interior space of a dollhouse or a matchbox car. Each of these spaces evokes a slightly different feeling and offers itself as a differentiated feature in the expanding landscape of the child's consciousness. Bachelard would probably demand that a good poet be a good topoanalyst, for only a differentiated understanding of the nuances of spatial experience allows a poet to create images that express intimacy and transcendence. And here is also the point where poetry and play meet, for it is in play that the child's mind engages and explores the spatial gestures of things and what they feel like.

Bachelard challenges our ordinary understanding of what feelings are. He differentiates them from emotions, such as fear, anger, happiness, which are much less subtle than the feelings that are evoked when we look into a bird's nest or take our teddy bear into the dark nook under Grandfather's desk. A feeling is not an internal, subjective state—it is, as Ricoeur said, a matter of "se trouver au monde," of finding oneself in the world. "Each feeling delineates a matter of situating oneself, of orienting oneself in the world" (1985, 69). A feeling is a perception of a particular world formation, and as such it resides in the thing as much as in the child. The poem, in turn, issues an invitation to step into a particular world by reexperiencing the feelings evoked by its differentiated images: "it creates or induces a new manner of finding oneself, of feeling oneself living in the world," and thus "renovates our horizon." On the other hand, maybe it takes the poetic extension of our everyday language, its allusions and ambivalences, its carefully crafted juxtapositions and surprises, to reclaim some of the feeling depth of our early childhood spaces: "I found a nest in the skeleton of the ivy / a soft nest of country moss and dream herb" (Yvan Goll, *Tombeau du pere*, as cited in Bachelard 1994, 90).

FROM SYNCRETISM TO LIVED DISTANCE

The mobile two-year-old is very much caught up in the movement a space invites. Waiting at a bus stop, I watched a two-year-old play with

the leaves on the ground, the dip of the gutter, the cracks of the wall behind us. He made a small doll move through these spaces, picked up
twigs and stones and old candy, carefully observed the wheel of a parked
car, and suddenly and determinedly walked off down the sidewalk, doll
clutched under one arm. He seemed completely absorbed and caught
up in the many facets of the sensory world. Another toddler, visiting a
neighbor's house with his parents, moved through the rooms, one after
the other, and spent much time opening and closing the shutters, the
doors, the toilet seat. He was compelled to move and caught up in moving features. He sensed and touched, followed the spatial flow to see
what he had not seen before, then returned to an earlier place to dwell
with and explore one feature for a while. These two toddlers were living out a *syncretic spatiality*, to borrow and modify one of Merleau-
Ponty's terms, where the child's consciousness is completely merged and
caught up in the spatial features of the environment. Children have not
yet achieved a unifying perspective on self and space that would create
distance and order. Everything at hand is still compelling and near.

But the three-year-old "stops confusing himself with the situation or
the role in which he might find himself engaged. He adopts a proper
perspective or viewpoint on his own—or rather he understands that,
whatever the diversity of situations or roles, he is *someone* above and beyond these different situations and roles" (Merleau-Ponty 1964b, 152).
Spatiality has a more intense quality at this time and is experienced now
not only in its syncretic here-and-there movement, which determines
the trajectory of the two-year-old's desire, but also appears in its aspect
of *lived distance*. Lived distance is the sense of seeing life unfold around
me, while its "ambient becoming" (that is, the movement toward the future of beings and things that are not me) is happening more or less independently of me:

> I see this life bursting out all around me, I participate in it myself,
> but it does not really "touch" me in an immediate way; I feel that I
> am independent to a certain extent, and there seems to be spatiality
> in this independence; there is a distance which separates me from
> life or, rather, which unites me with life. There is always *free space*
> in front of me in which my activity can develop. I feel at ease, I feel
> free in this space which I have before me; there is no *immediate con-
> tact*, in the physical sense of the word, between the ego and ambient
> becoming. My contact with ambient becoming is achieved across, or
> rather with the help of, a *distance* which unites us to it. (Minkowski
> 1970, 403)

Parents of three-year-olds, who have been through the terrible twos, notice a more relaxed attitude in their child's approach to people and situations (Fraiberg 1959). It is as if a sphere of ease opened up in front of the child into which she or he can step now with more comfort and freedom. Free space means that the touch of the world has somewhat receded and does not overpower the child's consciousness: activity can now develop its own pace. Perhaps the clearest appearance of this free space of lived distance is the space in which children play. The surprising is/is not of play, its dimension of make-believe combined with total absorption, is possible only when the sphere of ease of lived distance allows children to think, imagine, and act out their own projects without fear of encroachment or violation from the "ambient becoming" of the reality around them. Lived distance unites rather than separates me from the world because in it the transcendent world exists and moves independently of me (Minkowski calls this phenomenon *ambient becoming*), which leaves me free to pursue my own projects. The world is larger than myself, and the birds and the dogs and the clouds go about their own business, which has little to do with me. "Life," as Minkowski puts it, "which unfolds around us and in which we take part, has *fullness*" (1970, 406), and we live this fullness in an "organopsychic solidarity" between body and world:

> I go into the street and meet a number of people, but each of them, while forming a part of the whole, follows his own path and his own thoughts; we go in opposite directions, and yet we remain related to one another without "touching" in the strict sense of the word. Our life unfolds in space and is one life because of this fact; space thus contributes in making us into a society, but there is always free space between us, lived distance full of individual possibilities, which allows each one of us to live his own life within this space. The *fullness* of life emerges from this state of affairs. (407)

The fullness of life is the moving backdrop to all our personal projects and without it we could not live. Minkowski points out that disturbances in lived distance are at the heart of the schizophrenic's experience of reality. People and events are no longer situated in their own spheres of ease and with their own fullness; they are experienced as shrunken, compressed, and conglomerated in space: "ambient life 'touches' the individual in an immediate way, . . . it is in direct, almost material, contact with him" (410).[5] Lived distance is not a fixed, quantitative entity; it contracts and expands during a human being's lifetime and depends on a person's relationship to the fullness of life around him or her. For one-year-olds there is little distance between themselves and ambient life: everything is near and needs to be touched and incorporated. The two-year-old throws a temper tantrum when the parent enforces a lived distance that is culturally required. For the three-year-old the clearing of ease from which the world can be observed and loved is still small, and being touched and overwhelmed by the unknown plenum is still a real possibility. The anchorage of the child's being within the parental sphere assures that there is protection from many of the vagaries of ambient life as well as guidance so that the child's freedom can play itself out in an open and growing world space.

From the perspective of spatial existence, then, we see the three-year-old child achieve a growing awareness of anchorage, a rudimentary sense of lived distance, and the ability to live oneself as a particular, body-centered perspective, which now uses the word "I" to describe itself. However, the I does not yet have itself as a reflective theme and, as Piaget (1929/1951) saw, is still egocentric: for example, it lives in a magical, animistic, nondualistic, world-oriented manner. It lives, in Merleau-Ponty's terms, in a mythical space, in which reside "great affective entities" (1962, 285).[6] The ease of the three-year-old, the reprieve from the storms of feeling, does not last for long: when infant syncretism recedes behind the perspectival I and the child is able to distance him- or herself from immediate involvement in situations, "then human anxieties gather themselves unto him" (Langeveld 1983b, 16).

THE PLENUM AND THE MOODEDNESS OF LIVED SPACE

In her autobiography of her childhood in Pittsburgh, Annie Dillard (1987) captures the moodedeness of childhood spaces. The alley behind her house was the mysterious excavation place for old coins, a space that invited the child to dig deeper and deeper with her popsicle stick and dream of Roman treasure. But it was also the deserted backwater where a "terrible old man" and his sister, a "terrible old woman," lived above the darkest part of the alley in a "teetering set of rooms," and where the children, playing on the woodpile, were violently scattered by the old man's unintelligible rantings at them: "We looked fearfully overhead and saw him stamp his aerial porch, a raven messing up his pile of sticks and littering the ground below" (39).

Many childhood places can quickly switch moods from an engaging, safe, fun environment to one of mystery, strangeness, and uncanniness. The alterity of space—the dimension that conceals itself and yet remains present—waits on the other side of the familiar situation. The word *plenum* describes the plenitude or fullness of the web of spatial presence.[7] The plenum shows itself in Annie's excavation: the exciting promise that there is *more* to experience in the depth of a place and that it holds hidden treasure. But it also shows itself in the forbidding figure on the rickety stairs: darkness, uncanniness, and fear permeate the now-inhospitable place and repulse the child. "There dwells the anonymous being, the unperson. Watch out! Soon he will peek over the ramps and look at us" (Langeveld 1983a, 184).

Children's attunement to the mysterious depth of the plenum becomes more pronounced between the ages of three and four. It seems that with the experience of lived distance, which according to Minkowski results from the experience of visible, lighted space, the child also becomes more sensitive to depth and darkness. The hidden profiles of things, the dimensions of space concealed from view, are a normal aspect of everyday living, but children at this age are particularly attuned to them. Play and the plenum are intimately connected. The child intuits possibilities for play inherent in the concealed dimensions of the spatial plenum. They reveal themselves first in the affective life of the child, where they evoke strong feelings: the *excitement* of making a home or a fort in the large box that came with the new refrigerator, the *feeling of bravery* when the dizzy height of the apple tree branch could be reached, the *secretive* space under the overhanging hedge that makes for a perfect lookout spot. Imaginative play responds to the plenum and allows the child to perceive and realize some of its dimensions that are hidden from most adults.

But the plenum can also become the "unperson," that is, the alien and threatening face of space that intimidates and frightens the child. Many preschoolers fear the secretive, hidden spaces in their bedrooms. Our son was afraid that there were witches in his closet at night, and every evening we had to make sure that the closet door was securely fastened. Other children I know were afraid of monsters hiding behind the curtains or of wolves living under the bed, and I have heard of a parent who gave her daughter a squirt gun that had magical powers to ward off the mysterious unpersons that threatened her in the night. It seemed to have worked, but needless to say, some mornings her carpet was very wet!

Parents notice that preschoolers are now plagued with new fears: they resist going to bed at night, wake up with nightmares, worry whether they will wake up in the morning, and wonder where people or pets go

when they die. Thinking awakens in the child, and the sensorimotor relationship with spaces is overshadowed by the more symbolic relationship of mythical, animistic thinking. The child's emerging sense of separateness and perspective lets the plenum appear in all its formidable
otherness. While the animal has no fear of the dark, the child responds
to the emptiness and darkness of spaces: "here we experience the dialogue with nothingness; we are sucked into the spell of emptiness, and
we experience the loss of a sense of self" (Langeveld 1983b, 16). Fear of
the dark, fear of death, fear of sleep, fear of self-annihilation are all connected to the great dread of nothingness.[8] The barely achieved continuity of the spatiotemporal world, which is the central achievement of
the new self's unified perspective, is interrupted by the dark, threatened
by sleep, and extinguished by death. It is not surprising that bedtime is
often such a traumatic time for young children.

NIGHT SPACE

Lying in her bed at night, her little sister innocently sleeping in the bed
across the room, four-year-old Annie Dillard was visited by a luminous,
oblong, roaring monster that slid into the room, crept across the wall,
searched for her, but gave up right as it reached her wall: "After its fleet,
searching passage, things looked the same, but weren't. I dared not blink
or breathe; I tried to hush my whooping blood. If it found another
awareness, it would destroy it" (1987, 21).

The uncanniness of the spatial plenum becomes most apparent in
children's fear of the dark. Children are afraid to be in the dark because
at night the existential spatial continuum, which, as we saw, is the matrix for the continuum of the self, becomes alien and fragmented. The
journey from the womb has altered the meaning of darkness and the developmental entwining of senses and world is irrevocable: darkness now
threatens the fragile coherence of the child's sense of self; its intimacy
permeates, overwhelms, and negates the senses; and it threatens the developing being with regression to a more amorphous state of being. In
the dark bedroom the visible web of spatial connection between things
is dissolved and their distances from each other and from the child become vague. Moreover, the "I can do" body, tucked in under sheets and
blankets, relinquishes its upright posture and gives up its centering perspective. Sound becomes more intense because the dominance of the
eye does not overpower the other senses anymore. Consciousness be-

comes kaleidoscopic once again: "When, for example, the world of clear and articulate objects is abolished, our perceptual being, cut off from its world, evolves a spatiality without things. This is what happens in the night. Night is not an object before me; it enwraps me and infiltrates through all my senses, stifling my recollections and almost destroying my personal identity, I am no longer withdrawn into my perceptual outlook from which I watch the outlines of objects moving at a distance" (Merleau-Ponty 1962, 283).[9] In dark space the I loses its perspective and boundary and becomes merged and confused with the darkness. The unknown, the "unperson" faces us. "Night has no outlines; it is itself in contact with me and its unity is the mystical unity of *mana*." Dark space has power.

In its positive aspect, the obscurity of night opens up the mystery of being around us: it has *depth*. Dark space allows individual sounds and shadows to appear with full impact because the "besides" of light space—that is, the web of visible distances between things—dissolves and cannot be experienced anymore. Annie saw the movement and heard the roar of the oblong slicing into her bedroom, but she did not connect it with the headlights of cars that had stopped at a stop sign outside her window. She had a great moment of enlightenment one afternoon when she finally understood that the inside world of her room was connected to the outside world on the street, and that they were part of the same world. For a while, in the dark, she even amused herself by entering the "fiction" of the monster on the wall, and then replacing it with the chain of reasoning that restored the connective tissue of light space: "It's coming after me; it's a car outside. It's after me. It's a car" (Dillard 1987, 23).

The night space is mine, but it is not subjective or "inward," since we experience what occurs in it as "out there." "Nor will this space be a social space" (Minkowski 1970, 430), and I am alone within it: I do not know if others share it with me because I cannot see if they attend to the same things. It is through light that we achieve a social, shared world, and in the dark we find our solitude. Annie's sleeping sister is no help when the monster appears, and neither are her parents, whom she did not tell about her fear. "This was a private matter between me and it. If I spoke of it, it would kill me" (Dillard 1987, 20). As children we often have the sense that whatever addresses us in the night is meant only for us and demands from us that we deal with it alone and with all the reserves of our own courage and power. Rilke speaks of this in the *Third Duino Elegy* (1999, 93):

> his destiny, tall in its cloak, stepped back
> behind the cupboard, and his unquiet future, easily shifting,
> fitted itself into the folds of the curtain.

The dark figure behind the curtain or the oblong being sliding along the wall are mine, because *they are looking for me*. In them the world addresses *my particular being*, the plenum demands my attention and is so close that it could shatter me. But I do not shatter, and that, perhaps, is also part of my new sense of destiny and power. Alone, I can stand up to the night, and to its mystery I can add my own.

CLEARINGS OF FREEDOM

In his analysis of childhood spatial experience, the Dutch phenomenologist and pedagogue Martinus Langeveld distinguishes between *determined* and *undetermined* places in a child's spatial range. For the greater part of their days, children find themselves in spaces that have been designed and determined by adults. The family home, the street and the sidewalk, the school building, the baseball field: all have been preplanned for specific activities. As action spaces, they proscribe to the child what to do and how to behave within their confines. Undetermined places, on the other hand, are "open places" or "white spaces" that are not prestructured by adults (1960, 73) and in which children can freely choose their activity. I have interviewed over one hundred adults about their undetermined childhood places, and they are almost always spaces that were neglected and unwanted by adults. One child claimed the crawl space under the eaves, where he documented his childhood through doodles and paintings on the walls; another claimed a gully, which became "horse canyon" in the middle of a Pittsburgh ghetto; many had play forts in the woods behind the house, others claimed the top of a tree, and some had elaborate, furnished hiding places under hedges or became stewards of the wildlife along forgotten creek beds. City children often took over the unwanted spaces in their homes, and their secret places were under beds, in closets, or up in dusty, unused attics. Goodenough (2003a, 2003b) collected descriptions of childhood secret spaces from contemporary writers and found very similar features: children's book author Gerald McDermott claimed a secret staircase in the medieval section of the Detroit Institute of Art, which he roamed every Saturday; Joyce Carol Oates spied on the new baby through the planks in the barn floor; another child sketched stars and planets in the back of an abandoned bus among the factory ruins of a

Mexican town; and a boy who later became a noted landscape historian pressed a sweet fern leaf between the pages of his junior high math book so that its smell could transport him back to the favorite, sweet-smelling bank where the fern came from. What characterizes all these undetermined places is that they are *clearings of freedom*, where the undetermined nature of childhood can live itself out.

Throughout childhood the quality and the significance of the secret place evolves. The three-year-old does not yet claim a special place, but the four- and five-year-old will hide under the table and behind the furniture: it is a secret place but close to the adult world, and the child still tends to look outward and talk to others in the room. But at eight children begin to claim a place of their own, away from adult eyes, and create their own worlds: "Here one has escaped out of the world of grown-ups in which one is only 'just' a child. Here one is free from this world, and now one can create totally useless and wonderful and fascinating things out of odds, ends, and pieces" (Langeveld 1983a, 186). Between eight and twelve, children retreat to their secret place in order *to be by themselves*. When they reach adolescence, children have no need for the secret place anymore, are almost embarrassed by it, and give it up for the more personal, private bedroom, where they listen to music under the headphones, daydream, read, or write in their journals.

THE PUZZLE OF JUNG'S STONE

When Carl Jung was about nine years old he claimed a particular place as his own. A large stone jutted out of a slope, and he would go there and sit alone and engage in the following imaginary game:

> "I am sitting on top of this stone and it is underneath." But the stone could also say "I" and think: "I am lying here on this slope and he is sitting on top of me." The question then arose: "Am I the one who is sitting on the stone, or am I the stone on which *he* is sitting?" This question always perplexed me, and I would stand up, wondering who was what now. The answer remained totally unclear, and my uncertainty was accompanied by a feeling of curious and fascinating darkness. But there was no doubt whatsoever that this stone stood in some secret relationship to me. I could sit on it for hours, fascinated by the puzzle it set me. (Jung 1961, 20)

It is perhaps not surprising that even as a child Jung was particularly attuned to the dark, concealed dimension of human experience. His feeling of "curious and fascinating darkness" refers to Minkowski's discovery of dark space, which is not restricted to the absence of daylight but is a primary dimension of all spatial experiences. We see the boy struggle with the closeness and demand of a being other than human, and the diminution of lived distance. The stone addresses him, its presence can be felt under his body, its stony intentionality rises into the child's language and thinking. Intentionally Carl submits himself to the demand of and invasion by the stone, opens his consciousness repeatedly to the stone's being. He *plays* with the darkness, is lured by its secret promise, but also senses its uncanny quality. In the stone, the unperson of the plenum once again addresses the child's feeling life. But now, for the nine-year-old, it comes into awareness and speaks, and it raises puzzling questions: Who am I? Who is the stone? Where is the boundary between us?

A brief topoanalysis of the place of Carl's reverie reveals its particular psychological nature. The stone is ancient and immovable and has been embedded in the slope for eons. Through it the earth's bones poke through the soft ground, revealing and concealing a depth that goes on far below in the dark underground. It has patience and permanence and dwells in unchanging persistence in the swirling stream of changing seasons. Its strength and hardness support the body, stand under it solidly, but it also is an individual being and unlike any other stone. Its surface is warmed by the sun and inhabited by smaller creatures. The stone is the matrix for timelessness and time, visibility and invisibility, depth and surface, solitude and relatedness. The boy's contemplation allows him to step into this matrix and he is moved by it in feeling and thought.

Apart from the psychological dimension of this particular place, Jung's rock reveals the structural features that many of childhood's secret places have in common. It is unclaimed by adults and therefore *undetermined* in Langeveld's sense. *Full of secrets*, it promises that the child can discover unknown things there. Something impersonal and mysterious inhabits its confines, the "unperson" waits behind the appearances. Even though it is still in *proximity to the familiar adult world* and the child *feels safe* there, he claims the place in *solitude* and *peace, freed from the intrusions and demands of everyday life. Time in the secret place does not flow forward* with the march of measured clock time but shrinks and expands and curls up on itself in surprising ways. The child's attention is not caught up in things but is dreamlike and unfocused, and we witness the *silence of the child's being as it is by itself* (Langeveld 1983a, 1983b). "The secret place is, then, a home where one finds oneself at home, a place where one is with oneself. Its intimate character is determined, in the first place, by the fact that one finds oneself in the unexpected presence of one's own self without having tried to make oneself a project of study. Here, one has every opportunity by doing or dreaming to realize, to make real, a world of one's own" (Langeveld 1983b, 183–84).

The developmental function of the secret place is as a clearing where the child in free activity can create the world. But world creation here is not an activity that necessarily alters the world and leaves visible traces. By making a world, even if only in fantasy, the *I* finds itself reflected through its creations and *recognizes itself without taking itself as a theme of reflection.* The adolescent gives up the secret place because at this age the self does become a more direct theme for conscious contemplation.

SOMETHING OF DEATH IN THE SOUL

A childhood that takes place in a completely adult-determined spatiality is "personally malnourished" (Langeveld 1960, 73) because it denies children the opportunity to discover and express themselves through their own free and creative initiative. Children need open, undetermined places to truly have a childhood:

> Especially if you consider that in these "open places" children have the opportunity to express *themselves* or to be by themselves without a preordained task, it becomes clear that in those situations the child will appear especially forcefully *as child.* The undeterminedness of a place allows children the initiative to form the undetermined according to their own will. Being untouched by everyday usefulness and familiarity, the undetermined is full of secrets. It lures us—but it is not dominated by known determinants. There the soul is still free. (73–74)[10]

If children are deprived of the undetermined places that allow them to take up the world as their own free project, if we take away the places and activities where they can appear as a child, we produce adults who are incomplete: "for he who became an adult without having been solidly and calmly a child has already something of death in his soul, even before he could enter the full unfolding of human life. He is cool and distant toward the world around him, weak in his affects, inwardly without understanding for children and always ready to push them away or even overpower them" (Langeveld 1960, 71).

Implicit in Langeveld's argument is also a warning to contemporary adults. By more and more restricting the undetermined places where our children play—because we think that time can be better spent doing homework or in other adult-organized activities—we are limiting the child's ability and initiative to create a future world that has depth, fullness, and compassion. Children who are allowed to claim their secret, open places have the opportunity to develop empathy, imagination, creativity, and a true interest in the natural and the human world.

THREE

About Hens, Hands, and Old-Fashioned Telephones

Gestural Bodies and Participatory Consciousness

THE HISTORY OF BODY AND SPACE

In medieval illuminated manuscripts and pre-Renaissance paintings we find many depictions of the human body that strike the modern reader as odd. We come across the infant Jesus sitting or standing on his mother's lap: sometimes he is larger in size than the shepherds or other adults who are visiting.

At other times we find biblical characters in the midst of an activity—such as giving a present to the infant Jesus or presenting a sacrifice in the temple—but the length of their arms, legs, and torsos seems to contradict our expectations of anatomical correctness: the arms are too short, the legs are too long, and the whole formation of the bodies disturbs our modern sensibilities. We feel inclined to think that medieval artists did not know how to draw. But can it be true that the people who built Chartres—and carved statues that were placed thirty or even a hundred feet above the viewer and still looked lifelike and completely appropriate—did not know how to draw a human figure? Rather than dismiss the medieval representation of the human body as inadequate, I would like to take it on its own terms—and by way of this detour also arrive at a new appreciation of children's drawings. The depiction of the human body and its surrounding space in artists' as well as children's artwork reflects the ways human beings understand and conceptualize their experiences of embodiment and spatiality. Culturally and personally, a change in the representation of body and space also announces a change in how embodiment and spatiality are experienced and understood (Romanyshyn 1989).

This chapter will show that adults have not always and everywhere conceptualized embodiment and spatial experience in the same way contemporary Western adults do. Anatomical bodies and geometrical spaces as objective, measurable, and conceptual entities are inventions of the Western mind and have a rather brief history. They also contradict children's experiences and conceptions of body and space. The lived body along with the lived dimensions of space, time, and coexistence are no longer obvious to the thinking adult mind, but they come to expression in children's symbolic representations. The lived dimensions of existence have to be unearthed through a careful investigation into states of consciousness and forms of existence that are different from our own.

MAPS AND TELEPHONES

If you ask contemporary adults to draw a map of their house they usually assume that they see their house from a bird's-eye view and take great pains to construct the rooms in the correct measured proportions. Children, on the other hand, when asked to draw a map of their house, often begin with their own room, followed by everybody else's space. The size of the room is not geometrical; size is determined by the meaning this space has for the child. The following illustrations are children's drawings collected by myself and my students in the context of classroom assignments.

Children's bedrooms are often larger than other rooms, or a particular object dominates the scene and its size is out of proportion to the other things in the house. Scott, for example, incorporates a huge red telephone into his map (fig. 1), and Tela (eight) made sure that the basement full of boxes was in the picture.

Children's representations of their homes always have furniture in them, for the furniture stands for the activities that happen in these lived spaces. Sometimes the rooms seem laid out on the page as if seen from above, but the furniture is depicted in frontal view. The different rooms exist not as measured extensions but as meaningful spaces for human activity. Children feel perfectly free to ignore and even distort the geometrical extension of a space in order to represent the meaning that the space has for them: we can almost hear Scott say, "My own bedroom is

Figure 1. Scott (six years old): "A map of my house with the old-fashioned phone." Courtesy of the Simms collection.

the biggest, because it needs to be big enough to hold all my favorite things (and myself, too)."

Children share the preference for the depiction of the meaning of a space with medieval artists. Compared to the significance of one's bed or the telephone or the guinea pig's cage—or the birth of Jesus or the heavenly city of Jerusalem—how important is it to measure and draw a room or a landscape geometrically correctly? Medieval artists, like our children, looked at the world and saw not pure extension but a web of significances, symbols, and references to other lives.

When our son, Nicholas, was five years old, he drew a nativity scene that shows the traditional stable with Mary, Joseph, the Christ child in the manger, and the angel floating above. The most impressive figures in this picture, however, are not the angel or the infant Jesus but the huge shepherds with their crooks flanking the holy family. Their size is out of proportion to the rest of the figures. Why does the child draw large shepherds? For the five-year-old boy the most significant people in this Christmas scene are the shepherds: they are the ones who get to carry the big sticks!

LINEAR PERSPECTIVE AND THE MIGRATION OF ANGELS

In the previous chapter we investigated children's experiences of lived space, and I would like to add a short historical digression into the genesis of our modern concepts of space and light that will underscore the difference between children and adults. Scott, Tela, and Nick draw their spaces independent of geometrical spatial requirements. Space is organized around what has significance to them. It is shot through with psychological depth. Medieval spaces as well are organized in terms of depth: what comes to representation is not a literal picture of the physical world but a spatiality resonating with hidden meaning. Often the depictions, like the children's drawings, are very subtle and deceptively simple.

A very interesting phenomenon in the history of art is the Renaissance change in the representation of light. During the medieval period, illuminated manuscripts were inhabited by painted figures that *shone in their own light*. "The world is represented as if its beings all contained their own source of light. Light is immanent in this world of medieval things, and they reach the eye of the beholder as sources of their own luminosity" (Illich 1996, 19). Light, *lumen*, emanates from beings and expresses their spiritual nature. We still find this understanding of light in modern icon painting. The Renaissance functionalized light and invented the exterior light source: light began to be used to show the visible planes of things, and shadows showed their spatial depth. While the medieval artist revealed the *Eigenlicht*, the essential light, of a being, the Renaissance artist used a *Zeigelicht*, a pointing light, and showed us the three-dimensional surfaces of opaque objects (Illich 1996).

Beings become surfaces when the eye and its perspective dominate human experience. The world becomes an assemblage of things to be measured, mapped, and painted from a distance. Painting a being's essential light required intuition. Painting a being's surface appearance requires exact observation and analysis of the visible space and an awareness of the painter's own perspective.

The use of light and shadow in Western art is accompanied by a shift in the understanding of spatial reality. Medieval space, according to Panofsky (1991), was discontinuous: it "clung" to things and each being inhabited its own separate, qualitative space. Like the Eigenlicht, it was an intuitive space. With the advent of the Renaissance things acquired a shared and abstract space that could be measured in numbers and was the same for all beings. Cartography, beginning with the *porotlan charts* of the thirteenth century and developing into the exact maps of the fifteenth century, pioneered this new geometrical view of the world. In AD 1400 Ptolemy's *Geographia* (AD second century), and its cartographic system were brought to Florence, and in the following years more and more detailed maps were produced, which made the long sea voyages and the discovery of America in the fifteenth century possible. Mapping required the application of a uniform measuring grid upon the seen world. The mapmaker had to assume a disembodied "bird's-eye" perspective in order to produce a chart. The uniform measuring grid and the bird's-eye perspective of the viewer are two essential techniques that mapmaking shared with the other revolutionary Florentine invention of the fifteenth century: linear perspective drawing.

Linear perspective drawing was conceived by the architect Filippo Brunelleschi and a group of friends in 1425 and then articulated as a technique in Alberti's book *De Pictura*. The technique of constructing an exact replica of three-dimensional space on a two-dimensional plane with the help of a geometrical grid changed the history of painting. It also solidified a profound alteration in the outlook of the Renaissance adult's experience of the world (Edgerton 1976; Panofsky 1991; Romanyshyn 1989). Space became a quantitative extension and things were seen as physical and material objects. Angels have no room on a map: "there be dragons" *only* at the edges of Renaissance maps, where the grid stops. Their kind of light and Eigenlicht, and their particular nonliteral space, cannot be represented in the uniform, homogenous, and geometrical visual space the Renaissance strove for.[1]

Before Alberti's invention, space, as we know it, did not exist in medieval pictures. Space was conceived not in terms of measurable distances but as a meaningful arrangement for human action. Its key feature was not the distance between people and objects but the nearness and farness of living beings. Spatial arrangements depicted the quality and depth of lived relationships. With the advent of the Renaissance, space became an objective, quantifiable entity that was measured by a distant, objective observer. The new construction of spatial dimensions clashed for a while with the old medieval symbolic universe, where size was not a mathematical dimension but an indicator of importance, until linear perspective construction won the day. With the increasing conceptualization of space as a purely geometrical extension, the lived, pathic space that the medieval artists represented in their pictures withdraws from adult consciousness and representation. In the wake of this change, beings that easily had inhabited symbolic spaces gradually left the stage. Angels and saints and virgins with their halos and hovering bodies became an anachronism in homogenous, purely extensive space. Their cousins, however, are still surviving in the drawings of twenty-first-century children.

SHORT ARMS, LARGE FEET, NO HANDS:
BEYOND ANATOMY

Medieval art and children's drawings represent not only space in an intuitive, meaningful way but bodies as well: they are depicted for their gestural meaning rather than anatomical correctness. The biblical scenes carved in the door of a tenth-century church in Hildesheim, Germany, for example, show Joseph making an offering in the temple with his arms definitely too short. The same short arms appear in the relief of the three kings bringing gifts while they are pointing at Herod's city or clutching their cloaks tightly. The short arms tell us stories of failure: Joseph feels small and unable to reach toward God with his offering, and the gift of the three kings is tainted by Herod's rage against the "newborn king." The very shortness of the arms expresses the intensity of the characters' gestures and focuses attention on what the body means in this particular situation. Medieval artists spoke through the gestural language of the body, and their bodies were not objects separated from the scene in which they appeared. The symbolic space of medieval art was inhabited by symbolic bodies, or, to use a term coined by Merleau-Ponty (1964b), by "gestural bodies." The body as an anatomical object did not exist before the Renaissance, and to apply this concept to medieval representations leads to a false evaluation and dismissal of the artists' skills. In the greater scheme of things, anatomy was simply unimportant (Romanyshyn 1989).

In children's drawings we find the same disregard of anatomy or the laws of reality as it is described by physics. I saw a picture a nine-year-old girl drew of her "blended" family: Dad and his girlfriend with herself in the middle on one half of the page, and the same configuration with Mom and her new husband on the other. All characters were drawn in detail, clothes and all. The striking element, however, was that the little girl in the pictures was the only character with no hands at all. She seemed to cope, but actually she could not quite "handle" or "grasp" this new life. I have seen many drawings of young children where hands become larger than heads as soon as the depicted person tries to catch a ball. Hands and feet appear and disappear, and their size changes in relation to the meaningful action the character is engaged in.

With this comparison between medieval art and children's drawings I do not want to claim that medieval art is childlike and unsophisticated. Quite the opposite! I think that children's drawings can be understood more clearly when we look at representations of space and body by people who do not share the materialistic assumptions about the nature of space and body that have developed in the West since the Renaissance. The definition of the human body as anatomical and the insistence on anatomically correct representation is part of our contemporary habitual attitude—it is one of our unreflected assumptions and blind spots about the nature of reality. We seem to have trouble getting beyond the literalness of the body and dismiss as primitive and undeveloped the symbolic, gestural bodies drawn by children or medieval artists. The historical reflection on medieval art, however, shows us that there are other ways of conceptualizing reality: bodies are more than a mass of bones and tissue. The detour via medieval art allows us to approach children's art with renewed respect. Like the medieval artist, the child works beyond the boundaries of anatomical bodies and geometrical spaces. If we set aside the assumption that all bodies are anatomical and allow them to appear in their "gestural" or symbolic dimension, children's art becomes a medium for understanding a child's experience of the world.

THE NATURE OF TOOLS: THE HAND
AND THE WATERING CAN ARE ONE

During a class exercise for one of my developmental psychology classes, five-year-old Anna was asked to draw a picture of her family, and she used colorful markers to draw her mother and sister watering the flowers in their garden (fig. 2).

Figure 2. Anna (five years old): "My mother and my sister watering the flowers." Courtesy of the Simms collection.

First she establishes the space of the picture and delineates up and down, earth and sky. Then she introduces the figures of her mother and her sister. The two protagonists are obviously engaged in a happy event, for they are both smiling widely. There are two striking features about Anna's depiction of the human body: when we examine the mother, who is carrying the watering can, we cannot tell if we see her hand or the watering can; and the characters seem to float above the flowers.

As she draws her mother, Anna very carefully adds the blue of water in the shape of a container with a spout to the lower part of the mother's dress. The spout, however, could also be the mother's arm, and where the blue trickle of water ought to be we find orange lines in the same color as the hand on the other arm. These orange "fingers," however, point downward and extend the gesture of the blue water that will fall onto the thirsty flowers. Anna depicts the hand and the watering can as one. The tool and the hand merge in the act of pouring: the streaming of water becomes the streaming of fingers, the arm the extension of the spout. How is this possible? How does a child think when she does not distinguish the anatomy of an arm from the physical structure of a tool?

The bodies in Anna's drawing, like the bodies in the medieval pictures discussed earlier, are not drawn as literal copies of a physical reality. When Anna looks at the hand she does not see bones covered by skin but an active gesture that finds expression through the hand. When she imitates, in her drawing, what she has witnessed the day or the week before, she imitates not the literal details of the event but its global impact. The depicted body is not static, it is an "I can" body, an action body that appropriates the world in a particular way. Anna shows how this appropriation, the watering of flowers, is harmonious when the gesture of the hand and the gesture of the watering can correspond to each other. For the watering can as well is not merely an inanimate object, it is a thing that shapes the human hand in its own unique way. It holds the water and serves as its container, which the hand alone could not do, and only *through it* the joyous act of pouring out and nourishing becomes possible.

The pictorial space Anna marked for us delineates a reality where things and bodies exist as action bodies and action things, that is, as bodies and things interacting with each other in meaningful ways. The hand and the watering can are one when they share in the gesture of pouring. Only a mind unused to reading the *significance* of gestures could dismiss her depiction as "unrealistic." Quite the opposite: the reality she depicts is the *psychological* reality she—and we adults as well—experience all the time. We ought to admire Anna for the great economy with which she shows the amazing congruence of human gesture and thing gesture in the use of tools.

Five-year-old Anna does not yet accept the hand as a purely anatomical appendage completely separated from the inanimate objects out there. For her *the world of things is a world of gestures* that extend an invitation to the human body. She responds to and represents the physiognomy of human bodies as well as the physiognomy of things. The hand and the watering can are one: "The truth is that there are no things, only physiognomies," as Merleau-Ponty said (1963/1983, 168).[2] The world of physiognomies is a world of forces and actions rather than objects and concepts. To see the gesture, you have to see through the anatomical body and the self-enclosed object it interacts with. The hand belongs neither to the mother's body nor to the watering can—it exemplifies the gestural in-between space, the chiasm between body and world. Inside/outside, self/other, subject/object are distinctions that do not yet figure prominently in the world of the five-year-old, and so have no place in her drawing.

TIPTOE THROUGH THE TULIPS

The second striking feature of Anna's figures is the way they move across the page. At first glance they seem to be hovering in the air above the flowers, arms slightly outstretched. Their feet, especially those of the little sister, are triangular and pointing downward. From what we have learned before, we look at the gesture of these bodies and understand: care of flowers is a delicate process, and feet must tread daintily so that they do not crush the fragile blossoms. Mother and daughter happily "tiptoe through the tulips," floating like angels above the fragile, mortal things. As with the watering can, Anna perfectly caught the mood of care in the way she depicted the small, careful gesture of the toes.

This is not to say that she set out to draw pointy toes or hands and watering cans that are one. The details of the drawing are not planned as discrete elements; they arise out of Anna's attempt to represent a global experience, a mood, rather than a discrete and literal historical event. Mother and sister do not literally float above the garden, but in the child's experience and its pictorial representation they do. The child's drawing is not a copy of a visual reality but an *expressive* act, which attempts to catch the visual as well as the affective experience of an event (Merleau-Ponty 1994).

Merleau-Ponty notes that what we as adults would call unrealistic in the child's representation of bodies and things is actually an attempt to "bring the whole existing reality into representation" (1994, 215)—that is, to represent a thing from more than one perspective. The adult's mode of synthesizing experience, on the other hand, "must be interpreted as an abstraction, which ignores anything that we encounter in the world but which we do not see from a single perspective. . . . But while the adult sacrifices everything to visual appearance, the child sacrifices it in order to bring the object in its totality to expression" (my translation). Anna attempts to catch the sheltered, happy, caring, careful feeling of her family and put it on paper. In the world of meaning and expression the boundaries between bodies and things and the laws of gravity are suspended. She looks not with the anatomical, distant, measuring eye, but with eyes that penetrate beyond the surface and see things in their totality and from multiple perspectives. Cézanne said that a picture contains within itself even the smell of its landscape (Merleau-Ponty 1962), and if we pay attention, perhaps we can perceive the perfume of Anna's flowers.

Anna's tiptoeing bodies and the hand/watering can represent the world as it communicates with her directly and without the filter of reflection and conceptual thought. Erwin Straus (1966/1980) calls this immediate communication we have with things on the basis of their changing mode of sensory givenness the *pathic* moment of perception. The pathic refers to the "immediately present, sensually vivid, still preconceptual communication we have with appearances" (12) and is opposed to the *gnostic* aspect of perception, which filters what we encounter through our thought processes. "The gnostic develops the *what* of the given in its object character, the pathic the *how* of its being as given." The pathic is a "being touched" by a thing; the gnostic is a "touching" of it. The distinction between the pathic and the gnostic is a helpful tool when discussing the child's experience of the world. Buytendijk (1933) even goes so far as to say that the predominance of the pathic relationship with things is a character of the young not merely in the human but also in other animal species. In the young, because they lack a conceptual framework for experience and knowledge, the call and appeal of things is immediate and direct. The child's organism has an immediate connection and a preverbal communication with appearances. Things call to the body. While, for example, a balloon on a string makes us reach with one hand, a ball issues an invitation to *both* hands to rise in the gesture of catching. It begs to be rolled, its unpredictable bouncing and moving about excites the body to follow and anticipate its moves. The ball plays with us, as Buytendijk shows, because our pathic moment of perception communicates with the exciting thing-structure of the round object and follows it about. Later on we might invent rules for a ball game, or we study the trajectory of billiard balls in order to become better players, and so we elaborate the primary presence of the ball, its "how," by thinking about it and turning it into the *gnostic* "what." But the pathic connection with the ball is primary.

Anna's picture illustrates Merleau-Ponty's (1994) and Buytendijk's (1933) insight that the child encounters bodies and things not as epistemological, gnostic objects but as pathic, *affective* presences, and that the affective encounter is primarily represented in children's drawings. Anna represents not the concept but the ineffable experience of a moment in the garden. The watering can is a qualitative, emotional event.

It "gathers a world" that is fundamentally unspeakable but can be captured in pictures. Like any symbol, it contains a surplus of meaning that goes beyond representation and evokes the plural and complex experience of a particular world (Ricoeur 1985). Tied into the global, feeling aspect of perception, it defies conceptual rationality and can never completely be interpreted. We get a sense of Anna's participation in the joy of her family in the garden, but most of the world of her relationship with mother and sister remains hidden as the unspoken background to the figures on the page. The picture remains a trace of a little girl's experience, a historical artifact of her feeling on one sunny summer day. But it is also a palimpsest, a record of layers of experience that sediment her past life with her family into this one particular drawing.

"MOM, I'M GONNA MAKE YOU DIZZY"

The discussion of Anna's picture has revealed the pathic relationship between a child's experience of her world and how she brings it to representation in gesture and drawing. Even though pathic relationships characterize adult life as well (Lippitz 1997; van Manen 1999), they are particularly characteristic of the young child's interaction with the world. The child's consciousness, as Merleau-Ponty (1994) puts it, has a "different equilibrium"—that is, it interacts with the world in a more immediate and less distanced way—than adult consciousness.

In a central passage from the *Phenomenology of Perception* (1962) Merleau-Ponty places the early forms of human consciousness into a broad existential and philosophical context. The nondualistic, non-Cartesian rationality of infancy and early childhood "remains as an indispensable acquisition underlying that of maturity, if there is for the adult one single intersubjective world" (355). The experience of living in a world that is not distinct and distant from oneself, where the infant "is the world," as Piaget (1929/1951, 152) puts it, provides the possibility for the experience of a shared human reality and allows for the fundamental conviction that we adult human beings can bridge the gap of our personal and cultural differences and share a meal, a poem, or a landscape in mutual understanding. Following Merleau-Ponty, we can uncover the participatory, pathic structures of children's consciousness and show their importance for adult life.[3]

Young children often surprise adults when, with one brief phrase or gesture, they shatter our habitual assumption that they experience the world as we adults do. The boundaries between self and world, which we take for granted, are not drawn in the same way for our children. Let us examine the following little vignette (Simms 1999):

> Three-year-old Lea twirls around the kitchen, saying to her mother: "Mom, I'm gonna make you dizzy."

What kind of a mind does the three-year-old have that she can assume that her twirling and her mother's dizziness are intimately related? What is the nature of her consciousness so that she assumes that she immediately impacts another? How is the three-year-old making her mother dizzy?

Piaget has given us a conceptual framework and a terminology for the preschooler's style of consciousness. In his descriptions and examples in *The Child's Conception of the World* (1929/1951), he offers us a glimpse into the world-constitution of the young child prior to the formation of a distinct self. *Participatory* or *magical realism* is Piaget's term for Lea's relationship to the world that shines through her thinking and expressions. Participation and magic in children have their origin (1) in "realism," that is, "a confusion between thoughts and things, or between self and the external world" (150); and (2) in "ideas evoked in the child's mind by his relations with persons surrounding him" that then are translated into the physical world (151). Children's cognition, then, is not merely an a-logical thinking, it arises from a different experience of the world: the world for the child is not an external, objective, conceptual, hard "reality," it is suffused by the child's intentions and the feeling-tone of his or her social relationships. Young children have no interiority, and the world has no exteriority.

Let us take up Lea's example. She twirls around the kitchen, believing that her action can make her mother dizzy. She assumes that there is an immediate connection between her action and her mother's experience, that her experience of dizziness is also her mother's. Self and other are distinct people for the three-year-old—for she names herself ("I") and her mother ("Mom")—but they participate in the same experience. Lea has no self-reflection, and the other, too, has no separate interiority for her. Lea lives her life completely turned toward the world and tuned into what she senses there. People exist for her as they conduct themselves in situations, as participating actors in the unfolding drama of the world. If a stranger had been in the kitchen, I am convinced Lea would not have played the same game, for the other's strangeness would have permeated the space of the otherwise familiar room and turned it into a place with a more or less threatening feeling-tone: a space suffused and crowded by an alien presence; not a place where one could twirl with abandon!

Merleau-Ponty appropriates the term *syncretism* from the child psychologist Henri Wallon (1954) to conceptualize the young child's relation to the world: "Syncretism here is the indistinction between me and the other, a confusion at the core of a situation that is common to us both" (Merleau-Ponty 1964b, 120). Piaget's notion of *egocentrism* approximates Wallon's term but misses its key element: young children are not centered on themselves and do not introject objects and people into their perspective; they are completely focused on the events of a shared situation. There is no self, there is only participation in a situation. For Lea there is only twirling, and as she twirls, her mother participates, too. Self and other meet in a shared action.[4]

Early and middle childhood bring the gradual emergence of the child out of the syncretic, egocentric state, marked by an increasing awareness of self and other and their distinction. But as Wallon, Merleau-Ponty, and others have seen, it is never completely surmounted and remains the foundation of adult relationships and thinking. The implications of this are far-reaching. If syncretism is the foundation of children's consciousness, then *the situations children encounter are the very stuff their psyche is made of.* If children live in the actions of others, these others had better act as if they were a part of the child's psyche. The people, the places, the things, the rhythms Lea encounters shape her personality—are, moreover, an extension of who she is and will become. The environment, then, is not incidental but an essential aspect of child rearing and pedagogy. And so are the adults the child encounters.

In order to understand a syncretic or participatory consciousness, a different approach to the study of children becomes necessary: if the child is an unreflective, radical being-in-the-world, this *being in the world* becomes the focus of research inquiry. It is no longer enough to assess children's IQs or have them answer questionnaires in order to examine them as isolated, cognitive entities. We have to find methods that approach their lived world systematically. The shift from an epistemology ("I think") to an ontology ("I am in the world") of the child requires a shift in method. From the question "Can children at this age process that kind of information?" we move toward an understanding of how children experience the world and how this world influences their development. Borrowing from Martin Heidegger (1962) and Medard Boss (1979), we can develop methods that systematically investigate some of the fundamental dimensions of the child's existence. Applying the existential structures of embodiment, coexistence, spatiality, and temporality as a heuristic framework, we can take up a situation like Lea's twirling in the kitchen and ask: How does she live her *body?* How is *space* lived? What are *things* for her? How is *time* structured in her life? How are *others* entwined with her experience of reality, and how does *language* permeate her childhood? Much of the data we need, although interpreted in a different light, can be found in the growing body of research in developmental psychology. However, a fresh reading is necessary. We have to attempt to see the child not as a patchwork of discrete abilities but as a being who bodily, socially, spatially, temporally, and linguistically constitutes a world.

TO TAME WILD THINKING

The recognition that children and medieval artists share certain attitudes toward the visible world can lead to a number of claims. The first one is that medieval art is childlike and primitive, and that the history of art is the history of the Western mind rising out of the ignorance and superstition of the "Dark Ages" to finally achieve and represent the true picture of a scientific worldview. The second, and frankly the viewpoint I prefer, is that there are similarities between children's experiences and those of premodern people that are deeply rooted in human existence and that point to a way of thinking and experiencing the world that is the underpinning of all human development, even the development of advanced scientific thinking.

The equation of *childlike* and *primitive* has a history that permeates anthropology and the other social sciences, child psychology among them. Johnson (1995) traces the roots of the child as primitive from Darwin through Hall and Piaget. Arising out of the embryologists' concept of the recapitulation of earlier developmental stages of phylogenetic history in each individual and in different cultures, the child and the "primitive" were seen as savage, not fully developed, and therefore as insufficient adults. "For white, Western anthropologists, recapitulation provided a comfortable myth of the progressive perfection of the species, with Caucasians at the apex of development. In this account the 'savage races' appeared perpetually stuck in a primitive and childlike state. They could not be expected to reach the heights of civilization of the Western, Caucasian world and so required the paternal guardianship of the mature races; the savage took on the status of the child" (43).

The child, in turn, was measured against Western adult achievements in scientific thinking and found wanting. In Piaget's genetic epistemology the epistemological subject toward which all child development strives is the rational, logical, objective thinker. The preoperational child's thought has value only insofar as it prepares the ground for the triumph of formal operations over participation and animism. As Johnson so aptly summarizes: "For Piaget, the young child is a primitive *scientist*, with an immature set of hypothesis about the nature of reality" (1995, 47).

Why is the equation of child and primitive so persuasive and pervasive? I suggest that there are two reasons. First, there *is* something to see in the semblance of children and aboriginal peoples, and second, their differences are covered over by the identification of Western adult rationality with formal operational, logical-scientific thinking.

The terms Piaget (1929/1951) uses to describe children's thinking, like *participation*, *magic*, and *animism*, are borrowed largely from anthropology, specifically Lévy-Bruhl's (1966) work on the nature of primitive thinking. Combined with Piaget's epistemological project of showing the genesis of operational thought, the child's primitive constitution of the world *and* aboriginal magical, participatory, and animistic practices appear to arise from unfinished and insufficient world conceptions and seem deficient when compared to Western adult rationality. The imperialism that has marked the relationship between Western and non-Western cultures, which defines anything alien as flawed, has its parallels in the imperialism of formal operations with which we measure and repress children's thinking.

There is, however, a different way to resolve the semblance and difference between children and primitive cultures, which brings us to the second argument. Instead of assuming that the child is just a "miniature adult," Merleau-Ponty (1964a) proposes that we take the child's consciousness as a positive phenomenon and explore it on its own terms. The structures of children's rationality have a different organization and content than those of adults, and children experience the relationship between self and world in a different way. Merleau-Ponty suggests that the semblance between child and primitive has its roots in the child's "social polymorphousness," that is, the plurality of possibilities of world-formations present in the child:

> The child and the primitive resemble each other simply because the child lets us see a particular background which is common to all humanity, and from here the many different cultural selections will depart and realize themselves. In the child one can find all possible forms pre-drawn or indicated. . . . Certain of these formations will be inhibited during development, while we find them stabilized in

the primitive. This means simply that there is a plurality of possibilities in each infant, primitive or civilized. Different cultures
inhibit or choose in different ways. (1994, 173–74; my translation)

The implications are far-reaching. If different cultures inhibit or
choose in different ways, so does ours. Varied formations of rationality
can be understood through their grounding in the child's thinking. Investigation of the child's existence allows us to understand the common
ground for all possible variations of adult thinking, be they primitive or
scientific. Merleau-Ponty thus gives primacy to childhood rationality
over the rationality of logic that Piaget advocates. The child's "wild
thinking" hence is not the inferior that has to be tamed, conquered, and
subjugated by the hierarchy of formal operations; rather, it contains its
own rationality, which will be differentiated into various adult cultural
formations (Meyer-Drawe 1986).

Much of the debate between Piaget and Merleau-Ponty centers
around the definition of rationality and the place of perception in the
constitution of reality. For Piaget, "the qualitative givens of perception
are gradually repressed through a rational reality which seems to contradict them, but which ultimately explains them. Thus the world
changes its architecture—a new reality elaborated by the intellect re-
presses finally the reality of perception" (as quoted in Meyer-Drawe
1986, 259; my translation). Against this understanding of development
as the intellectual repression of the child's perception and rationality,
Merleau-Ponty places a lived reorganization of the field of experience
that implies and contains the processes of perception as they constitute
rationality. Crises and regressions are part of the picture, and development is not merely optimistically oriented toward the increase of rationality. He argues that the achievements of abstract rationality are ambivalent: the acquisition of a univalent, adult perspective also means the
loss of a baroque and multivalent world (Meyer-Drawe 1986).

Rationality in its deeper sense is not equated with formal operational
thinking; it is the very process of structuring the world in a meaningful
way. The child's thoughtfulness in engaging and ordering the perceived
world cannot be dismissed as irrational. The care, for example, that the
young child in Piaget's interviews reveals when he thinks through and
makes sense out of questions like: "why does a boat float on water whilst
a little stone, which is lighter, sinks immediately?" (Piaget 1929/1951,
223) reveals that his mind is engaged in detailed observation and sense
making. Six-year-old Vern reflects for a moment, then says: "The boat
is more intelligent than the stone." Asked for his definition of the boat's

intelligence, he replies: "It doesn't do things it ought not to do." Vern's answer is not arbitrary; it follows a logic not encompassed by our modern definition of intelligence. For us, inanimate matter is not intelligent. Vern's answer, however, is not so very strange in the history of Western philosophy. As Piaget himself points out, there are Aristotelian parallels in the child's conceptions of nature and in the distinction of things that are compelled to physical activity by either necessity (nature as an obstacle of activity; the stone does not float by its own will) or by moral obligation (intelligence; the boat floats by its own desire, no one makes it so; if it sinks it is not a boat anymore). Another parallel between children's thinking and Greek philosophical conceptions runs as a subtext through *The Child's Conception of the World:* Piaget glosses frequently on the semblance or analogy between the thoughts expressed by children and pre-Socratic philosophers.

The child's "wild thinking" is "wild" only from a perspective that does not appreciate its rationality. It appears as perfectly ordinary when seen from a pre-Socratic, medieval, or "primitive" perspective. Alone among twentieth-century philosophers, Maurice Merleau-Ponty appreciated and tried to rehabilitate the rationality inherent in the child's conception of the world. Against the logocentric subject, Merleau-Ponty describes the child subject as multiperspectival; instead of skimming the world of things and presupposing the fixed identity of objects, the child's consciousness inhabits things and situations and is truly in the world; instead of repressing perception of the world, children's thinking arises out of the constant restructuring of their field of experience. "This rationality is of another type, which does not reveal itself when measured against the external patterns of reality of the object-world of an adult physicist" (Meyer-Drawe 1986, 270).

And do adults truly think like scientists? Does the understanding of world and self of adults in Western civilization necessarily follow a progressive, linear developmental history from childlike naive forms to "adult," rational world-concepts?

> Don't we as adults have to admit that, in our everyday lives, many
> successful actions and interpretations remain naive and childlike
> and do not orient themselves by the high rationality standards
> of thinking and acting which are applied in the science centered
> developmental psychologies of Piaget or Kohlberg? . . . The
> pre-rational, pre-symbolic and representational and more or less
> picture-like structures that dominate the development of children
> also play an irreplaceable and constitutive role in the adult, and not

only in the separate area of aesthetic experience but also in the experiences of science and in our everyday lives. (Lippitz 1997, 270)

Adult existence is broader than the confines of Descartes's *cogito*, more complex than what the limitations imposed by the natural scientific method can circumscribe. The strictures that the myth of scientific rationality has imposed on adult life become even more significant and dangerous when adults unquestioningly apply them to the education of their children.

It takes more than a decade of schooling to restructure children's participatory experiences of the world and replace them with the critical, uncompassionate, disembodied eye of the scientific observer. I am constantly surprised that in most of the mainstream psychological and pedagogical literature and praxis Piaget's description of the presymbolic and prerational structures of children's experiences are either ignored or dismissed. This is probably due to Piaget's own haste in getting to the "good stuff" of the structures of operational thinking, and psychologists and educators followed suit. But there is a telling anecdote: when Piaget was asked by American educators if it was possible to speed up the transition into the concrete operational stage, he responded: "But why would you want to do that?" His bafflement hearkens to a time when early childhood was associated with play and not with preschoolers preparing themselves for Harvard. Even Piaget wanted to give young children the time to develop their sensorimotor and preoperational abilities. Where do we have preschool programs that respond to and cultivate the intuitive, world-centered thinking of the young child? Do we even know what abilities of feeling, imagining, creating, and sensing we squash and stunt by the early introduction of literacy and logical structures into young children's lives?

In the following section I want to pick up the example of a young child's act of imitation and show the complexity of the process and the depth of transformative learning that can be accomplished by such a simple, free childhood activity. We have only to learn how to see it.

THE HEN IN THE BASKET AND THE ORIGIN OF ETHICS

The pathic link between a child's body and the things of her world becomes visible in an old photograph included in Buytendijk's (1933) book. We see a little girl (perhaps three years old) sitting on a footstool, delightedly gazing at a hay-filled basket that contains a hen. It is obvious that the basket is a nest, even though we can only assume that there are eggs hidden in the hay under the mother bird. The child is not touching the basket, but her feet are pulled back under the stool and her toes are slightly curled to gently place her weight on the floor. Her hands are brought together in her lap. The obvious delight she feels at seeing the cradling and protective gesture of the hen is mirrored in her own gesture: her large smile comes from a face that is pulled in, chin to chest, and that forms a nestlike semicircle with arms and lap. She is not reaching out to touch the bird, is not trying to pet it or use her hands to investigate what lies hidden in the hay. Rather, she holds herself back, lets her body imitate the nesting hen.

The astonishing capacity of children to imitate the gestures of adults is extended here into the nonhuman world. Imitation, as Merleau-Ponty (1994) has shown, is not point for point copying of what is literally there:

> The third element between the other and my self is the external world of things: the other's action as well as my own refer to it. This profound idea is fertile: at first we do not have a consciousness of our body, but a consciousness of things. There is a kind of ignorance of action modalities, and yet the body moves toward things. We can understand imitation hence as the *encounter of two actions that circle around the same object*. Imitation does not mean to do something just like the other, but to *get to the same result*. (47; my emphasis)

The gestures of the child and of the hen circle around the same object: caring for and protecting something fragile. As carefully as the hen reclines on her eggs, the child gently sits on her stool, her toes touching the ground only as much as they are needed to keep her upright. The protective circle of the nest finds its counterpart in the cradle of the lap with the small hands nesting there together. Her indrawn chin and straight back are a response to the possible danger that threatens from the nest: the hen will pick at anything endangering her eggs. The child feels her way into the hen's world of careful rest and alert attentiveness. Her body, caught up in the drama of the nesting bird, does not "play chicken" but conforms itself to get the same results as the hen.

The photograph of the little girl and the nesting hen illustrates, like Anna's drawing, the nature of imitation: the child imitates the *results* of an observed action *with her own means*. This is possible because even the very young child has an empathic understanding of other gestures and their relation to the world. The understanding of gestures is a global phenomenon and does not require the perceiver to deconstruct the gesture into its discrete elements. The little girl does not have recourse to mental associations or previously learned schemata in order to intellectually construct an action that resembles the hen. What we witness here is an *incarnate intentionality* (Merleau-Ponty 1962), an intentionality of the lived body that cannot be reduced to purely intellectual phenomena. The intention of the other (the nesting bird) inhabits the body of the child without her being aware of its details. Pathically the child understands the bird. The animal outlines a way of being in the world with its gestures, and the child feels herself into this particular world through her own gestures.

The capacity for imitation, which is not restricted to the human species, is an a priori of embodiment. It cannot be reduced to mental or intellectual phenomena. It indicates the place where body and world entwine and where the basic meaning structure of human existence becomes possible. Things have meaning because their gestures become possibilities for the child's body and provide new horizons for her being in the world. While the little girl can develop her conceptual grasp of the nesting hen and learn the facts of animal biology in the course of her future education, her pathic and empathic encounter with the hen is of a profoundly *moral* nature: the being of the mother bird discloses itself to her because she lends herself to its call and inhabits its world. Some of the world of the bird is now her own, is a cared-for and familiar horizon of her own being. The otherness of the animal has partly relinquished its strangeness, and a bond of familiarity and kinship between human and animal has been established. In this free, imaginative, playful act of a young child, we can find hope for the future of our and other species.

FOUR

The Child in the World of Things

> Show him how joyful, how innocent, how much ours, a thing can be,
> how even the lamenting of sorrow resolves into pure form,
> serves as a thing, or dies into a thing—and when it crosses over
> blissfully flows out of the violin.
> *Rainer Maria Rilke*, Ninth Duino Elegy

THE GESTURES OF THINGS

Worlding

More than any other existential form (such as space, time, and other human beings) things are present, tangible, and near in the environment of the body, but they also withdraw from philosophical reflection. They are close and distant at the same time. Things are so ordinary that they do not seem worthy of philosophical thought. Should we not leave them over there, in the separate sphere of the "real" world, where they are defined as empty, indifferent objects over and against us as internal subjects? Heidegger, in the late essay *The Thing* (1971) pointed out that we cannot afford this luxury of indifference toward things anymore. The objectification of things is a direct antecedent of the atom bomb and, I would add, of the destruction of the earth through global warming and the extinction of species. He warns us that the scientific enframing and redefinition of things as *objects* makes the thing into a nonentity "in not permitting things to be the standard for what is real": "Science's knowledge, which is compelling within its own sphere, the sphere of objects, already had annihilated things as things long before the atom bomb

exploded. The bomb's explosion is only the grossest of all gross confir-
mations of the long-since-accomplished annihilation of the thing: the
confirmation that the thing as a thing remains nil. The thingness of the
thing remains concealed, forgotten. The nature of the thing never
comes to light, that is it never gets a hearing" (170).

The word *Thing* in German refers to a gathering, a coming together,
while the Latin word *objectum* describes what stands opposite or against
us. When we live in a world of "objects," we live in a world without nearness. We have forgotten the gathering of things. The thing, because it
does not get a hearing, does not lay claim to thought, nor can we think
about what it gathers. This does not mean that things have no existential significance. On the contrary: things are deeply woven into the
structures of the human body and, as we saw before, determine locations in the web of lived space. But the way we think about them misses
the subtlety and power with which they lay hold of our psychological
life. In the language of psychoanalysis, I would say that objects dwell in
the light of consciousness, but things are active in the darkness of the
unconscious; they exert a dynamic power in the deep structures of the
psyche.

Heidegger calls us to vigilance—the first step toward a philosophy
and psychology of things is a step back from a thinking that merely represents and explains presences—and urges us to cultivate "the thinking
that *responds* and *recalls*" (1971, 181). Phenomenological thinking is
faithful to the response and the recall: to co-*respond* with what is there
and create a clearing in our attention so that the thing can address us
and we can hear its appeal; to *re-call* means to remember the fullness of
the world, for which every thing is a gathering place. Sometimes this
process requires the transformation of our habitual use of language
(which explains the many hyphenated words of existential philosophers)
in order to grasp phenomena that are outside the range of established
concepts.

There is a great anecdote about a lecture the young Privatdozent Heidegger gave in Freiburg on a gray February day in 1919. The students
expected him to talk about "experience" and with anticipation they
probably thought: "is that not a label for hidden secrets, for the black
sack from which metaphysical treasures may, after all, be conjured up?"
(Safranski 1998, 94). But instead of giving them metaphysical razzle-
dazzle, Heidegger stepped up to the lectern and for the next two hours
talked about the lectern. He spoke about what the students saw when they
entered the room, how the lectern appeared to the speaker, how it is

more than a geometrical box, and how it gathers a world around it. He finished with the insight that the whole environment of the lectern comes to bear upon it: the lectern "is all of this world, it is worlding" (as cited in Safranski 1998, 95).

The lectern is worlding. It gathers sensory, spatial, social, and temporal meaning around it, and without this gathering it would make no sense to the speaker or his listeners. To identify the lectern as an object would mean to deprive it of its full presence. The thing's worlding is an aspect of our primary experience, even if we do not notice it. Safranski asks us to put this to the test: "If at some later time we recall something like this lectern experience, we shall discover—and since Proust we do so especially well—that at the same time we recall an entire life situation. We dredge up the lectern, and a whole world comes up with it. Proust dunks his madeleine in his tea—and the universe of Cambrai unfolds. The madeleine, that sweet shell-shaped cake, 'is worlding'" (1998, 96).

Like the lectern or the madeleine, early childhood things, such as blankies, dolls, teddy bears, and so on (and I would never call them objects!), are worlding, and they give us a glimpse of things that are still near, before they are forgotten and relegated to the limbo of an objectified world. In the following we will try to respond to and recall the thingness of things through encounters with some of the worlding things of our early lives.

First Things First: The Cradle and the House

In chapter 1 we followed Gaston Bachelard's (1994) meditation on the house and looked at the fundamental sense of housedness and "living from" (Levinas 1969) that characterizes the primary experience of human infants. Before human beings are "cast into the world," before they acquire an attitude of reflective distance, they are "laid in the cradle of the house" (Bachelard 1994, 7). The very structure of the world makes it possible for a human being to be nourished, and human existence is fundamentally woven into the fabric of the sensory world. As Bachelard puts it: "Life begins well, it begins enclosed, protected, all warm in the bosom of the house," and "it is as though in this material paradise, the human being were bathed in nourishment, as though he were gratified with all the essential benefits." The first maternal house, this first experience of containment, becomes the blueprint of all later forms of inhabitation and is deeply inscribed into the structures of human existence. The first things an infant encounters, such as blankets, baby bottles, pacifiers, rattles, and toys, are part of the house in a literal and metaphorical sense. They are elements of the "material paradise" that surrounds the newborn. Winnicot (2002) calls this the "holding environment."

The first things human infants encounter are determined by the presence of the mother and are part of the maternal field. The mother's hands, face, breast come to the infant and call forth reflexive, involuntary responses: cradling into the adult's arms, rooting, sucking, swallowing. Milk is the first nourishment, the lifeline that ties the infant body to the body of the mother. The chiasmic form of cradling provides us with a beautiful example of the flesh as it is shared by infant and parent. Healthy newborns, when placed into the arms of an adult, will conform the contours of their bodies to fit along the groove between adult arms and chest. They "snuggle" into the adult, maintaining the closest possible bodily contact. The gesture of cradling an infant encircles the newborn body and supports the head. It provides an intimate and immediate sense of warmth to the skin, the perfume of milk and sweat to the nose, the contours of the father's face to the eye, the sound of the other's heartbeat or the lilting of a familiar voice to the ear. The cradling arms re-create the warmth and support of the primal enclosure of the womb. They are the prototype for the deepest comfortings of later life: we step into human arms to celebrate intimacy and joy, and we huddle there in times of mourning and distress. Being cradled in their shelter returns us to the possibility of happiness and reconnects us with the foundation of being that is well-being.

Many of the things in an infant's life are variations of the gesture of cradling and evoke its moods. The swaddling cloth recalls the warmth and tightness of the womb, the cradle the circle of the arms; the blanket, the pram, the crib, the car seat, the infant carrier are all variations of the same theme. For adults the bed is probably the thing that comes closest to the cradling arms, and where, once again, love and despair are most often celebrated or endured. The world of things in which infants find themselves shifts its focus from the mother's body to a widening field of other things that at first echo the first containment but then transcend it in ever-differing variation of forms: at four months babies reach for rattles and toys, at nine months they follow the line of a pointing finger, at twelve months the house needs to be "childproofed" because the allure of the varied thing-world is irresistible. But when babies hurt themselves in their forays of exploration among things, they return to the "secure base" (Bowlby 1969): the safe shelter of familiar, cradling arms for comfort.

Among things the house is probably the most comprehensive extension of the original, cradling maternal space.[1] The chiasmic relation between infant and mother is mirrored in the relationship human beings have with their houses. In Bachelard's phenomenology of dwelling, the house appears as a thing that is entwined with human being, a thing that in Langeveld's sense is not merely inhabited and peopled *by us* but *lives within us* (1984). Bachelard recognized that the cradle of the house, in which we spent our early years, is not merely a place in the past. It is *present* in our gestures, *inscribed* into our bodies, *inhabits* our imagination, is part of our chiasmic heritage: "But over and beyond our memories, the house we were born in is physically inscribed in us. It is a group of organic habits" (1994, 14). The word *habit* does not quite satisfy Bachelard: "the word habit is too worn a word to express this passionate liaison of our bodies, which do not forget, with an unforgettable house" (15). I think that the word *gesture* captures some of that "passionate liaison." The gestures of the house evoke a corresponding gesture from us: the rise of the old steps is immediately familiar to our feet, the slightly sticking door handle tells our fingers still how it wants to be turned smoothly, the attic window with the view of the tree outside invites us to linger and dream. The lived body of the child is educated by the structures of the first house. All later houses "are but variations on a fundamental theme." Bachelard calls us to reimagine being prior to the dualisms that come with the upright posture, and his "topoanalysis" is an attempt to evoke the *worlding* of things and places. The topoanalysis of a nest, a cupboard, or a dollhouse describes the worlding of things not from the perspective of human consciousness but as if things had their own voice. From the perspective of Merleau-Ponty's late work, Bachelard attempts to speak the nonhuman voice of the flesh of the world as it coils into and constitutes our psychological lives. Things "truly people and inhabit our souls" (Langeveld 1968, 156).

The "well-housed infant" encounters the world of things and people within the framework of the "good enough" family—to use Winnicot's term (1971)—which describes the family that gives appropriate, predictable care. Children who grow up in institutions or in families that neglect them show the effects of the loss of the primary gestures of housedness. In their development we can see how important the foundation of early infant well-being is for the years that follow. Institutionalized children carry the early world of things they experience written into the very structure of their senses. They frequently suffer from "attachment disorder," which refers to disturbances in social relations (James 1994). Severe isolation in the first years of life produces "sen sory integration disorders," which means that these children are unable to see, hear, smell, taste, and touch the world appropriately and smoothly (Ayers 1979; Greenspan and Benderly 1997). If, as an infant, you are kept permanently in a white crib in a gray room and deprived of loving social interactions, that particular world-structure becomes the norm for your senses. Your body does not know what to do with a world of color or spatial depth. You will come out of a place like that not knowing how far your hand has to reach or how it has to conform itself to pick up a ball or a crayon. Your eyes cannot structure wide-open spaces and, if you can walk at all, you run into cars in the parking lot or crash into door frames. Food is a horribly confusing sensation on your tongue and your throat refuses to swallow it. When the call of things is severely restricted, the body does not know what to do with the world. The flesh restricts itself to the horizon of the familiar white crib. The child's intentionality exhausts itself in autistic activities, like rocking for hours or continuously flicking a light switch. In infants who are deprived of the "material paradise," we find that the foreclosure of the thing-world has long-term consequences for brain development. The brain, especially in the first years of life, is an interactive organ: the development of its structures is profoundly entwined with the child's experience of the world. The separation between brain and world is an artificial construct: the brain is part of the lived, chiasmic body.

In our psychological life the primary forms of cradling become an archetypal image of containment. To be within an enclosure that is safe, large, and full is the prototype and root metaphor for a concept that Western philosophy and psychology have adopted without much question: *interiority*. The illusion of human interiority is so compelling because it echoes the experience of containment of our early wild being: "O happiness of the gnat, who still leaps *within*, / even on its wedding day: for womb is all" (Rilke 1999, 127).

Gestural Presences

Seeing a house, or any other thing, not just as an object-in-itself composed of mere matter but as a *gesture* alters the way we understand its presence in psychological life. For Bachelard the house becomes a shelter for human imagination, the location that makes memory possible. The forms of housedness are forms of intimacy that constitute those who inhabit them in particular ways. The floor as a gesture is understood as a relationship of support. The roof shelters us from the elements, the walls are an embracing gesture that encloses our world and provides intimacy. Horizontal and vertical variations of buildings are also variations in the psychological response to the space. Our lived bodies inhabit a coal mine differently than a cathedral, and our feeling life resonates accordingly: "The truth is that there are no things, only physiognomies" (Merleau-Ponty 1963/1983, 168).

Deliteralizing a thing—like the house above—and describing it not as a purely material object but as a gestural presence, as a "physiognomy," as "the flesh of the world" that calls for a corresponding response from human beings, helps us to understand infant perception. It also provides a foundation for reinterpreting the findings of developmental research. Meltzoff and Borton (1979), for example, blindfolded three-week-old infants and gave them one of two different pacifiers to suck on: one had a standard spherical-shaped nipple, the other a nipple with nubs protruding from various points around its surface. The babies were allowed to touch the nipple with their tongue and mouth and suck on it for a while. Then the pacifier was removed and placed next to the other one. The blindfold was taken off. After a quick visual comparison, infants looked more at the nipple they had just sucked. The researchers interpret the results as an indication that infants can perceive across different sensory modalities without the need for learned correlations. Furthermore, they assume that infants store "abstract information about objects in their world" that allows for "recognition of objects across changes in size and modality of perception" (404).

Cross-modal perception baffles many psychologists in the empiricist and constructivist tradition. How can an infant who has never seen a particular shape but only felt it show a visual preference for the one felt and *immediately connect the felt and the seen*? How can babies connect the visual and tactile schemata without experiencing them together? As Daniel Stern put it so aptly: "On theoretical grounds, infants should not have been able to do this task" (1985, 48). They could not have gone through the intellectual steps of construction because they had no way of associating felt and seen through prior experience. Stern infers that newborn perception has the "innate design" to yoke tactile and visual experiences. In other words: babies are born with this ability. This, however, begs the question of how babies do it.

If we think of the pacifier not as an abstract representation in the infant's mind but as a thing that presents a physiognomy or gestural presence, the infant's preference for looking at the pacifier just sucked becomes clear. Newborns follow the gesture of the nubby pacifier first with their tongues, then with their eyes. *Its* spherical shape fits into the baby's mouth and leads the tongue to travel its ridges and grooves. *Its* gesture invites the complementary gesture of the human tongue. When the eye traces the ridges and grooves, it is called by the same thing gesture, which inscribes itself into the gesture of vision. The tongue, the eye, and the pacifier are one: engaged in the flesh, caught up in the coiling over of the visible and the tactile, their gestures perform the seamless dance of perception. If we understand infant perception in this way, we do not have to have recourse to theories about "mental schemas" and "internal representations" (Piaget 1962) of external objects. Things belong to perception, are the other side of the flesh.

It is within things that a fundamental stability and permanence of the world is found. The gestures of things, more so than the gestures of human beings, are not contingent and chaotic but conform to themselves. The nubby pacifier always evokes the path of the tongue in the same way, its faint taste of rubber remains constant, its surface shadows guide the eye up and down its form. The flesh of the world is predictable, the contours of things remain relatively permanent. The gestures of things invite the infant to respond and conform to their texture. *Their* order becomes the order of infant perception, inscribes in the infant body— as it lends itself to perception—the truth of their constancy.

Only when the flesh is unrecognized and denied, when the tongue and the pacifier are placed in "subjective" and "objective" worlds that never meet: then we are forced to bifurcate perception; then things become silent, immovable, and closed in on themselves; then infant perception becomes solipsistic, internalized, and an impossible miracle. Once we recognize that what is seen is integral to perception and that the perceiver and the perceived are a chiasmic form, the miracle of infant perception is no longer impossible to understand. It testifies to the perfect dance between the body and the world and to the original housedness of human flesh in the flesh of the world.

OBJECT PERMANENCE: THE CASE OF THE VANISHING STORK

In the constructivist-cognitive framework, the duration and order of things is approximated by the term *object permanence*. Object permanence means that objects are perceived as having "substance, permanence, and constant dimensions," and a universe of permanent objects is "a universe both stable and external, relatively distinct from the internal world and one in which the subject places himself as one particular term among all the other terms." The absence of object permanence produces "a world of pictures each one of which can be known and analyzed but which disappear and reappear capriciously" (Piaget 1954, 1–2). Early infancy is marked by this world of pictures that vanish and reappear, and the constancy of objects becomes "constructed little by little" in the infant's mind. Recent research findings (Bower 1977; Maratos 1998; Meltzoff and Moore 1998), as we saw above, challenge the conception that infants have to construct all the coherent structures of the world and indicate that at least some forms of object-understanding are, from the beginning, inherent in the structures of the perceiving body.

Piaget, when observing his infant sons and daughters, was puzzled by their peculiar response to hidden toys. The following observation shows Piaget's daughter Lucienne in a typical procedure that Piaget and his followers later adopted for testing object permanence in infants:

> At 8 months, Lucienne is seated and tries to recapture a celluloid stork (containing a rattle) which she has just held and shaken. I place the stork beside her right knee, covering it with the edge of the cloth on which the child is seated; nothing would be simpler than to find it again. Moreover, Lucienne has watched each of my movements most attentively and they were slow and clearly visible. However, as soon as the stork disappears under the cloth, Lucienne stops looking at it and looks at my hand. She examines it with great interest but pays no more attention to the cloth. (1954, 41)

Lucienne's behavior, which is typical for infants her age, raises the following questions: why is she not searching for the hidden toy—which an older infant would do—and what does this tell us about her consciousness and experience of the world of things? Piaget interprets this observation as indicating that infants under nine months of age have not established object permanence. As soon as the toy vanishes behind the screen, it ceases to exist to the infant: out of sight, out of mind. The soft toy is merely a discontinuous picture in the infant's mind, "a mere image which reenters the void as soon as it vanishes, and emerges from it for no objective reason" (Piaget 1954, 11). Piaget assumes that Lucienne's experience of the stork is a purely internal event; for her, the stork has not yet acquired the true permanence of the outer physical world. By nine months of age Lucienne will eventually come to believe that the stork is part of a stable, external, and objective universe that is distinct from her internal world. When the child has finally achieved a permanent and objectified sense of herself, the world around her rearranges itself into the permanent shape of Cartesian *res extensa*. Piaget's concept of object permanence forms an essential part of his version of the genesis of the Cartesian subject, which has the human infant at twelve months already well entrenched in an interior world of images and concepts divided and distanced from the exterior assemblage of objects.

From a non-Cartesian, existential phenomenological perspective, the infant's action appears in a different light. Let us perform an imaginative variation and—applying what we know about infant perception—describe what this experience might be like for the infant. First we will give an expanded redescription of Piaget's scene and then interpret it *without the assumption of a separation between inner and outer world.*

Lucienne's father is playing with her, moving the stork about. For Lucienne, the act of playing with the stork is not an act separate from her father's presence. The celluloid stork comes to her when father's hand approaches, and it is woven into the playfulness and excitement of his *engagement with her.* Rather than a separate, distinct "object" that has abstract properties, the plaything is woven into the field of meaning and moodedness that surround the presence of her father. The toy is worlding, and the father's presence is one of its constant textures that return and conform to themselves (Merleau-Ponty 1968). The toy is the bridge between Lucienne and her father, the token of shared activity, the place where their intentionalities entwine.

The texture of the celluloid stork invites the senses: it feels smooth, cool, rigid, and its elongated legs guide the hand in an expansive gesture. To the mouth it slightly gives when it touches gums or teeth, and it faintly smells of plastic. It rattles when she turns it upside down. The pathic qualities of the thing invite exploration and guide the senses in predictable ways. All the senses are involved in exploring the toy, are "pulled along" by what else there is to trace.

The father interrupts the infant's activity and takes the toy away. The stork vanishes, the arc of exploration is broken. Lucienne's gestures have lost their complement. Breaking an infant's activity with a thing leaves the cycle of activity and response to the thing only half complete. In variations of this experiment (Cole, Cole, and Lightfoot 2005), the infant looks *dumbfounded* when the toy is taken away and placed behind a screen. Lucienne had heard the next invitation of the stork/hand and anticipated its movement: she was already living toward a particular future. When her father suddenly makes the stork vanish, she needs time to catch up and collect her tattered gestures and an interrupted future, which now have no complement in the flesh of the world.

Piaget presents the toy again but, in full view, he places it under a cover. Lucienne pays attention not to the stork but to the relational field surrounding it. Once again the hand makes the stork move, brings it closer, makes it vanish. Instead of being caught up in the attractiveness of the stork, she stares at her father's hand as it rests on the cover. She hears the stork's rattle as the hand shakes it. Now she looks at his hand, is caught up in its *texture, movement, noise, and activity.* The stork as a thing exists only as an *action,* as a presence that engages her senses, as something that does something with her. It is not an "object" in itself, that is, a conceptual, independent entity. In her world of meaning the invisible stork has transferred its appeal to the attached hand. The gestures of the stork as it appeals to her are continued by the gestures of her father's hand. In her experience the stork and the hand are one. As the stork becomes invisible, she shifts her engagement to the next connected thing: the hand that continues the cycle of playful invitation.

Lucienne and her friends, then, do not present to us evidence of the absence of object permanence, they invite us to deliteralize things. A thing is woven into a larger meaning structure—in this case the presence of her father—and not an object "in-itself." Things gather a world around themselves. The stork, despite its inorganic celluloid nature, is an *active* principle in the field of perception. *It* engages Lucienne's attention, guides her senses, and complements her gestures as long as she is uninterrupted in her play. *The thing calls to her, engages her, plays with her.* A thing to a young infant is present as the action that unfolds between the player and the toy.

We cannot conclude from the object permanence experiments that infants have no sense of the structure of the universe and that they completely live in tattered images. But we can conclude that young infants' attention moves in a different pattern than the attention of older children. What we witness with Lucienne is the absence of an *intentionality of act* (Merleau-Ponty 1962). In the dance between Lucienne, her father, and the stork we find the web of *operative intentionalities* that lies beneath the *intentionality of act* that we usually associate with human volition and judgment. Operative intentionality implies the natural and prethematic unity of the world and of our life. It appears most directly in our desires and in our immediate grasp and evaluations of situations (Merleau-Ponty 1962). Eight-month-old Lucienne is caught up in the totality and immediacy of sense impressions and is primarily responsive, rather than active, in her way of engaging her environment. When Lucienne is about nine months old, she will reach for the cover and search for the stork under it. The gestures of things and the infant's operational intentionality begin to be modified at this time by the achievement of a more active intentionality.

A phenomenon related to searching behavior is pointing. Pointing, like the child's understanding of the permanence of things, becomes reorganized toward the end of the first year. Similar to the patient Schneider discussed by Merleau-Ponty in *Phenomenology of Perception* (1962), the infant at eight months of age can grasp various things but cannot follow his or her father's hand as he points at things in the room (Stern 1985). Lucienne would continue to stare at his hand, missing the larger protosymbolic gesture that is meant to direct her intentionality beyond the immediate sensory realm. Like Schneider, Lucienne's intentionality is caught up in the phenomenal, submerged in the operational intentionality that ties the perceiving body into the landscape of things. Her "projects" are mainly sensual engagements. At nine or ten months, however, she will understand that the finger points beyond itself, and that the ready-made sensory world can refer to things and events beyond their immediate presence. The stork keeps calling her even though it is invisible. Intentionality of act comes into being when the infant engages in "projects" or "summonings" beyond the phenomenal. What Merleau-Ponty says about Schneider can also be said about young infants:

> The world exists only as one ready-made or congealed, whereas for the normal person his projects polarize the world, bringing magically to view a host of signs which guide action, as notices in a museum guide the visitor. This function of "projection" or "summoning" (in the sense in which the medium summons an absent person and causes him to appear) is also what makes abstract movement possible: for, in order to be in possession of my body independently of any urgent task to be performed; in order to enjoy the use of it as the mood takes me, in order to describe in the air a movement formulated only verbally or in terms of moral requirements, I must reverse the natural relationship in which the body stands to its environment, and a human productive power must reveal itself through the density of being. (112)

When Lucienne understands the pointing gesture, her "human productive power" reveals itself and she reaches beyond the immediately visible. By the time she is a toddler a few months later, her world has already a future horizon: "a host of signs" appears that structure the fullness of sensory perception and guide action beyond what is present. The worlding of things has expanded. Children *summon* a particular part of the plenum and leave others aside as their active projects shape what they see (this is not a conscious but a "magical" process—even for adults!). But the plenary world also expands beyond the purely sensible and becomes multiplied by gestural and then linguistic significances. With this the infant takes up her or his place in the human, symbolic order (Merleau-Ponty 1963/1983) and becomes a *creative* participant of her or his environment.

"Object permanence" is achieved when the immediate and pathic call of the senses can be reorganized and points beyond itself toward a world of projects for self and others. Babies follow now another's intentions when they follow the trajectory of the pointing finger, and their own "summoning" reaches beyond the grasp of their hands. They will search for the hidden toy even though its presence is not visible or audible. Things appear permanent *over time* when the child's action space is extended beyond the visible, when the first acts of referential, symbolic activity appear. Then a future space structured by language becomes possible. The gestures of things call now from a physical as well as a symbolic distance and invite complementary responses: Lucienne will walk into the other room to find the stork, she will cradle the baby doll instead of sucking at its foot, and she will speak her own name.

TRANSITIONAL THINGS

In Praise of Blankie: Beloved Things

I do not want to give the impression that operational intentionality becomes lost in the process of development. It is the permanent substratum of all human experience and the foundation of all later symbolic activity (Merleau-Ponty 1962). Operational intentionality, the call of the flesh of the world and my own complementary response, are part of the ground upon which the figures of human projects and their volitional intentionality are drawn. The transition from the infant's immersion into the sensory world to the emergence of a symbolic, active intentionality can be traced through another powerful phenomenon of the first year: the baby's acquisition of and attachment to a particular thing, which often becomes the child's essential companion throughout the trials and tribulations of early and middle childhood.

When our son, Nicholas, was born he received a small white fuzzy blanket with satin lining from his godmother. At night, in his crib, we covered him up with it. At six months he would suck his thumb and rub the edge of the blanket against his nose. When he began to walk at ten months, he often dragged the blanket around with him. When he was eleven months we had to take it everywhere: to the mall, on walks, across the ocean when we visited my family in Europe. He called the blanket "num-num," and my husband and I referred to it as "nummi." Without num-num he could not go to sleep, and sucking his thumb and rubbing the blanket against his nose worked as an immediate sedative when he was upset. At fourteen months he began visiting a daycare center for a few mornings a week, and num-num had to go, too. There he met other children who also had their special things, and num-num acquired a new name, borrowed from one of the other children and the teacher: "blankie." One day we lost blankie in the mall, and I remember clearly his crying and *my panic*, and how we searched high and low for it until we found it in the security guard's office. Over time blankie became more ragged and dirty, and we bought another blanket as a substitute, but it would not do. Nicholas refused to touch it. I snuck blankie into the washing machine a few times, and when he discovered my transgression he would sit before the washing machine and watch blankie go round and round behind the glass bull's-eye. When it came out of the drier, he would hug and sniff it and cry, and then wipe it across the floor to get it dirty again. I finally gave up washing the thing because it upset him too much.

By the time he was six years old, blankie was a bundle of shreds held together by a big knot, and it lived almost exclusively in his bed—the only time it left was when he went to a sleepover party and blankie went into the backpack. He told me that all the boys had their blankies or teddies tucked away in their packs, too, and got them out before they went to sleep. This went on for two years, during which the boys seemed to have an unspoken agreement that they would ignore the others' need for a blankie. By the time he was nine blankie had become an embarrassment and had to be hidden in the closet when friends came over. There, tucked away, it was forgotten until we cleaned out the closet when he was a teenager. I left it to him to decide, and we never asked: blankie might have ended up in the trash, but it also might still live in a dark corner of his cupboard.

Between Inside and Outside

Blankie was, in D. W. Winnicot's terms (1971), a "transitional object." Toward the end of the first year many infants form a passionate attachment to a soft thing, which they claim as their own, give a name, and hug and fondle at times of transition (sleep) or stress (illness, travel, new situations). This first possession accompanies many children through their early and middle childhoods. (I have been surprised how many of my undergraduate students admit they still have their bald teddy bears, or the rabbits without eyes, in their dorm rooms!) For Winnicot, the psychoanalyst, the transitional object exists in a middle realm between the infant's magical, omnipotent control over the mother's breast, and the older child's ability to project internal experiences onto an external world. Transitional objects and transitional phenomena inhabit a place where things are neither external nor internal. They exist in "an inter-mediate area of *experiencing*, to which inner life and external life both contribute. It is an area that is not challenged, because no claim is made on its behalf except that it shall exist as a resting-place for the individual engaged in the perpetual human task of keeping inner and outer reality separate yet interrelated" (2). Winnicot understands this inter-mediate place between inside and outside, subject and world, ego and object as a necessary but illusory space where play, art, and religion can flourish in later life. The transitional space delineates the area that Freud (1953–74) assigned to fantasy and the arts: an illusory realm of subli-mated pleasure that protects the psyche—at least temporarily—from the harsh demands of necessity and the reality principle.[2] The use of transitional objects seems to vary by culture.

Winnicot's transitional object is an event in the process of ego for-mation. It is a way station between the infant's primary narcissism and the formation of the ego. At first the child does not distinguish between ego and external world and lives in the illusion of total control over the mother's breast. Through encounter with reality, where desires are not met, the ego is forced to accept that it is not everything and all power-ful: "In this way, then, the ego detaches itself from the external world. Or, to put it more correctly, originally the ego includes everything, later it separates off an external world from itself" (Freud 1989, 724–25).

The story that psychoanalysis tells about ego formation is one of vi-olent disappointment and final resignation: the ego is the organ of com-promise that scans the real to make sure that the unbounded desires of the id do not destroy the organism. Fantasy and transitional phe-nomena are the secret, unclaimed spaces where the ego allows the id some measure of sublimated pleasure against the demands of a cruel, overbearing, censoring civilization. Freud and the psychoanalysts who follow him unquestioningly accept the Cartesian/Kantian distinction between an inner subject and an outer real world of objects, and they use psychoanalytic theory to give an account of the genesis of the Cartesian subject. The concept of the unconscious becomes necessary within this solipsistic personality theory (and undermines Descartes's cogito without challenging its dualisms) because, as Freud said, the ego "is not even master in his own house" (Freud 1924/1953, 296) and is continually disturbed by objects and events that the id wants but is not allowed to have. The ego-subject, struggling to keep the unconscious in check, is faced with a meaningless world of factual objects that it uses as the canvas for internal projections of desires and fantasies. In the psychoanalytic model we have a clear separation between psyche and world, where the only contact with things is via projection—that is, the solipsistic process of assuming that my internal picture matches the world. The psychoanalytic schools of object-relations theory (see Klein, Fairbairn, Bowlby, Mahler, Winnicot, Guntripp, all in Buckley 1986) also assume the fundamental dichotomy between human being and world, even though object-relations theory focuses on the interpersonal realm: the *other person* is identified as the *object* of the infant's projection of subjective needs. An *external object* (breast, blanket) is invested with internal psychic energy, and an *internal object* (the introjected maternal object) is a mental representation of an outside object. Winnicot's transitional phenomena are an attempt to claim an intermediary space between inside and outside while maintaining the fundamental dualism between what he calls "inner reality" and "outer reality" (1971, 2). Despite his attempts to bridge the gap between "inner" and "outer" reality, Winnicot, like most psychoanalysts, does not question the fundamental dichotomy of inside and outside, object and representation, that is part of his underlying Cartesian worldview.

Transitional Objects and Transitional Things

However, with this critique of psychoanalysis I do not want to dispute the sophistication of psychoanalytic theory or its appropriateness for clinical practice. On the contrary, many of the phenomena that psychoanalysts (and here I include object relations practitioners) have discovered and described in the last hundred years of practice have great importance for clinical work and developmental theory. They became visible because the psychoanalytic lens was trained on them. But through psychoanalytic theory only a part of the full spectrum of their meaning emerges, while it forecloses other discourses, other ways of seeing, and other forms of practice.

Let us return to a phenomenology of the transitional object and apply some of the earlier ideas we developed about things. First a caveat about terminology. The term *transitional object* reflects a conception of things as distant, dead, and disconnected. Because of the very feature of nearness and passionate animation, "transitional objects" are actually *things* that, for the infants, are worlding in very powerful ways: they gather meaning around them. Therefore I will discard the word *object* and call them from now on "transitional things," maintaining Winnicot's term *transitional* until further reflection. The second caveat is that transitional things are culture bound: American infants are much more likely to use objects for soothing than are infants in Korea or Guatemala (Morelli et al. 1993), and particularly in cultures where cosleeping is the norm, the use of transitional objects seems to be less frequent (Burnham et al. 2002; Hobara 2003). A transitional thing is not an enclosed object but a field of meaning that varies in the context of an infant's relationships with his or her caretakers and the spatiotemporal arrangement of sleeping and comforting patterns in the family.

Keeping these caveats in mind, we will proceed by looking at Winnicot's description of the phenomenon he labeled "transitional object," examine its features and qualities more closely, and reinvestigate transitional things from a nondualistic, chiasmic perspective. Following our previous strategy of examining phenomena by beginning with sensory appearance and bodily engagement, I want to rearrange Winnicot's sequence and stay more closely with the description, rather than begin with interpretation. Transitional things are the first "not me possessions" (Winnicot 1971, 5) of infants and have the following features:

1. The thing is affectionately cuddled as well as excitedly loved and mutilated.
2. It must seem to the infant to give warmth, or to move, or to have texture, or to do something that seems to show it has vitality or reality of its own.
3. The infant assumes rights over the thing, and we agree to this assumption. Nevertheless, some abrogation of omnipotence is a feature from the start.
4. It must never change, unless changed by the infant.
5. It must survive instinctual loving and also hating and, if it be a feature, pure aggression.
(6. It comes from without, from our point of view, but not so from the point of view of the baby. Neither does it come from within; it is not a hallucination.)
7. Its fate is to be gradually allowed to become decathected, so that

over the course of years it becomes not so much forgotten as relegated to limbo.

Chiasmic Physiognomies

Nicholas's blankie had all the features Winnicot mentions: it was soft and cuddly and his first claimed, named, and respected possession; it had its own vitality and personality; and it became, over time, relegated to the limbo of the closet. Not all things lend themselves to becoming transitional objects, especially those that are acquired in the first year of life. Softness is one of their key features. Most infants adopt a soft toy or cloth as their transitional thing, and very few, if any, choose a Tonka truck, a rubber duckie, or a ball for their early passionate attachment. The reason for this is that the sensual structure of the transitional thing needs to fit into the structure of the infant's body. The child, alone in the crib at night, has to be able to hug and cuddle the blanket. Its sensory texture must conform to the baby's body as it is held close. It must not resist the contours of arms and chest, but at the same time it must be substantial enough to give warmth.

The physiognomy of the transitional thing mirrors the gestures of the maternal field: close bodily contact, warmth, responsive touch, unwavering presence when needed. At the same time, as Winnicot remarks, the blanket *is not* the mother: the desire for the perfect fusion with the maternal world has been "abrogated," the "omnipotence" of Eden has been given up, the gestures that constitute wellness and happiness have been transferred from the mother to a thing. This is possible only if a thing echoes the quality of the first experience of being housed and calls the child's body to interact with it in similar gestures. The blanket's pathic quality shapes the infant's arms into the primal cradling gesture—and that is why you hardly ever see a Tonka truck chosen as a transitional thing: it cannot be hugged without pain. On the sensory level transitional things are an extension of the maternal field. In the baby's engagement with the transitional thing we find, once again, the operational intentionality of the body and its dialectical relationship with the world of things.

And, like the mother, the transitional thing is experienced as alive and full of intentionality: it gives warmth to the infant's chest, or it moves and fits itself against the body, or its texture tickles and soothes the nose. Blankie is not an "object in itself" but a locus of action that proves itself over and over again. The child treats the blanket as a living being because it can do things: it responds to hugs and it soothes one's fears. Blankie is an *active being*, an Other who is never completely comprehended and who holds aspects of itself in reserve. Winnicot calls this experience of the otherness of the transitional thing the "abrogation of omnipotence" because blankie has power, too, and its absence can be experienced as painful. Faced with the thing's magical intentionality infants accept that they share power with this other being. It is this reserved otherness, the plenary fullness of this particular blanket or velveteen rabbit, its quality as an independent, active being, that merits a name.

From "Num-Num" to "Blankie": What's in a Name?

Naming the blanket "num-num" was our son's first onomatopoeic evocation of the pleasure it provided as he was being comforted, and initially this sound fully existed in the presymbolic, sensory realm. Like the sound "mmm" we make when we express our pleasure over food, "num-num" is the intersection of pleasure and breathing, a pure expression that communicates with nothing but the world itself. But soon "num-num" became the calling cry for the comforting thing, and suddenly the blanket was named because it stood out and endured among other blankets (which smelled differently and did not do the same things). Naming the transitional thing made it special and gave it its separate place in the world. As when Adam and Eve named all beings in Eden, naming num-num is the invention of a cosmology in which the name delineates the essential nature of a being and places it among others. It can now be called by its name, and it inhabits as an invisible presence the discourse between parent and infant. "Num-num's" phonology changed into "nummi" because Nicholas's parents did not want to mumble when they asked him where the blanket was. The magic of this name lay in its power to make the blanket present in our conversations while it was actually not present. The name gave it permanence beyond the present sensory realm. "Nummi" gave the blanket status as a privileged member of the Simms family, because we would not go anywhere without it (while even our dog had to stay home).

"Nummi" became "blankie" in the daycare center during Nicholas's first few weeks outside the family world. Language is a shared reality, and he took on "blankie" because it is a name shared by other blankets he encountered. It was also closer to the conventionally correct term "blanket": when he asked for blankie, any stranger could understand what he was talking about. One afternoon (he was about eighteen months old), as I picked him up and asked where nummi was, he said that it was now called "blankie," and that blankie was in his lunchbox. That was that, and we all called it blankie from then on. As soon as Nicholas had learned gendered pronouns, he announced that blankie was a "he." And there was no doubt about it: "he" was a powerful actor on the stage of our child's life and comforted him for many years in darkness, illness, and strange situations. Blankie allowed our child to go to places that were new and strange and face reality more openly and with greater courage and independence.

Naming the transitional thing was a "summoning" in a number of ways. The first mumbled sound of comfort and pleasure became the auditory sign "num-num" for the blanket *when Nicholas was looking for it.* Summoning the absent thing into presence was one of the functions of its name. It also allowed for a summoning of the parents' shared attention, because we all would look for the blanket. The word "nummi" was a repeated summoning by the parents of a shared language realm where a thing has its own particular name that is used by all language participants. It was no longer fully tied to the baby's primary sensory pleasure: it became slightly censored and abstracted while still maintaining some of its original sonorous phonemes.

The shift to "blankie," which was a total renunciation of sensory origins, summoned a cultural world into which the child and the transitional thing had to fit.

The First Possession

In the psychological space of the family, it is understood that the transitional thing is surrounded by a privacy fence: no other family member is allowed to play with it or change it in any way. It is the human being's first true possession and as such it is not merely an engagement with the phenomenal nature of a thing (its sensory lure, so to say), but it becomes a symbolic agent. The infant alone is allowed to determine what happens to the transitional thing. And families usually respect it. I gave up washing blankie when I noticed the distress this caused. The laundry detergent had destroyed one of blankie's essential features, its smell, and I finally gave up my cultural ideals about cleanliness and body odor and accepted a germy rag in my child's bed: his passionate need to have blankie unchanged by anyone but himself won out in the end. It was his to do with as he wished. To have a possession like blankie means also to have the freedom to determine what happens in its particular part of the world. That first freedom is granted or violated by the parents.

When we consider the transitional thing as a worlding event, its possession is not merely the material possession of an inanimate object. The physiognomic presence of the blanket is a gesture of nourishment that alleviates the fear of the dark or the unfamiliar. The infant's control of the blanket is also a control of the gesture of nourishment and the world it evokes. By owning the blanket, the baby can own and produce the mood of the first housedness—never perfectly, but still upon command. The family respects this gesture because it testifies to the infant's growing independence: baby can now soothe him- or herself to a certain degree, and the safe base that the mother represents becomes more "portable" when it is diffused into a thing. It is striking that institutionalized and neglected infants usually do not adopt a soft thing and at a later time even seem to have an aversion against soft toys (Bowlby 1969), as if the reliance on anything outside of themselves were a threat. When the original ground of housedness has been destroyed, the child cannot bear to see its reflection in other things.

As a possession with a name, the transitional thing is a first cultural creation: it has value within the family and it is protected by unspoken rules. Perhaps here we see the human origin of property rights and a code of laws? Through the transitional object the infant carves his or her world out of the world of the family and exercises a small amount of freedom. In Merleau-Ponty's sense, the transitional object is a sign of emerging active intentionality and human creativity.

Changes

The transitional thing has some qualities that transcend the maternal field. Its relative constancy and invariant structure is more predictable than the mother's varied and human activity: it stays where it is put, and "it must never change, unless changed by the infant" (Winnicot 1971, 5). This astute observation shows us the tension between the persistence and duration of things but also their quiet assent to human control. Blankie, unlike Mother, allows itself to be dragged around and mutilated by persistent rubbing and fondling. Violent loving and aggression are absorbed into its soft body and it bears what human culture censors. There is no guilt or shame attached to the frequent violation or slow destruction of the transitional thing. Its quiet persistence reflects back a nonhuman world of silent endurance. The worst response it can give is to passively get lost and vanish out of the child's world. This, however, is also one of the most traumatic experiences for children who are attached to a thing and leads to panic, anxiety, and grief.

The transitional thing is small enough to be easily handled by the toddler and hidden in the older child's backpack. It can go where the mother cannot go. It goes along in the forays into the worlds of mall and airplane, daycare and babysitter, hospital and sleepover. It accompanies the child into darkness and sleep every night and dwells in places that are inaccessible to other humans. It is a companion in worlds that the child experiences in solitude. Things like blankie exist at the intersection between dependence and independence because they allow the child to carry a sense of housedness and safety into strange and unfamiliar settings.

Unlike organic beings, the transitional thing does not resist decay but gradually fades and falls apart and assumes the metamorphosed shape of shredded fabric and bald velveteen. It carries the traces of early life in its decaying folds and is a record of the years of passionate childhood history.

MAGIC AND PARTICIPATION

"It's alive": Participation, Realism, and Twisted Strings

As we saw in previous chapters, child consciousness is marked by an immersion in the world and the absence of self-reflection. A young child's fear of the dark is experienced as the menace of witches in the closet, not as something that is personally and internally owned. Until late childhood, the attention of children is focused on the exploration and creation of worlds, rather than thinking and reflecting about the self (Langeveld 1960). Transitional things with their names and genders come into being for a mind that locates power in things and events, not in human consciousness and the self. In *The Child's Conception of the World* (1929/1951), Piaget calls the nondualistic, syncretic attitude *participatory* or *magical realism*. "Participation" refers to the assumption that two beings or phenomena are partially identical or influence each other without direct physical or causal proximity; "magic" refers to the belief that things can be used to influence each other through participation (132). The young child experiences things as alive and endowed with consciousness. Vel (nine years and five months), for example, is convinced that a twisted string has intentionality and knowledge of itself "because it wants to untwist itself, it knows it's twisted" (176); Nel, two years and nine months old, worries at seeing a hollow chestnut tree: "didn't it cry when the hole was made?" (213). Both children assume that the world is full of feeling and intentionality. Their thinking is what Piaget calls "realistic" because they do not distinguish between "thoughts and things, or between self and the external world" (150) and have ideas that are immediately evoked by relationships with the people around them (that then are translated into the physical world, as he puts it). One of Piaget's great findings is that children's cognition is not merely a-logical thinking; rather, it arises from a different experience of the world: the world for the child is not an external, objective, conceptual, hard "reality" but is suffused by the child's intentions and the feeling-tone of social relationships. There is neither interiority nor exteriority in the child's experience.

If we interpret the child's realism from an existential-phenomenological perspective, it appears that Vel and Nel are open to more of the multiple facets of the worlding of a twisted string or an injured chestnut tree. Their thinking is not a-logical but follows the *logos* in a much more fundamental sense: the word *logos* means "relation" or, more precisely, the "laying open of a relation" (Held 2002, 83). Vel and Nel look at the world and their gaze lays open relationships. They see the ordered cosmos and are "*permitting things to be the standard for what is real*" (Heidegger 1971, 170). They *live in a fuller slice of the plenum* which, on their way to becoming Western adults, is gradually reduced, redefined, and mostly made unspeakable.[3]

The Color of Pebbles and the Little Brown Horse

The ability to experience the symbolic dimension of things lies in the child's capacity to grasp the many dimensions of the plenum that are rooted in sensory presence but also go beyond it. By the time children are four years old, their capacity to act in the symbolic realm is strongly developed. Children's animism and magical thinking elaborate connections between things and themselves that are beyond surface causality and visibility. A little girl of six secretly gathered white, round stones to throw into the lake, but close to the shore, in the hope that the next day water lilies would grow out of them for her to touch. Another child very carefully chose the shape and color of the pebble that goes in the bottom of a clay flowerpot because she thought the life of the plant depended on it (Piaget 1929/1951). Young children see an overabundance of signs in everything. Their world is full of connections. But, according to Piaget, they "confuse the sign with the cause of an event" (143)—that is, they assume that there is a causality that does not follow the laws of adult logic. The order that governs children's causality, however (and Piaget concedes this), is not ruled by physical laws but by *moral laws*. There is an affinity between the smooth, round, white stone and the rare, white water lily, and the care that goes into selecting a pebble for the bottom of a flowerpot will also have a beneficial effect on the plant. The moral law of connection and care supersedes physical causality. Magical participation assumes a continuum between the mind and world phenomena, so "that thought can insert itself directly into the real and thus influence events" (155). In turn, things have a profound influence on human beings and the world around them.

Among the many examples Piaget gives of children's participatory magic, none is more powerful than the recollection of Mlle. Vé, and it beautifully shows the depth and range of the symbolic, plenary dimension of a thing.

> One of my most distant memories relates to my mother. She was very ill and had been in bed several weeks and a servant had told me that she would die in a few days. I must have been about 4 or 5 years old. My most treasured possession was a little brown wooden horse, covered with "real hair." . . . A curious thought came into my head: I must give up my horse in order to make my mother better. It was more than I could do at once and cost me the greatest pain. I started by throwing the saddle and the bridle into the fire, thinking that "when it's very ugly I shall be able to keep it." I can't remember exactly what happened. But I know that in the greatest distress I ended by smashing my horse to bits, and that seeing my mother up a few days later, I was convinced that it was my sacrifice that had mysteriously cured her and this conviction lasted for a long while. (Piaget 1929/1951, 139)

It is clear from the start that the toy horse is not a simple wooden object. In the economy of the child's feeling life, the horse is a treasure of the greatest value, not merely to her but to the whole universe. Its polymorphous nature changes from being the special, beautiful, and treasured possession of a pampered little girl to a bargaining chip with the invisible powers that rule life and death.

We can only imagine how the little girl spent time with the toy horse before her mother's illness. Because it had "real hair," its sensuous qualities invited touching and stroking, and its replicated horse morphology called the child to pick it up and gallop it along the floor or the windowsills. She probably brushed it and fed it and daydreamed about riding across the meadows. All we know is that she must have *spent time* with this toy and must have *derived great satisfaction* from her encounters with it. Otherwise she would not have formed such a strong affection for it, and it could not have had such great value for her. As a small wooden structure it was definitely overdetermined, and it truly inhabited and peopled her soul. But she also took it for granted.

The presence of death changes everything. Her mother's illness threatens the very foundation of housedness in which the little girl can play with her horse in safety. The child realizes a semblance between mother and toy: they are both beloved. But the mother is loved more, and her impending loss, announced to her by a servant, will be unbearable. Against this background the toy horse's true value appears. Maybe in the irrational moral world ruled by death it can tip the scales in favor of her mother: can the grief over the loss of the horse be thrown into the balance? So the small brown horse changes from a favored toy into a sacrificial offering that must be given up.

The child's ritual of dismantling the toy gradually by throwing first the saddle, then the bridle into the fire is a cosmic act of bargaining. Perhaps the gods only want its beauty? No, it was not the beauty they wanted. They want its very essence. She finally smashes the horse—wood and hair and all—and destroys the very form that holds it together. She annihilates the thing to give the gods something very much loved so that they may spare her beloved mother. The gift she makes to free her mother from the clutches of death is not merely the gift of an inanimate object: she gives her love and attachment that animate a physical thing and the depth of her grief upon its loss. Thus she wants to provoke a change in the invisible equation of fate. The toy horse reaches into the invisible and is a placeholder for a part of her own being, which she will give up for her mother.

The small brown toy horse is, to the little girl, a wonderful thing—that is, something that inspires wonder. But wonder also is marked by a deep ambivalence. On the one hand, it is the attunement to the larger ordering of the world: "we are overtaken by a joyous wonder that the single, all life-world encompassing world is 'there' at all, rather than not being there" (Held 2002, 88). The horse is beautiful: it has order and is connected to other things in the child's life. There is joy in its presence and simple "being there" for play and comfort. "In this elevated attunement, wherein this wonder at the opening of the world overcomes us, we sense at the same time that the fact of the world's being there, rather than there being nothing, *is not in our power*" (my emphasis). The shadowy abyss of nothingness stands behind the beloved mother and the beloved toy, and life and death and the larger order of destiny are not in the child's power but in the hands of invisible forces. Destroying the wondrous thing pays homage to their power. Before the dark background of nothingness the mother and the horse grow luminescent in their full significance, until they have become so clear that the child can make her choice to let one of them fall into extinction.

Mlle. Vé's recollection of this very touching and complex act of childhood magic shares one feature with such acts of other children: they go unremarked by the adult world and are hardly ever talked about. Perhaps their secrecy lies in the different nature of things and language: we know from play therapy that children find some traumatic events unspeakable, but these same events can be symbolized and resolved through playthings. Much of our emotional life finds its abode in the playful cosmology of things and lives a much richer life there than in our articulated language. Things are worlding, while language is trying to catch up.

Things and Philosophy

Socrates, in his conversation with Theaetetus, thought that philosophy begins in wonder—moreover, that wonder is the key *feeling* a philosopher ought to have.[4] Without the feeling of wonder, and the initial speechless awe it produces when faced with the large order of the cosmos, the process of human inquiry and growth will be stunted. Perhaps a child's wonder is not philosophy or science, but it certainly contains the seeds of future philosophical and scientific inquiry. It awakens the passion for inquiry and grounds it in the sense of deep ethical connectedness with the larger world.

Wonder is a child's ability to be open to the surprising otherness and fullness of the things of the world. As with Heidegger's lectern or Proust's madeleine, wonder arises when a child "spends time" with a thing and begins to notice its many possibilities. Wonder begins in the engagement with simple things such as balls, dolls, and anthills. We have a simple word for this "spending time" in its plenary fullness: play. The ball is worlding in ever-surprising vectors and bounces. The doll needs to be fed and cared for or disciplined and punished for one or another transgression against social norms. The anthill reveals itself as a complicated hub for incoming and outgoing creatures whose life underground is a great mystery. With the acquisition of language the horizon of worlding expands dramatically, and the summoning of possible worlds becomes more individual. Like Annie Dillard, a child can experience wonder when she finds a buried dime in the alley and spend the rest of her life digging for the layers of deeper history behind the appearance of things. Annie's parents were probably baffled by their five-year-old daughter's sudden passion for digging, but they were also tolerant and told her about buried layers of past civilizations (Dillard 1987).

Rachel Carson told us that the only way to teach children stewardship of the future of the earth is to keep alive their original sense of wonder and cherish the emotional link between their participatory consciousness and the things of the natural world. Adults have the power to open up children's sense of kinship with the natural world and cultivate it, or they can bury it under layers of facts:

> I sincerely believe that for the child, and for the parent seeking to guide him, it is not half so important to *know* as to *feel*. If facts are the seeds that later produce knowledge and wisdom, then the emotions and the impressions of the senses are the fertile soil in which the seeds must grow. The years of early childhood are the time to prepare the soil. Once the emotions have been aroused— a sense of the beautiful, the excitement of the new and the unknown, a feeling of sympathy, pity, admiration or love—then we wish for knowledge about the object of our emotional response. Once found, it has lasting meaning. (1956, 45)

FIVE

Playing at the Edge
What We Can Learn from Therapeutic Play

States parties recognize the right of the child to rest and leisure,
to engage in play and recreational activities appropriate to the age
of the child, and to participate freely in cultural life and the arts.
  Article 31, Convention on the Rights of the Child, United Nations

The psychology of child's play, the psychology of the child in general
is a psychology of his little room, the garden and the kitchen, it is a
psychology of the garret with its trunks, boxes and dark corners, of
the cellar with its significant smell and chilliness, of the cupboard
without tangible boundaries, of the space under the table, where
the legs of the parents and of the guests invited to the family feast
have their lively play. Thus, and in no other way, is the psychology
of the child a psychology that does not forget the child.
  *J. H. van den Berg, "The Human Body and the Significance
  of Human Movement"*

By the end of the twentieth century the connection between early
childhood and play seemed well established and generally accepted
in the humanities and social sciences: philosophers, poets, educators,
and psychologists seemed to agree that early childhood is the "play age,"
and that play is the child's work, as the philosopher Rousseau (1762/
1979) had stated in the eighteenth century. Politics followed suit: in
1990 the United Nations ratified and legally protected child play in the
International Convention on the Rights of the Child. It seems ironic
that just as child play has achieved internationally protected status it be-

gins to vanish from American public life. Since 1990 the number of academic books published on play has fallen dramatically. Preschools and kindergartens are trading in their play corners for worksheets and desks, elementary and middle schools reduce leisure and playtime on the playgrounds, parents are too afraid of traffic and abductions to let their children play in neighborhoods, and free indoor play has been taken over by adult-produced television and computer games. Finding time and space for free play, unregulated and unstructured by adults, has become difficult for most children, especially in our educational institutions. Indeed, play seems to have become antithetical to the goals of Western education.

In this chapter, I will illustrate the critical role of play in children's affective and cognitive development through a phenomenological-structural analysis of play. We meet Niki again, the young child who was severely neglected during her infancy and early childhood (see chapter 1) and follow the course of her play therapy. We will witness Niki's courageous struggle to work through her feelings of abandonment via play therapy, and in so doing, learn much about the vital role of play in children's lives. I have chosen the somewhat extreme form of therapeutic play because it brings into focus some of the structural elements of play that are present but concealed in ordinary play situations.

THE CUPS OF SAND: FROM AUTISTIC
TO SENSORY PLAY

Psychotherapists who work with children understand the transformative power of play. Rather than enjoyment and leisure, which are the hallmarks of ordinary play, pain and suffering are the driving forces of therapeutic play. This kind of play has an existential urgency: it provides a lifeline back into a world shared with others. Therapeutic play is play with an edge, stripped of all but its essential features.

The following passages by therapist Eliana Gil (cited in James 1994) introduce us to her work with Niki who, as we saw before, suffered from *failure to thrive* as a result of profound parental neglect. In addition to malnutrition and untreated rashes and infections, Niki, at four years of age, could not walk, could barely talk, and was not toilet trained when she entered the foster care system: "The foster mother reported that Niki was lethargic and passive. She did not cry, even when soiled or hungry. She preferred to stay in one spot, apparently uncomfortable with being out of her crib. She didn't seem interested in toys and usually clutched her blanket in her hands. Niki flinched when her foster mother came into the room in the morning" (142). In the therapy room, her therapist found her to be passive and unresponsive for many months, unattached to anyone and uninterested in the activities of other people: "Sitting next to her I would make sure she watched as I rolled a ball, cut a cardboard into shapes, played with water, built blocks, and built a variety of other things. She usually sat staring, with fingers of both hands in her mouth."

As we saw in earlier chapters, in the absence of caring adults the horizon of a child's world is severely restricted. Neglected, uncared-for children will not cry when hurt or upset because they do not expect a response from the world anymore. They do not investigate new situations or play with unknown things. Their trust in themselves, others, and the world has been damaged (Erikson 1950/1963), so that their openness to engage with people and things is severely stunted. Unable to be a true participant, Niki becomes a distant spectator of other people's play. She creates a predictable narrow horizon within which she knows how to function and which keeps the threatening, alien, and confusing world at bay.

Within this semiautistic horizon, play is replaced with repetitive, self-stimulating activities: rocking, head banging, flipping a light switch, or waving the fingers before the eyes. Unlike play, these activities are not modulated and varied but are monotonously pursued without change in their structure. Normal play investigates the qualities of things as the child encounters them, but autistic playlike activities limit the multiple possibilities inherent in a thing to action on just one exclusive feature. *Sensory defensiveness* implies that the horizon of possible modes of activity between self and world has been severely restricted. The senses shut down and allow only a narrow range of stimulation to penetrate. In autistic and traumatic play the child feels the compulsion to repeat the same act over and over because it is a small act that the child can initiate and control him- or herself. In true, nontraumatic play the plaything begins to interact with the player and changes the play (Buytendijk 1933). The autistic player, on the other hand, does not have the capacity to put up with the unpredictability of the toy. Instead of open-ended, mutual engagement with things and people, one gesture is seized upon and totalized, and it dominates the perceptual field to the exclusion of everything else. It is a defense against the unpredictable intrusion of the plenum and an inability to bear its presence.

For four months Niki remained unresponsive. She watched the therapist handle toys but kept her own fingers in her mouth. When her first self-initiated play activity appeared, it consisted of the very basic act of "pouring sand from one cup into another and pouring water on the sand, watching it absorb and dry" (Gil, in James 1994, 142). It is not incidental that her first play is repetitive and focused on sensory experience. Even though it looks simple, Niki's initial sand play leaves the semiautistic activity loop behind and heralds a profound shift in her relationship with the world.

Sensory experience in the interaction with water, sand, blocks, scissors, and other things gives the young child the opportunity of being shaped by and shaping her particular environment. But to do so requires the courage to be challenged: water slips away, sand runs to nothing between one's fingers, scissors cut, and things resist. This type of play, which Piaget (1962) termed sensorimotor play, stimulates sensory and brain development. Rather than mere observation of the properties of objects, it entails direct experience, which in turn deepens the child's self-awareness. The child *discovers* his or her fingers as they try to contain the sand or stack the blocks and discovers their limitation when the sand is spilled or the block tower collapses. The most fundamental requirement of any type of play is the experience that a child can change the structure of the world through his or her own engagement with it—and that he or she is changed in turn.

Initially, Niki's therapist models simple forms of play and tries to coax her out of the narrow circumference of her life in the crib by showing her that a playful engagement with things is safe. She opens up the possibilities inherent in the sand: it can be dug up or smoothed, hollowed or stacked, filtered or packed together. A precondition for play is the ability to experience the multiple possibilities for engagement inherent in things. This openness sets play apart from other human activities such as work or structured learning. In play, as we saw in earlier chapters, the other, concealed dimensions of things beckons. The sand in the sand tray "is worlding," that is, it reveals itself as the nexus of a full field of meaning, and hence of possible engagements. To a child deprived of a holding environment the uncanniness and fullness of plenary possibilities can be overwhelming: the sand tray is strange and threatening. To play with the sand tray would mean to venture into the unknown and leave traces of herself, which this little girl has learned not to do. Her life was marked by the severe restriction of her intentionality. When the sand responds to the touch of the hand, it makes suddenly visible the child's very own gesture and reveals her as an actor on the world's stage. It becomes a possible location for self-expression and self-experience and makes the child's intentionality visible: "Here *I want* to have a hollow in the sand . . . and there . . . Do I want it to remain smooth?"

Play becomes the location where *agency and selfhood are exercised without direct annunciation of the self* (Gadamer 1996).

For a long time Niki merely watches the therapist play with all kinds of things, withholding all traces of herself. The therapist is very aware that Niki needs the adult's constancy and the sameness of the small play-room, and she is content to establish the human warmth, spatial constancy, and temporal rhythms that mark a good holding environment and re-create a primary sense of housedness. Finally, Niki picks up two cups and pours sand from one into the other, a gesture that is followed by pouring water onto the sand. Filling and emptying, giving and receiving are two primary forms of human experience. The satisfaction of sensory sand play, its visceral pleasure, is enhanced by this primary experience of emptiness and fullness that Niki herself can now create.

The sand flowing from the cup is more than an object to Niki. Sand has its own gesture and physiognomy, which interacts with her. The outpouring and receiving of the cups makes visible the cycle of fullness and emptiness that has been an overwhelming theme in Niki's previous life. Interaction with things condenses the complexity of human emotions into a simple form, which then can be re-created and reproduced in drawing, play, language, and other symbolic expressions (Langeveld 1968). At the intersection between the child's gestures and the gestures of things, symbols are born. *Symbols arise in childhood not out of cognitive processing but from the active, affective entwining of the child's embodied existence and the sense-world.*

Niki's initial inability to play despite being in the "play age" highlights a number of structural elements of play. Play is a bodily, emotional, and mental engagement with the *possibilities* inherent in the physical world. These possibilities can be taken up and explored only when the child is *held* by a trusting and inviting relationship with adults (Erikson 1950/ 1963; Winnicot 2002). Adult neglect leads to autistic-type narrowing of the horizon of engagement, as the child fearfully avoids playing with the possibilities of things. Once the child takes up a playful relationship with the physical world, *symbolism* begins in the sensory-affective realm, only secondarily leading to cognitive understanding. The *self* is displayed and affirmed without directly announcing itself.

SYMBOLIC PLAY

After playing with the sifting cups for quite a while, Niki achieves a significant breakthrough in the sand tray: *she brings a mother pig with seven piglets into the sandbox.* Out of the hundreds of figures on the shelves in her therapist's office she chooses these particular ones. This moment is a turning point: before her the sand is transformed into a landscape. The presence of the piglets and their mother alters what the sand can be, and whole new horizons of possible activity open up before the child. Placing the piglets in the sand tray is a founding event and a commitment to step into a particular world and engage it. I have intentionally chosen the word "world": "We understand by this the totality of that to which human comportment can be related and we assume that this 'totality' can be viewed as a whole" (Held 2002, 83). The sand becomes a world—a *kosmos*, as the Greeks would have called it. It has a particular order, a certain web of relationships that are concealed but nevertheless present. The sand tray is no longer an empty yellow expanse; it is the location where the drama of a mother-child relationship can be acted out. Niki's play in the sand tray seems to have now some inevitable paths to traverse. It is committed. She steps into this world, and over time its web of significances unfolds.

Niki's commitment required courage. She had to break out of the narrow, repetitive, sensory experience of the sand and allow herself to become an actor in the unfolding of her own inevitable drama. She tells us: "Out of all possibilities, the piglets and their mother are the first to inhabit my world, because their particular possibilities most closely mirror my need." The world she chooses is *her* creation, and she chooses it because *its* possibilities are *her* possibilities. Niki is awakening to the potentialities of her environment, and she steps into the clearing, allowing herself to be reflected back through her toys. She does not know yet what is coming, but by the choice of the mother pig and piglets she intuits and prefigures a particular narrative theme or plotline. The future is no longer undetermined; it is already marked out with possible themes that are compelling and, once opened up, inevitable.

Niki's play from then on has a particular logic, which means that she is striving to gain insight into the relationships that make up her world. Play therapy makes use of the implicit web of relationships or meanings that constitute the child's life-world and tries to let the child illuminate them. It reconnects with the ancient Greek sense of logic: "the fundamental meaning of the word *logos*, which it also has for Greek mathematics, is 'relation,' or more precisely, the 'laying open of a relation'" (Held 2002, 83). Play therapy is a logical activity, but it involves a logic that goes deeper than cognition or even verbal expression. This also can be said for play in general: *it lays open relations*.

With the piglets in the sandbox, the curtain upon the unfolding drama of mothers and babies has been opened, and the child cannot help but take up the narrative in her particular way.

> From this time forward her play took on different characteristics, becoming repetitive and exact. At every session for about three months, she buried the mother pig in the left hand corner of the sand tray. The piglets were placed in the opposite corner, and they took turns trying to find the mother pig. The child said nothing during this play, yet appeared to be absorbed in what she was doing, frequently showing a low-range affective variance. The piglets would go looking for the mother and would alternately fall in water and drown, climb and fall off a tree, fall off a bridge, and be unable to climb fences, mountains, or other obstacles. (Gil, cited in James 1994, 142–43)

The endless journey of the piglets in search of their mother has a deeply tragic quality. Niki has stepped into the world of symbolic play, and its affective power carries her along. Despite its almost unbearable sadness, Niki perseveres with her script over and over. The young in search of mother fall and drown, get stopped by mountains, trees, fences, and streams, and it seems as if the whole world prevents them from getting what they need. The exact repetition of this painful script points to one of the key elements of play: play is an emotional or *pathic* activity. Unlike cognitive or *gnostic* activities, which are articulate, process oriented, and focus on what we know about something, *pathic* activities are a feeling-toned communion with playthings. The pathic child experiences an immediate connection with her world (Buytendijk 1933). Her affective intentionality determines the course of play, and its goal is not necessarily pleasure and happy excitement (which we usually associate with contented children's play) but the completion of an emotional form. She strives to grasp the hidden order of her world. Niki is not talking to her therapist to figure out how to live her life better (which would be a later, cognitive/gnostic activity); she is shaping and reshaping the affective dimension of her life. Like a musician, she plays through the variations of her theme of "getting lost"; like a sculptor, she goes over and over the layers to peel away the emotional form that lies under the surface. Her play differentiates the affective domain, and her toys help her find containers or gestures for the pain in her life. Unhurried play makes it possible for the child to learn a *silent symbolic language*, prior to speech or even alongside the spoken word, which shapes and brings to visibility the affective threads that bind her, however tenuously, to things and people in her life.

"We play only with what is pathic in our presence" (Buytendijk 1933, 129), that is, with things or events that addresses our feeling life. The primary motivation for play lies in its power to let the child move in a feeling world that has become accessible to the senses: pain takes the visible form of the mound over the buried mother, the auditory form of the swishing sand as the piglets are pushed through it, the haptic form of the smallness of piglet bodies. The plenary fullness of a play situation evokes a world that is ineffable and profound. The complexity and depth of the feeling world that the child makes visible through her toys goes beyond verbal articulation. Play displays the affective life of the child but, as in theater, there are some scripts that are more differentiated and satisfactory than others. It takes Niki three months to perfect her "searching for mother" script. The first act, burying the mother, remains constant, but there are so many ways to get lost on the way to her!

After founding and stepping into her world, Niki gets stuck in one of its most powerful relational themes. She cannot see the rest and compulsively repeats the traumatic feeling form. But then we see a second major turning point in Niki's play. The child startles herself when one day the familiar script moves into a different direction: "One day there was a major difference in Niki's repetitive scenario: None of the piglets drowned, fell down, or otherwise faced an overwhelming obstacle—they instead found and uncovered the mother pig! *Niki stopped abruptly, almost surprised by what she had done* and quickly moved away from the sand-tray, indicating she was done for the day" (Gil, as cited in James 1994, 143; my emphasis). Niki is so surprised by what opens up before her that she cannot engage with it and, at least temporarily, abandons the world she has created. This moment is a moment of wonder or awe. What has happened?

One of the essential features of play is that we continue to play with something only *if it plays with us* (Buytendijk 1933). The unpredictable response of the bouncing ball, the wiggling and giggling of the other players collapsed in a heap at the end of ring-around-the-rosy, the piglets exploring possible paths through the sand tray: all illustrate how playthings interact with the player and change the game. Niki is *surprised* when the piglets find and uncover their mother because the possibilities inherent in the sandbox go beyond the fixed game she has set up. At this juncture the sand tray becomes uncanny because the new constellation of playthings implies affective possibilities that are overwhelming. Niki arrests her symbolic play because she does not know if it is safe to step into the new world that has opened up where piglets are *with* their mother. This is a fearful moment, an instant where the child gets a glimpse of the future: the piglets cannot go back now to getting lost. They must engage their mother. In Niki's pathic world, the heroes find the grail, but they get more than they bargained for. Finding the mother is not the end but just the beginning of another leg of the quest. It ushers in a new set of affective play gestures that symbolize the troubled relationship between mother and child.

Niki's surprise when the piglets find their mother is a moment of wonder in the truest sense. Wonder, as Held (2002) has shown, is of an ambivalent nature. For the Greeks it was a *pathos*, a suffering.

> We are overtaken by a joyous wonder *that* the single, all life-world encompassing world is "there" at all, rather than not being there. In this elevated attunement, wherein this "wonder" at the opening of the world overcomes us, we sense at the same time the fact of the world's being there, rather than there being nothing, is not in our power. In the happy occurrence of wonder, the darkness of nothing is concurrently present as a shadowy abyss. Therefore deep wonder leaves us speechless and calls forth questions. (88)

Niki's wonder is more of the awe-full nature: the totality of the world opens before her, but what she glimpses is the shadowy abyss of *no relationship*. The darkness of nothing is in the foreground and overwhelms her. Even though she created the play script, ultimately it is not in her power because it reflects the order of a larger world. Her moment of deep wonder means that she cannot continue her play as it has been. A question has arisen, and it demands answers: what happens when the babies find their lost mother?

> During the following session one piglet began the "search for the mother" ritual and found and uncovered her quickly. This time the child put the piglet next to the mother, looked up at me, and said: "titty no milk." She seemed genuinely sad, and her eyes watered up. I said "No milk for the baby," and the child responded tearfully, "Baby sad." She held a big stuffed rabbit in her lap for the rest of the session and rocked it and fed it with a plastic bottle. From time to time a single tear would fall on her cheek. (Gil, in James 1994, 143)

Niki's first verbal communicative act is the phrase "titty no milk." It sums up her mother's greatest failure: "no milk" signifies the absence of nourishment and intimacy, the loss of a basic housedness and well-being that is the foundation for the baby's full future. It also evokes the loss of the bond between mother and baby and reverberates with a young child's profound loneliness. This is the tragic disappointment at the core of Niki's life experience. "Titty no milk"—it seems that from the beginning her play with the piglets has been moving toward this scene.

The progression of Niki's response mirrors the archetypal progression of wonder, speech, and curiosity: "As is well known, wonder makes one initially speechless. But what is peculiar to this attunement is that it does not wish to abide in speechlessness, but demands that the things that show themselves in the newly appearing world be brought to language. Thus deep wonder transforms itself into a curiosity about things now seen anew" (Held 2002, 89).

Niki, for the first time, comes to speech because a world is opening before her *that demands to be spoken*. Speech arises because it is now possible to speak to someone. The relationship with another human being is the foundation of the speech act: *someone speaks because there is someone who might hear it.* The silent play in the sandbox had allowed Niki time to elaborate the emotional ground of her trauma beyond spoken language, but finally words break through: "Baby sad." How insufficient these first words seem compared to the full emotional impact of her play script! But now her play changes as well and assumes a more fluid and expressive form. As if to restore the emotional fullness of her drama, she picks up the stuffed rabbit and comforts it by *rocking and feeding* it. Taking up the maternal gestures herself, Niki changes perspective and supplies to another being what the pig failed to give the piglet, what her mother failed to give to her: she holds it. The paradox of nurturing and abandonment is borne fully in Niki's pietalike cradling of the rabbit, while "from time to time a single tear would fall on her cheek" (Gil, in James 1994, 143).

Niki retreats from the affective form of the piglets into the sphere of the stuffed rabbit because it is more intimate and immediate: the cloth rabbit can be hugged and touched; it is closer to all the senses than the toys in the sand tray. Holding and feeding are sensuous experiences and more primary than symbolic play. Niki's play narrative is eclipsed at this point because she needs more than symbolism. Her regression to holding the rabbit is a regression to a familiar experience: the blanket she used to clutch in her crib. But as she hugs the soft toy, she also feeds it, and hence maintains the symbolic play-space. She is not retreating into mute self-enclosedness as before.

This moment is deeply significant. Earlier, with the sifting cups, she discovered her power to change the sensory world, and she uses this power now as she hugs the rabbit close to her body. But she also maintains a symbolic distance where the rabbit is more than a comforter to her senses. Niki plays not only with material, sensory objects but with the full affective dimension of the relationship between mother and infant as it is evoked by these particular toys. In the world of play she can assume the maternal gestures herself while at the same time empathizing with the baby rabbit. We witness here the dynamic relationship between the sensuous and the symbolic and how one or the other dimension has a preferred place in play at one time or the other. And there are times when they come together: Niki is comforted by the sensuousness of the rabbit's touch as she herself symbolically comforts another infant being. Play augments that which cannot be spoken because in play the child can begin to represent symbolically the totality of her world as it appears in wonder. Symbolic play is one of the way stations of world exploration: an expression of human curiosity and a striving for knowledge that transcends spoken language.

Conceptual language has great difficulty unraveling the complexity of Niki's affective gestural symbols. Her therapist Eliana Gil, in an unadorned way, allows for a very simple language to describe the events that are visible. Her sentences—"The mother pig is buried," "The baby pig fell from the tree," or "No milk for the baby"—offer no other comfort but the communication that another human being is fully present and witnessing the drama unfold. Her language—which restricts itself to straightforward statement sentences without adjectives or other linguistic embellishments—lifts into words the mute play of the child. It is unobtrusive and lets the child's own intentionality unfold. It simply describes what is seen and respects the child's right to express her own suffering. But the subtext that the therapist enacts lies in the reassurance that even unspeakable things can be shared and that there are other, compassionate human beings who are welcoming her into their community. Through her simple speech the therapist signals that she has heard the child. While Niki's previous play was primarily solipsistic, the exchange of spoken words necessitates the active engagement in the interpersonal realm. Language is symbolism as it is shared, reflected, and elaborated in the space between people.

In the next therapy session Niki repeats the same theme a number of times: the piglet finds the mother, there is no milk, the rabbit is stroked and fed. "When the piglet found no milk the third time Niki did this play, Niki reached over and placed a mother giraffe in the opposite corner of the tray. She then picked up the baby giraffe, and the baby giraffe and the piglet seemed to nestle together next to the mother giraffe. 'This mommy gots milk!' the child exclaimed. She again held the rabbit and stroked its head, saying 'There, there, . . . you awright'" (Gil, in James 1994, 143). After this session Niki's relationship with her therapist and foster mother became more engaged, and her play went beyond the piglets in the sand tray and included a whole variety of new forms. The narrative line of babies in search of mothers had come to its conclusion: the piglets, the baby rabbit, and Niki herself will be "awright."

Niki's case highlights the potential of play to shift the feeling life of a child and to create a world that she understands and inhabits in a fuller way. Play is the creation of a symbolic world in all existential dimensions, and it allows for fluid experimentation with embodiment, coexistence, objects, spatiality, temporality, and language. The *body* can be strong or delicate, young or old, animal or human, and do or pretend to do the impossible. *Others* can be real people who are imitated, or they might be purely pathic figures who are given an anthropomorphic form. *Things* transform from one into the other in metaphoric splendor, pushing the edge of what a particular thing is. *Space* allows for an imaginary world to be created and enacted, and yet there is a faithfulness to the most essential and archetypal spatial forms (journey, abyss, corner, nest, and so on). *Time* curls in on itself: it is nonlinear, past and future weave together, it is intuitive and unfettered by the need for timed production. Play follows the spell of the sensuous, is the lining, the curling over between natural and symbolic forms. It is an essential activity for children at an age when they are not reflective but learn by engagement.

EARLY CHILDHOOD AND THE STRUCTURES OF PLAY

Play, because of its affective, magical, prelogical relationship to things and people, is the perfect activity for a nondualistic, egocentric mind. Piaget's insight that the young child does not separate self from world and has very little understanding of an "inner" life has far-reaching implications for how we deal with Niki and other young children. For Niki, the world is not a panorama "out there"—its openness and closedness, its invitations and refusals are entwined with who she is. As an "egocentric" consciousness in Piaget's sense (Piaget 1929/1951), she initially has no distance from her environment, and the influence of the social world is immediate and profound. We understand the smallness of her world as a direct reflection of the smallness of her psychological life: no invitation from the world = no person there to be invited. The activity of play creates a clearing where the empathic fluidity of a non-dualistic consciousness can display itself. It holds open a field of action *between* reality and illusion, necessity and fantasy.

The analysis of Niki's case has revealed a number of characteristic features of play that I want to reiterate:

Play requires a safe, predictable, and caring adult presence in the background. Without this the child's horizon becomes constricted. Loving caregivers provide the sense of safety that emboldens the child to explore his or her environment and to risk being changed or shaped by it. In their strange-situation experiments, Mary Ainsworth et al. (1978) demonstrated clearly that toddlers' rate of comfort and inquisitive exploration behavior in a strange playroom is directly related to the quality of attachment to their parents. Children who are securely attached, who have a sense of housedness, also have less anxiety in a strange environment and are more willing to explore. Housedness extends beyond the walls of the home and is one of the preconditions for creative play. Creative play happens when the existential ground of housedness and nourishment makes the world and relationships trustworthy. We see Niki's therapist patiently work on establishing this ground by her dependable and calm presence in the same place, at the same time, for every session. In nontherapeutic play the adults don't necessarily have to be there: their background presence is reflected in the open safety of the play situation and the child's absence of apprehension or fear.

Play follows the invitation of the sensuous world. We find here a reversal of our common dualistic attitude, which sees things as distant objects out there, waiting to be manipulated by masterful adults. For the egocentric child, things have their own intentionality: *things play with the child.* Hence, it is important to think about the qualities of play materials and what kind of play they invite. Is their structure and texture pleasing or exciting to the senses? Do they call for narrowly defined play scripts, or are they generous in what they allow the child to be?

Play explores the fullness of the world's hidden possibilities. Niki's exploration of the lost-piglet script reveals the close attention she pays to her playthings. She explores the plenary possibilities inherent in the sand and the piglet figures, and out of their imaginary interaction new possibilities for action arise. In play the mind is engaged without effort, but engaged nevertheless. The contemplation of a plaything's sensory and symbolic possibilities makes the mind more fluid and extends the range of what is attended to and known. A more varied and fuller world will make the child's thinking more expansive and will provide for a more nuanced verbal expression. It is "logical" in the sense that it lays open the concealed relations inherent in the world. Because young children do not have the preformed cultural explanations and concepts about the world that characterize adult thinking, their playful "magical" thinking is in fact a free, unprejudiced investigation into the structure and symbolism of things.

Play is an exercise in empathy. Play fosters an empathic relationship with things and people: playing children allow themselves to be touched by the world. The child probes being, and so probes her or his own being. The piglets are like Niki, and their victory draws a possible horizon for her own future victory. Play fosters empathic observation, and it establishes an affective-ethical connection between the child and the physical/social world.

Play explores and elaborates the affective dimension of the child's lived world. For young children there is not a "physical world" out there, only physiognomies: affective life is spread out over things, and things invite an emotional response. The egocentric mind does not see things as other; it experiences them as extensions of itself. As children playfully rearrange the visible and tangible world of things, they are also rearranging their feeling lives. The young child's egocentrism offers adults a wonderful opportunity: by the toys we offer, the stories we tell, the work we show them, the environments we create, we can influence our children's affective lives immediately and profoundly. Young children absorb what they see without reflection, critique, or distance. Parents and teachers either issue the invitation to the child to step into a safe world and make something of it or, in varying degrees, they foreclose the affective bond between the child and the world, as we saw in Niki's case.

Play fosters the discovery of symbols through the emotional/sensory contact with things and people before they become cognitive or linguistic. Language is often insufficient to address the complexity of the affective domain, but play displays this complexity tangibly, over time, and in all its paradoxical features. As Niki attaches her feelings to the piglet figures, her interaction with these toys changes her feeling life because the lost piglets become a symbolic affective form, which is particularly suited to carrying out Niki's emotional project. It allows her to explore the subtleties and range of possible feelings as they are narrated through the pigs' adventures. The imaginative manipulation of toys restructures children's experience of their own emotions. The landscape of feelings that ties them to people and things becomes elaborated and refined through play. It seems to me that this is one of the most profound functions of play:

it evokes, represents, and differentiates the child's evolving emotional life in symbolic forms.

Play involves the creation of a meaningful, coherent world with ordered locations and scripts. The play scripts Niki developed, like the play scripts of kindergarten children playing prince and dragon, or mother cat and kittens, are of an archetypal nature. Mother/father–baby, venturing forth into a dangerous world, getting lost in the woods, rescuing people, fighting against evil—these are all typical plots for young children's play. By elaborating and individualizing these scripts, children traverse a universal emotional human landscape and in the process differentiate and articulate their feeling and thinking lives.

Play is an open, undetermined activity that allows the child's capacity for active intentionality to develop. The self is revealed and affirmed in the play-world without directly announcing itself. We saw Niki display and affirm herself by developing and inhabiting a world of her own creation. She chose the pig and piglets; she made the trees, ditches, and walls. Play makes her emotional intentions visible. It allows for a symbolic space where the prereflective child can show her self without directly announcing it. Play thus honors the child's egocentrism by allowing awareness without self-awareness, self without self-reflection. The pleasure of play is driven by the satisfaction that the world I have created in my play reflects myself. Its failings in apathy and boredom, or in the extreme form of autistic repetition, are also a failing of the child's active intentionality and sense of self.

Play, to paraphrase Rousseau, is truly the child's work, because in play the child changes the world and his- or herself. Play requires that adults give children the freedom to build their own imaginary worlds free from adult expectation and instruction—but never too far removed from a protective adult presence.

FROM PLAY TO LITERACY

The structural analysis of Niki's play has revealed that play has an important function in educating the child's feeling life. Play in a preschool or kindergarten is not a waste of time in the antechambers of literacy but an activity appropriate for the egocentric, nondualistic young child. It teaches the child attention, observation, and empathy; it awakens symbolic capacity and provides images for a varied emotional life; it strengthens the child's sense of agency, intentionality, and selfhood; and it keeps the child's sense of wonder and curiosity alive.

The neglect or even disdain for play in American education has deep roots. As we saw in chapter 3, decades ago Piaget was asked by American educators how to speed up the developmental process in preoperational young children. This has become known as the "American Question." Piaget's reply was: "But why would you want to do that?" I share Piaget's puzzlement, as do other child researchers (Bruner et al. 1976; Elkind 1987/2000; Greenspan and Benderly 1997; Healey 1999).

Yet Piaget himself, despite his careful attention and understanding of early childhood thought, often disparages young children's mental activity. From the beginning of his research work, Piaget found children to exhibit forms of thinking that threatened adult logic. He evaluated the young child's egocentrism mostly in negative terms when compared to adult cognition and described is as a failure of the formal operational mind. The child adheres to observation of the physical world without distinguishing it from the self, which leads to a form of realism that Piaget characterizes as illusory. Even though Piaget showed much sensitivity to the texture of child thought, in the final analysis he dismissed it as merely a step to a higher adult logic. Piaget's attitude has clouded the minds of educators who, against Piaget's own advice, try to hurry our children through this "preoperational" stage, which, they mistakenly believe, is merely a waiting room where the child wastes time on the way to the good stuff. Play is the first casualty in hurrying up our children because on the surface it seems to be an unproductive waste of time. According to this approach, time would be better spent in adult-structured, educational activities so that we can give our children a head start in the three Rs.

But let me reformulate the question from the perspective of an existential developmental psychology: in the rush to teach our children academic skills, especially reading when they are four or five years old, are we foreclosing and stunting the development of mental and emotional abilities that need this sensitive period in early childhood to flourish? Teaching children how to read is not merely the acquisition of a skill, it is a restructuring of the psychological life of young children.

In their social and historical studies Ong (1982) and Eisenstein (1979) have shown that the acquisition of writing technology transforms human consciousness. This is true not only in the cultural acquisition of print but also in the lives of our young children. The cultural shift from orality to literacy is mirrored in each child's experience when he or she learns to read (Egan 1988). A competent reader has to develop the following abilities: the capacity for physical, emotional, and mental self-restraint; a tolerance for delayed gratification; a sophisticated ability to think conceptually and sequentially; a preoccupation with both historical continuity and the future; a high valuation of reason and hierarchical order (Postman 1994). On a practical level, children who learn to read have to sit still and restrict physical and mental attention to a small space, memorize arbitrary symbols, stay focused on a purely mental activity, think and see sequentially, give up their social interactions, pay attention to their teacher, and enter a purely symbolic world that is not mediated by human voice or presence. In order to teach young children how to read, the teacher has to set up a particular environment that limits social interaction and forces the child to be focused on the teacher; play corners and toy stations give way to desks that restrict spatial movement; the child's attention must be recalled again and again to follow the linear sequence of print and to memorize arbitrary letter shapes and sound patterns. In order to be competent readers, children have to restructure the way they live in the world.

The shift from audible interactions to visual text brings more subtle changes in the way reality is experienced. Oral and literate cultures are profoundly different from each other. Orality has its own sophistication and depth, which most people in literate cultures cannot perceive. Let me quote Walter Ong (1982, 73) because he shows so clearly the difference between a world shaped through the activities of the ear and a world shaped by the activities of the eye. The shift from orality to literacy also applies to the transformation of oral child culture:

> In a primarily oral culture where the word has its existence only in sound, with no reference whatsoever to any visually perceptible text, and no awareness of even the possibility of such a text, the phenomenology of sound enters deeply into human being's feel for existence, as processed by the spoken word. For the way in which the world is experienced is always momentous in psychic life. The centering action of sound (the field of sound is not spread out before me but is all around me) affects man's sense of the cosmos. For oral cultures, the cosmos is an ongoing event with man at its center. Man is the *umbilicus mundi*, the navel of the world. . . . Only after print and the extensive experience with maps that print implemented would human beings, when they thought about the cosmos or the universe or "world," think primarily of something laid out before their eyes, as in a modern printed atlas, a vast surface or assemblage of surfaces (vision presents surfaces) ready to be "explored."

The process of learning to read decenters the child from the "umbilicus mundi," the participatory, egocentric oneness with the world.

Reading and the educational rituals that accompany it send children on their way to becoming the rational, distanced, analytical observers whom Piaget had in mind as the endpoint of development: the stage he labeled *formal operations.* But with the shift to literacy we also foreclose other possibilities for learning that are inherent in the oral world.

Reading is an essential aspect of Western human development because it produces a particular self who functions relatively well in our technologically sophisticated societies and knows how to handle the vast array of symbolic material that characterizes a literate culture. But it is also clear that the qualities required of a good reader are in stark opposition to the egocentric nature of young children's thinking and experiencing. *Our children need time in the "oral" world to develop the mental and emotional capacities that will turn them into creative, self-reflective, socially responsible adults who have the motivation and will to realize their projects.* To be a good, advanced reader does not mean to acquire the alphabet and phonic systems at an early age. It means to acquire them *at the right age,* when attention, memory skills, fine-motor development, and emotional development are ready. It also means a person who has the ability to engage cognitively and empathically with what is read and who understands the varied conventions of language use and human expression, all qualities that are practiced in oral exchanges. Reading does not begin with the alphabet but with the opportunity to practice language forms in preliterate, oral activities that honor young children's short attention span and their need to move about, be social, and play. I have found the most careful attempt to respect and nurture the child's oral play culture and its cognitive and emotional potential in Waldorf education.

As we saw in our earlier reflections, play is one of the most profound and sophisticated activities that young children engage in. It differentiates the child's emotional landscape and connects it to symbolic expression. Through imaginative empathy, play fosters a fuller connection with the body, other people, and the physical world. It educates the mind and the heart, and it empowers children to approach their worlds with courage and creativity. The oral world is a playful world where work is done, but carried lightly. By pushing literacy into the kindergartens and preschools and by eliminating time and space for play, we prevent our children from developing emotional sophistication; intelligence that relies on its own observation; ethical bonds with the people, things, and the natural world around them; and faith in their own will and ability to create worlds—perhaps with better scripts than the ones we provide them with today.

SIX

Because We Are the Upsurge of Time

Toward a Genetic Phenomenology of Lived Time

CLOCK TIME AND LIVED TIME

Einstein's Question

At a conference in Davos during the late 1920s, Albert Einstein posed a set of questions to the philosophers and psychologists who were present: "Is our intuitive grasp of time primitive or derived? Is it identical with our intuitive grasp of velocity?" Jean Piaget, who was in the audience, heard the questions and set out to investigate how children understand time (1970, ix). He wanted to reply to Einstein by contributing data about the developmental unfolding of the child's conception of time. In the following years, he experimented in his laboratory with children's grasp of motion, sequencing, succession, simultaneity, and synchronization, and he also interviewed children about the concept of age.[1]

Piaget devised a set of ingenious experiments and interviews to test children's understanding of synchronization and temporal duration (1970). In his laboratory he constructed two parallel tracks on which two toy snails (Yellow and Blue) could be moved forward, their velocity (speed) and stopping points controlled by the experimenter. Both snails started at the same point and time, moving at different but continuous velocities, which meant that Blue stopped further down the track (D1) than Yellow (C2). When Piaget asked the younger children if the snails stopped at the same time ("before or after lunch"), they insisted that

Yellow had stopped first because Blue "went on longer because it was further" (87). Even when he made Yellow move from B_1 to C_1 while Blue was already stopped at D_1, the children still insisted that Yellow had stopped before Blue because Blue "went on longer." The children obviously understood time as a function of spatiality and insisted that something that covered more ground also must have taken longer to get there. The younger children equated time and space, understood duration as the distance traversed, saw time as tied to specific events and locations, and experienced it as discontinuous.

After concluding his research in the 1940s, Piaget (1970) reported his findings as a reply to Einstein's questions. Here is a summary of the main points:

1. Children initially confuse the temporal order with the spatial order and duration with the path traversed. In the beginning, time is localized and discontinuous.
2. The concept of time is not given to primitive intuition but needs to be constructed during childhood through an operational synthesis by which the child abstracts time from its qualitative context.
3. Children's conceptual understanding of abstract and uniform time coincides with their conceptual understanding of abstract and uniform velocity (which means that velocity, as well, is not intuitively grasped by all human beings but derived).
4. When children achieve concrete operational thinking in middle childhood (they "decenter," that is, can hold more than one observation in mind, and they can reverse their thinking process), time becomes homogenous and continuous, even on the qualitative plane. Without "operational time," time remains discontinuous and local.

Piaget gives us the impression that in the course of "normal development" all children achieve operational time and set aside the more primitive "egocentric" time of their earlier years. The achievement of an abstract, homogenous, continuous time that is valid for all locations, all people, and forever is, according to Piaget, the inevitable trajectory of child development.

Beginning with Piaget's own research and writing, in this chapter we will unearth children's experiences of *lived* time, which often resist and undermine operational time. We will look at the different ways the present, the future, and the past come to children and challenge Piaget's view that the homogenous and continuous time of physics rules the temporal understanding of adult human beings.

Lived Time and the Alphabet

When we look at cultural time concepts we find that time, as it is lived by human beings, is not homogenous: it flows differently in different places. As Eliade (1954) has shown, most indigenous peoples inhabit a cyclical, mythical time that is regenerated, together with the life force of the culture, through recurring ritual acts. Here time is experienced not as a line going from past to present but as a circle in which the past returns eternally, and the future cycles backward into a mythical present. Time is experienced in a dynamic interchange with the flow of spatial presences. Sunlight and shadow, the movement of the moon, the smell of the changing seasons, the color of the river water, the flight of birds, the sounds of predators at night: all are indicators of the world's changing activity as it moves through time. It is essential for a people to understand lived time in their particular place and adapt to its requirements in order to survive the next season.

Beyond Piaget's operational time concept, which defines time by scientific parameters, there is *lived time*. In our experience we live time pre-reflectively and often without particular awareness of its manifestation. Our heartbeat and our breathing measure out the rhythmic passage of organic time, our steps leave past places behind, and our eyes scan the horizon for things that are not yet present. We remember the past and anticipate the future, and sometimes we mourn what has been and dread what is to come. Our foods, festivals, and moods are determined by the turning of the seasons. An hour can stretch and seem eternal, while the years can fly past. Lived time is ever present to us as a primitive, vital phenomenon that permeates personal and cultural life. The fluid mass of lived time provides the existential foundation for any elaboration of a rational, scientific concept of time. Once we begin to pay attention to lived time, we find ourselves in "that shifting, mysterious, imposing, and mighty ocean that I see everywhere around me when I think about time" (Minkowski 1970, 18).

Piaget's genetic epistemology of the time concept portrays the developing human being as increasingly logical-operational and surmounting the more prereflective, perception-based thinking of an earlier age. Time as a logical, linear construct that moves homogenously from past to present to future dominates our Western articulation of the time concept. The development of this conception of time might not be innately predetermined but rather culturally produced. Abram (1996) argues that the acquisition of the alphabet and its accompanying style of linear notation changes a culture's experience of time from a dynamic, animate, and emergent sense of local time to a uniform conception of progressive, abstract, universal time. In a nonliterate, oral culture time emerges as the dynamic experience of an "emergent environment," as Abram calls it, that is, an environment whose essential quality is its continual transformation in time. Linear, homogenous time requires abstraction from the cyclical, repetitive time patterns of everyday life and the construction of an idealized, logical time frame that is valid for all. Literacy, as Ong (1982) has shown, restructures the life-worlds of oral people, and with it their sense of time and space, and this is true for children as well, as we saw in the last chapter. Egan (1988) has argued that schooling brings with it the same shift: from a primarily oral sensibility and experience of the world, children are inducted into the symbolic world of literacy, which restructures not merely their thinking but their embodiment, spatial presence, coexistence with others, and their sense of time. Could it be that the cognitive changes that Piaget saw as genetically predetermined are due not to biological changes but to changes in schooling and literacy? That the developmental appearance of abstract time concepts arises not automatically but is culturally produced? This might explain why many children in nonliterate cultures fail to conserve volume or number or cling to their magical thinking—as many adults do as well. Linear time and homogenous space might not make sense in their life-worlds and have no personal or cultural function.[2]

Cultural Time and the Duration of Loneliness

Lived time permeates cultural practices and varies widely across the globe. The social psychologist Robert Levine (1997) studied the fastness and slowness (velocity) of different cultures by measuring the walking speed of pedestrians, speed in the workplace, and the accuracy of bank clocks in downtown areas. He made the following observations: the healthier a place's economy, the faster its tempo; the more developed the country, the less free time per day; bigger cities have faster tempo; hotter places are slower; and individualistic cultures move faster than those that emphasize collectivism. He cites the example of the Kabyle people of Algeria, who despise speed in any of their affairs and regard hastiness as a lack of decorum and a sign of diabolical ambition. They refer to the clock as "the devil's mill" (19). Cultures are embedded into their own flow of time, and even though we regulate it through timepieces and rules pertaining to temporal rhythms, much of cultural time permeates our life without our awareness and reflection. Cultural time is *lived time*, and clock time is only one of its versions.

The unified, homogenous time that Piaget presupposes is a product of time as it is lived and conceptualized in Western culture. In our search for a healthy, fully developed economy, where life is centralized in air-conditioned big cities and where we prize the individual over the collective, cultural time is lived as an ever-increasing rush forward, and individuals feel that they have less and less time for themselves. When *time is money*, the relationship between care (time spent) and value (what has importance) has been reduced to purely material economic factors, and time becomes a scarce commodity to be counted, and hoarded, and exchanged for material wealth.[3] As a political tool, homogenous time allows for the homogenization and control (*Gleichschaltung*) of labor, education, and information dissemination. It is essential for coordinating activity in an increasingly global and technological economy, but it also standardizes and levels cultural differences wherever it is imposed. Homogenous time is a construct that exists because we have articulated it, believe in it, educate our children into it, and reinforce it through cultural practices and technologies. It has proven to be a powerful tool in the production of material wealth.

Levine (1997) cites a passage from Alan Lightman's book *Einstein's Dreams*, which illuminates the difference between clock time and "event" time as it is lived before the clock has homogenized cultural time:

> In a world where time cannot be measured, there are no clocks, no calendars, no definite appointments. Events are triggered by other events, not by time. A house is begun when stone and lumber arrive at the building site. The stone quarry delivers stone when the quarryman needs money . . . trains leave the station . . . when the cars are filled with passengers. . . . Long ago, before the Great Clock, time was measured by changes in heavenly bodies: the slow sweep of stars across the sky, the arc of the sun and variation in light, the waxing and waning of the moon, tides, seasons. Time was measured also by heartbeats, the rhythm of drowsiness and sleep, the recurrence of hunger, the menstrual cycles of women, the duration of loneliness. (81)

In economic terms, event time is not very efficient because the coordination of individual productive activities on a larger scale is almost impossible. Time here is tied to events and submits itself to *their* sequence and duration. It does not stand above events as the great conductor and taskmaster. Time technology, however, has reversed this relationship and forced the meandering brook of event time into the straight canal of numerical hours, minutes, and seconds. What we have gained in efficiency, however, we have lost in vision: no longer the careful observation of the night sky and the surrounding plant and animal habitat to determine spring planting time—eyes glued to our wristwatches, we miss the nonhomogenous, but nevertheless shared, time of the natural world around us. When my friend Dick Knowles was a boy he used to spend his summers at his uncles' farm in Ireland. He often worked with them in the fields. When lunchtime approached Uncle Davie would say: "Hey, Dickie, what time is it?" and wait for the boy to pull up his sleeve and check his American wristwatch. "It's 11:35," Dickie would say. The uncle would turn to his brother: "Is that correct, Mickey?" Uncle Mickey would raise his hands as if to weigh something and reply, "Nah, it feels like . . . mhmm . . . yes . . . 11:37." Uncle Davie would then squint up at the sun in concentration, wrinkle his brow in deep calculation, and finally say: "Nah, Dickie, your watch is wrong. Tis exactly 11:37."

As with so many phenomena that the natural sciences have investigated, the abstract, mathematical understanding of homogenous time has dominated our public discourse to such a degree that all intuitive understanding of time has lost its credibility. When no one speaks for a phenomenon, it eventually falls out of language, and after a while we lose the capacity to differentiate its nuances and think about it clearly. The task of phenomenology is to reconnect the fullness of phenomena to thinking and speaking, so that our psychological life can flow through a subtle and varied world. When we believe in Piaget's concept of adult, homogenous time, we forget that time is a mystery and full of depth, and that we are more than homo economicus working around the clock. J. H. van den Berg (1972) has shown that in lived time the causal sequences of the space-time continuum do not hold up: the past does not come before the present, and the future does not follow the past. No one gets out of bed in the morning, goes for a swim in the river, or travels to another country unless they were already in the day, in the river, on the journey and were meeting themselves in that particular future. The relation of present and future is such that the present envelops the future. And the past is coming to meet us out of the future. Minkowski argues that the idea of homogenous, geometric time that modern culture imposes upon us is a form of slavery from which we must free ourselves: "It is not a question of having free time but of learning how to live and to breathe freely and spontaneously in time." The problem of time, then, "becomes a very vital and personal problem for each one of us" (1970, 5).

Perhaps it takes extreme circumstances to awaken contemporary Western people to the strange depth of time. When Robert Levine had a teaching job in Brazil, it took him months to adjust to the Brazilian sense of time: he would show up to give a lecture at the appointed time, but none of the students were there. They trickled in over time, but then assumed that the class would continue at least half an hour beyond scheduled time, which would make Levine late for his next appointment, and so on. All the clocks on walls and watches on people's wrists gave different times, and nobody minded but him. But being later than a superior for a scheduled appointment and making her wait was seen as an arrogant insult! "Brazil made it clear to me that time was talking. But understanding what it was saying was no easy matter" (1997, xvi).

Sixty years before, Eugene Minkowski found himself in the trenches of World War I, enduring a monotony that deeply disturbed his sense of time and made him and his fellow soldiers forget the date, or even which day of the week it was. To the soldiers in the trenches, boredom, the infinite stretch of empty time, was the "other enemy": "all our suffering, outside the devastation sown by death, came from time" (1970, 14). In a calm sector of Aisne in a relatively comfortable shack in the winter of 1916–17, Minkowski drew up the ground plan for what later would become his great book, *Lived Time*. There, as Piaget's homogenous, measured Western time lay splintered and broken all around him, he worked on such poignant themes as "memory and oblivion," "the phenomenology of death," and "how we live the future."

THE LIVED PRESENT

Beyond the Proud Kitchen Clock

Lived time does not follow the rules of physics. In our experience of lived time, an hour can be an eternity when we are waiting for a medical test result, or it can shrink to nothing when we are playing a musical instrument with great intensity. It stretches ahead of us as the infinite summer after school lets out, or it vanishes behind us as the years wasted in an unsuitable job or relationship. We wonder sometimes why a year in childhood and youth seemed so long, and why now the months fly past and it is the next year in the blink of an eye. Time, as Merleau-Ponty (1962) discovered, is not really a river that flows forward with an inevitable, homogenous momentum from the past through the present into the future; it is not a flowing substance that carries everything forward in its wake. "Time is not a line, but a network of intentionalities" (417). In lived time past, present, and future overtake each other, reverse their order, and weave together their intricate web of becoming. The past is nothing without the future, the present does not exist without the past, and the future determines how we experience the past and the present. "Hence time, in our primordial experience, is not for us a system of objective positions, through which we pass, but a mobile setting which moves away from us, like the landscape seen through a railway carriage window" (420). Lived time rearranges itself continually because we flow along with it.

When Piaget, in his reply to Einstein, lays out the structure of children's *conceptual understanding of time*, he also gives us some clues to the *genetic structure of lived time.* Before the child applies operational, logical thinking to time phenomena, and apart from what children learn from adults, time is grasped by the young child in a prereflective, perception-centered, nondualistic way. The following two examples illustrate the typical features of young children's sense of time. One afternoon when Piaget's daughter had missed her customary nap, she remarked to him: "I have not had a nap, so it isn't afternoon" (Piaget 1930). She tried to correct her father's time concept, which contradicted her temporal experience. Minkowski begins his reflections on lived time with a very similar example: "When my son was six years old, I usually accompanied him to school. We had breakfast together, then I smoked a cigarette, and then we left for school. One day I got up later than usual. I said to my son, who was calmly drinking his milk, 'Hurry up, little one, or we'll be late.' The answer came at once: 'But father,' my son said, 'we can't be late; you haven't smoked your cigarette yet'" (1970, 14).

Adults, used to the temporal homogeneity of all afternoons, smile at the precausal reasoning of the child. It is 3:00, and therefore it is afternoon. It is 7:55 A.M., and therefore we are running late for school. But both children in the above anecdotes tell time not by the hands of the clock but by the remembered sequence of events. As Piaget discovered in his dialogue with Einstein, young children have experiences and concepts about time that differ from adults. They live in event time—that is, an experienced time that is not ruled by clock time. Even Einstein acknowledged the difference between lived time and time conceptualized by physics. He thought that there was something essential about the present (the "Now," as he calls it) that lies just outside the realm of science: "Once Einstein said that the problem of the Now worried him seriously. He explained that the experience of the Now means something special for man, something essentially different from the past and the future, but that this difference cannot occur in physics. That this experience cannot be grasped by science seemed to him a matter of painful but inevitable resignation" (Carnap 1963, as cited in Savitt 2002, #236, 2).

Despite Piaget's interpretation of children's understanding of time as primitive, their sense of time is not chaotic or undifferentiated. Time comes to the young child not as an abstract concept but as a lived, pre-reflective encounter with temporal phenomena that pervades her or his daily life. Time surges up, and the past, present, and future coil into each other in such simple events as a missed naptime. Piaget's daughter tells us that she remembers the sequence of events in her life, and within that sequence it cannot be afternoon because afternoon is *always* after naptime. The events that *have been* (the past) stand behind her protesting outcry in the form of sedimented temporal habits, and what is coming to be (the future), is suddenly uncertain: if it is afternoon but there has been no nap, what is coming next? How does she move into this strange afternoon that has no right beginning now, that feels different and disconnected from what came before and from all the other afternoons she has known? How does Minkowski's son feel as his morning becomes hurried and unpredictable because the sequence of events that marks the familiar flow of the present into the future schoolday cannot be relied upon? I have talked to a number of preschool teachers who told me that when a substitute teacher changes the sequence of scheduled events (which are usually strictly followed), the children become agitated and aggressive and out of sorts. They cannot articulate their intuitive understanding of time, but they respond anxiously when it is disturbed.

The young child's "intuitive time," as Piaget found, "is limited to successions and durations given by direct perceptions," unlike "operational time," which requires operational logic (1970, 2). Piaget's interviews with young children help us to unearth the beginning of time *perception* as it precedes the more abstract time *conceptions* of later years. The child's intuitive grasp of temporal phenomena arises from the prereflective, perceptual domain of the lived body.

Unlike Piaget, who sees the perception-based, intuitive sense of time as a primitive developmental phenomenon that has to be superseded and erased by the logical operations of the adult mind, Merleau-Ponty

(1962) argues that the prereflective, perceptual experience of lived time is not vanquished and supplanted by operational time but remains the central mode of experiencing time in adulthood as well. As Erwin Straus put it: "objective time, as it is symbolized by the image of the line, is not a primary datum of experience. It is a product of reflective thinking, a concept for the natural sciences" (1956, 31; my translation). Intuitive time, though perhaps not thematized and articulated, is with us as long as we live in a body and perceive the world, and it remains the pre-reflective foundation for mature thought. It is also the foundation for the cultural elaboration of adult time concepts, which can vary widely from the homogenous, linear, operational time postulated by Piaget.

Spatiotemporal Solidarity

We have a strong indicator of the depth of conviction that arises from children's experience of lived time. In Piaget's experiments with the blue and yellow snails, all the younger children claimed that the snail that traveled further also stopped later, despite the experimenter's careful arrangement of the opposite fact. "It went on longer because it was fur-ther" was the consensus among the children. Piaget wondered: "Why do they obstinately assert that II stopped 'first,' 'sooner,' or 'before' I?" (1970, 87).

The children's "obstinacy" is an indicator of a deeply held belief, and they hold to it even when Piaget demonstrates to them that snail II is still going while snail I has already stopped further down the path. The children believe that duration is tied to the distance traveled, and that clearly the snail that went further also *must have* taken longer. Time is measured by the amount of space covered. The children, as Piaget noted, do not differentiate space and time: "the child simply confuses time with velocity." "In other words, since it is at noon that you gener-ally come home for lunch, the fact that you have not reached home by then, far from implying that you are late, simply means that *time itself cannot possibly have reached the hour of lunch.* This is why children use the terms 'before,' 'first,' 'earlier,' etc., arbitrarily in their spatial and tem-poral senses, and why they equate the failure to reach a place at the nor-mal time with failure to reach the normal time itself" (Piaget 1970, 88; my emphasis).

Before and after in time are determined by spatial succession. It can-not possibly be afternoon since naptime has not happened yet, and we cannot be late for school since Father has not smoked his after-breakfast cigarette. Time is local and embedded in the unfolding of events. Rather than standing above spatial phenomena, it is intimately entwined with them. Lived time and space exist in a fundamental "spatiotemporal solidarity" (Minkowski 1970, 23).

The child measures time by *action sequences.* As *action space* is the prominent feature of lived childhood space, as we saw in chapter 2, *action time* characterizes the child's experience of time as it is tied to particular events and their succession. Temporality comes to children not as an abstract, homogenous, conscious construct; rather, it weaves through their felt sense of experience and expectation in the activities of everyday life. As if to a life raft, the young child clings to the succession of action time as the same action sequences unfold from last month to last week to yesterday to today. Month, week, yesterday do not exist apart from the repeated action sequences and, as words, do not make much sense until middle childhood.

In child psychology, we call these familiar action sequences "scripts" (Nelson 1981) or "frames" (Elkind 1987/2000). Scripts or frames describe the child's understanding of formatted events: how action unfolds, who participates, where it is going to happen, what kind of objects are present, and what the child's own role is. They allow the child to know what to expect and how to act in a social situation. Typical scripts are taking a bath, going to bed, having a snack, taking a nap, playing in the playground, going to a restaurant. They are generalized in the sense that children condense their past experiences into a structural format that transcends any single event. Elkind believes that frames have a very compelling quality and that children become very upset when a frame is broken, for example, when a parent leaves out words in a bedtime story: "it is a breaking of the order on which they begin to depend for security in a changing and often frightening world (131).

The naptime script, to which we saw Piaget's daughter cling, brings together the events after lunch that have been experienced repeatedly and arranges their content into an ordered plot, which the child understands and can narrate: "First we eat, then Daddy takes blankie and me to my bed, then I lie down and he covers me, then he kisses me, then I sleep. Then I wake up and my sister is home from school and we have a snack, then . . ." The past has become a memory of events that are enacted every day. In the now of the present the child expects the world to arrange itself into the same sequence: lunch, blankie, tucking in, kiss, sleep, waking to the voices of siblings are landmarks along the road of time. Each evokes a slightly different mood, and together they form the narrative "naptime," which comes before "afternoon." The sequence of "naptime first, then afternoon" provides consistency and order and allows the child to move into a future that is already predictable.

Our examples from Piaget and Minkowski show not only that children have scripts but that they often combine them into larger temporal frames. "Afternoon" is determined not by the clock but by the unfolding of scripted events, which act as beacons of consistency in an always-changing world. Children rely on the rhythm of events, and time is measured by their ordered appearance. This sense of rhythmic time is intuitive rather than cognitive, affective rather than rational, implicit rather than articulated.

Ambient Becoming

Not all events, however, are sequenced together into coherent temporal scripts, especially when they happen without a regular rhythmic order. One characteristic feature of preschoolers' thinking is that they focus on individual events but do not connect them into a larger structure. A typical feature of the "house-tree-person" drawings of four-year-olds, for example, is that even though there is a house, a tree, and a person in the picture, they seem to be disconnected from each other and look as if they are floating in space. An older child, on the other hand, will organize space and show the ground below, the house, tree, person, and the sky above (preferably with birds flying above the house to make the invisible sky visible). In the younger child's picture space clings to each thing, but there is no cosmology that orders them all into a single, universal space. We find a similar feature with respect to time phenomena. Piaget found that instead of a homogenous time that links events in a temporal sequence, children think that *everything has its own time*, and that time is directly tied to a particular location or event (1970). Yellow and Blue, the two snails from Piaget's experiment, each have their own time in which they travel the track, and the children do not think that there is a universal time that links them both. There is not yet a cosmological narrative that places events into a general, ordered time frame. Time is, to use Minkowski's term, kaleidoscopic.

What might the world be like, when everything has its own time? Minkowski introduces a concept that describes this phenomenon at the level of adult lived time: "*ambient becoming*." Ambient becoming describes the experience of time as life bursts out and unfolds around me for other people and things (1970, 403). A kaleidoscope of things and people, each with their own time, moves alongside the child: some slower, some faster, but each with its own temporal intentionality. Clouds move through the sky in a different time than the horse galloping in the meadow. Even the mountains move, albeit very slowly, and the moon lives its time in a steady, curious presence: does it not follow us as our family drives home through the night? Because of children's initial absence of self awareness and their egocentric sense of nondistinction from the world, ambient becoming features probably much more prominently in their experience than self-becoming.[4]

And yet, as the child gives each thing its own time, there is also a shared presence in the kaleidoscope of ambient becoming. Here and now we move together toward the future. The moon has its own space and time, but it also moves along with me. Langeveld (1960) describes our lived sense of the present as "the experience of what is cotemporal" (47). For the child this means primarily that the experienced, cotemporal structure of the present lies in the "doing together" of action time. During naptime blankie sleeps *with* me, but my sister away in school is not cotemporal. Her action time does not overlap with mine. She is outside of the kaleidoscope of ambient becoming until the afternoon, when I hear her voice in the kitchen.

The present in the child's lived experience is characterized not only by the word *now* but also by the preposition *with*. What is not with me (in whatever form) is not there. It falls out of time. When Mom leaves her son at the daycare center and goes to work, she is no longer cotemporal, and her loss is intensely felt—for a short while, until other cotemporal events claim his attention. This also explains why children very rarely hold grudges for a long time, and how they can go from anger one minute to best buddies with a friend the next. What is no longer with them here and now has less hold over their attention. The present lets go and falls away into the past, and the child moves on toward the new engagement and mood of the next action sequence. Because children's sense of time is intimately tied into what is actively present, they have only a vague sense of "last week" or "the day after tomorrow" until they acquire a narrative structure that links the perceptual now step-by-step with past and future events.

But there is another, more profound sense of the present that is sometimes experienced in childhood. In the *deep present*, time ceases to move, and only when we resurface after an intense involvement in contemplative play or musical and artistic practice do we notice that time has still happened around us. We are embedded in the being and unfolding of a world with which we are cotemporal. But, fully engaged and fused with this world, the child can participate, for a short while, in the deep duration of being. The poet Rilke (1999, 102) evokes this in *The Fourth Duino Elegy* (my translation):

> O hours of childhood,
> When behind the figures was more
> than the past, and before us not the future.
> We were growing up, of course, impatient at times
> To grow up more quickly, half to oblige those
> who had nothing anymore but being grown up.
> And yet, in our ambient solitude, what delighted us
> was duration, and there we stood
> in the space between world and toy,
> a place that, from the beginning,
> has been consecrated for the pure event.

The deep present is eternal because there being, as Parmenides said, has no beginning and is whole, still, and without end (Wheelwright 1960). It simply is. "And suddenly the measured time of the proud kitchen clock appears shallow, distant, and coldly factual" (Langeveld 1960, 47).

THE FUTURE AND WHAT IS COMING TOWARD US

As psychologists, our general tendency when looking at temporal phenomena has been to examine time in terms of the past. We have studied memory sequences, unearthed past childhoods, looked to the past for causes of pathological behavior. The future has found a small place in developmental psychology in terms of expected stages that a child has to achieve on the way to adulthood. But the lived future, the experience of what is coming to be, has been mostly overlooked. How does the future figure in children's lives?

Discontinuous Futures

The future for the child is conceived not as a continuous unfolding process "but rather [as] a process of change tending toward certain states: time ceases to flow when these states are attained" (Piaget 1970, 202). Children believe, for example, that people get older up to a certain age, and then stay that way forever, or that age differences between siblings are not maintained in the future: "when growing stops, time apparently ceases to operate." Piaget thinks that this conception of time is reminiscent of the ancient Greek idea of becoming, which, in his estimation, is as "static and relatively un-operational" as early childhood thought.

It is not clear which ancient philosophers Piaget refers to (since there were even in pre-Socratic times deep divisions among philosophers about the difference between being and becoming), but once again we get a glimpse of an "unoperational" *adult* thinking as Piaget likens it to the child's temporal sensibility. Adult time concepts have not always been tied to geometry, as they have since Newton. Heraclitus saw time as an infinite process of *becoming*, where all beings change forever in the flowing river of time. Parmenides, on the other hand, spoke of the eternal negation of time in the great presence of *Being*.[5] For these "unoperational" ancient thinkers, time was not a simple linear progression forward but a phenomenon of great complexity.

Piaget's children saw time as discontinuous: when something reaches its full growth, it does not change anymore. When it comes into its full being, time ceases to exist for it. In the children we find the curious admixture of being and becoming that split ancient thinkers. As we saw in our discussion of the lived present, there are phenomena in children's lives that support a Parmenidean view of time as subordinated to being: every being has its own time, ambient becoming is eternally cotemporal, and time submits itself to the order of being: "I have not had my nap, so it can't be afternoon," "I was there before my older brother was born." But there are also phenomena that support the Heraclitean sense of time as the process of continuous becoming: children are oriented to the future and are ever ready to reach for things and events that are mere possibilities in the present time. Elements of timeless being and continuous becoming exist side-by-side in children's lives without philosophical contradiction or logical impossibility. I would like to follow Langeveld's (1960) dictum that the child experiences not "time" but future, past, and present in three distinct but overlapping ways.

The Desire for Coming Things

For children time is not primarily an experience of the past, as it is for many older people, but "an *experienced* desire for coming things," and "an *experienced* directedness toward the future" (Langeveld 1960, 45). We find this desire for coming things in the earliest weeks of a human being's life: newborns already turn their heads to a location where they expect something to be. The looking behavior of three-month-olds is guided by their expectations about where an interesting thing will occur, and by four months they will reach toward it in the projected place, rather than where they perceived it first: "Infants are oriented toward the future, as well as the present, from the first days outside the womb" (Siegler 1998, 111).

In DeCasper and Spence's (1986) research on fetal perception of maternal speech, which we briefly discussed in earlier chapters, newborn babies recognized the rhythmic and melodic pattern of a poem they had heard for the last six weeks in utero. While they could not understand the meaning of the words, they remembered the temporal sequence of rhythm and the unfolding of the language melody. Past experience provided the newborns with the memory of a repeated structured pattern. This pattern guided the infant's outlook in the future. Newborns *desired* to turn on the tape deck with the correct poem on it: they sucked faster to hear the rhythmic pattern they preferred. They desired "a coming thing," directed themselves toward a particular future, and acted to make it happen.

Preference, which is the foundation of all habituation studies, always indicates that the child is already living in the future. Yet the future is not blank and neutral; the infant looks for the coming of a particular thing or event and chooses to step into this future because it is continuous with an already-known past. The past comes to call us out of the future. In the future, new and old, familiar and unfamiliar, past experiences and anticipated events are woven together into a dense and inextricable web.

The Other and the Élan Vitale

The vastness of the world before infants is not empty; it is already structured by their unique experiences and intentionalities. The future, we can say, is already inscribed in the direction the human organism takes at birth: toward the voice, smell, touch of familiar persons. From there, cotemporal and copresent with other human beings, the future, for a long time, has a particular shape: to be as close as possible to those the infant is attached to, to desire and explore the world from the safe base of parental care.

Spitz (1947) and Bowlby (1969) discovered that, over time, institutionalized infants can lose their desire for the future, with grave consequences for the well-being of the child. Deprived of attachment relationships, they become deeply sad and lose the will to live. Many do not survive illnesses that another child would have weathered easily. The future is colored by the affection and safety that parents provide and when deprived of them, the infant has no desire for coming things. The horizon of social and physical activities becomes narrower and narrower because there is nothing that calls strongly enough to be heard over the drone of grief. What these children have lost is their *élan vitale*, the force that gives them direction and creates a future before them. "In life everything has a direction in time, has *élan*, pushes forward, progresses toward a future. In the same way, as soon as I think of an orientation in time, I feel myself irresistibly pushed forward and see the future open in front of me. . . . I tend spontaneously with all my power, with all my being, toward a future" (Minkowski 1970, 38).

We see the élan vitale in the infant's voracious appetite for recognition in the face of the other, in the toddler's exuberant exploration behavior, in the preschooler's determined inquisitiveness. It is the force of expectation, hope, and openness that allows a child to vanquish his or her fear and mistrust of what is coming and create a future that transcends what the child already has, knows, and is. Erik Erikson (1950/1963) sees the challenge of the first year of life in the infant's ability to trust in self, other, and world, and this is the foundation for the openness of the older child and adult to allow people and events to touch them and create a richer life. Hope is the virtue that Erikson associates with this stage. If, through neglect and unpredictability of the caregiver, the infant learns to mistrust, then despair and withdrawal from social contact are the consequences. The élan vitale of a young child is not an individual, solipsistic force; it is always embedded into the social relationships between baby and caregiver. Infants move forward into a safe and promising future because they are cotemporal with caring adults, who structure the world to be an inviting place. My husband, Michael, has made it a practice throughout the years of our family life to tell our children what to expect from new situations, and also what is expected from them. The three-year-old needs to know what is coming at the first day of nursery school, while the sixteen-year-old needs to know what is coming in his relationships with women or with his new employer. Many of Michael's conversations with the children have been deceptively simple, like explaining what a lunchbox is for, or that most women like a man who talks to them. Adults usually assume that the future is just like the present and already known, but for children much of it is uncharted territory. The parent's straightforward words make the path into a confusing future more clear. The parent can provide the sign-posts, but it is up to the child to see and follow them. The future opens up before human children because we are coexistential with other human beings. Out of the future, the human community beckons to us.

Sometimes, though, the future desired by the child and the one planned by the grown-ups do not overlap. From a temporal perspective, the young child's temper tantrum is a response to two clashing futures: the one desired and the one determined by adults. As parents we are often taken off guard by the violence of this clash. It is our job to rein in the toddler who crumples the magazines at the grocery checkout, to stop the toy truck on its trajectory to another toddler's head, or to make sure that the belt of the car seat goes over the head. It is in the nature of children to desire things that are too dangerous, too expensive, or too disruptive because they might want, *but they do not know* what the future brings. Sometimes the power of the wanting itself can be divorced from particular things, and the child finds her- or himself drowned in a sea of desire.

When our son, Nicholas, was two years old, we visited the toy aisle of a local discount store. He was immediately attracted by a toy truck and pulled it off the shelf. "I want it," he said, but I refused to purchase it and he put it back with the other trucks. He hurried over to the next shelf, pulled down an action figure, and called: "I want it." When I refused again, he ran into the adjacent aisle, yelling, "I want" as he passed the shelves. I tried to keep up with him as he ran down the other aisles of the store, screaming and flapping his hands: "I want, I want, I want." When I caught him, I picked up his squirming little body and said, "It's okay," rubbing his back. He put down his head and started to sob. The future pushed around him as so many possibilities for action, and my prohibition foreclosed some of these possibilities repeatedly. After a while he was unable to reach for a particular thing. He desired coming things but did not know any longer what kind of things he wanted. He felt overwhelmed by the infinite possibilities of all he could want. His initial exuberant reach for what he desired went beyond the possible and became a mindless, goalless wanting that left him running through the aisles without direction. "I want, I want, I want" had no "it" in it any-more. His élan vitale had gone haywire, rushing madly into the entire universe, wanting it all and exhausting itself in the process. He could not step into a future with *resoluteness* and let other possibilities go.

This little example illuminates an important aspect of a young child's relationship to the future: the possible futures are not solely the child's own, they are safeguarded and to a large degree determined by adults.

We already saw that adults provide the trusting foundation for a child to step into the future, but they also determine the direction of the child's desires. The younger the child, the stronger the influence a parent has on the world in which the child lives out his or her own projects. In the preoperational, egocentric, magical stage, the adult functions as the child's "ego," protecting from injury, setting limits, seeking out possibilities. One of the most difficult processes for parents is to figure out what kind of an "ego" we have to be for the child. We can become too restrictive, and our children lose their own initiative and courage to explore. We can be too permissive, and our children become demanding little terrors who are disliked by peers and teachers. We can be too careful in planning their lives and training them to be successful, attempting to mold children into our particular idea of who they should become. Safeguarding the freedom of children means not to give them all kinds of choices (which is the mistake most American parents make)[6] but to allow for safe and stimulating places and social interactions where children can create their own worlds in play, conversation, daydreaming. *Freedom is not a matter of choice for a child (as it perhaps is for the adult mind) but a matter of depth: to be granted the opportunity of meeting oneself in a future that is created, in safety, through one's own initiative and imagination.* There must be areas in the child's life that are not completely dominated by adult planning and control so that children can discover the unexpected in themselves, surprise adults, and bring renewal and creativity to our future culture.

Toys: Meeting Oneself in the Future

Play, as Rousseau (1762/1979) remarked, is the child's work. It is one of the *free* areas in children's lives, and as such it should be unencumbered by the demands of economic production and academic performance. Toys are the gatekeepers of this free domain because they promise a particular pleasurable future. More than other things, they elicit the child's desires because they belong to the imaginary dimension of existence: a whole future action world stretches out before the player. New toys are exciting because they promise not-yet-experienced worlds of play. Old and familiar toys invite one to step again into a familiar action world, explore it, and live its variations more deeply. Within the horizon of the toy the child is seeking for possible ways of being. But there is a difference between the promise a toy makes and what it delivers.

When our children were young, their desires were easily captured by the surface appearance of a toy. Its color, its shape, the picture of a playing child on the box, the commercial on television compelled them to make a beeline for it in the toy store and want it.[7] Like many young parents, I initially fell into the trap of fulfilling all their desires. I bought trucks and action figures, dress-up clothes and Barbie dolls, and anything else the media presented as must-have toys that they requested. But soon we discovered that the whole expensive arsenal was attractive for a few minutes, but few things had the staying power to engage their imagination for a prolonged period of time. Toys were discarded almost as soon as they were out of the box, never to be played with again. Throughout their childhood, we figured out that it was the simple toys that our children returned to again and again. Nicholas fell in love with a plastic knight outfit from the dollar store, and we also bought one for his friend. For two years they wedged their heads into the too-small helmets, figured out how to untangle the straps of the breastplates, wielded their plastic swords in mock battle, or sat for hours, armored, in the cherry tree outside. Lea's best toy was a set of square silk cloths, which became tents, blankets for a picnic in the hallway, a princess's headdresses, a knight's capes, doll carriers, skirts, dresses, and various other garments during dress-up play.

A toy is an invitation to step into the future. It is like a closed gate that promises to provide a wonderful landscape of possibilities once you open it. The toddler in the toy aisle, wanting everything, became caught up in the ornate surface of that gate. Every toy promised a great adventure, if it could be taken home. Nick wanted *to be* the children in the commercials, who can perform magic and are transformed into the powerful action figures they play with. He wanted to be in a circle of friends, crashing dump trucks together and having a splendid time. The packaging promised him an exciting, fun- and friend-filled future. He wanted it all. The reality, however, proved to be different: behind the initial invitation of many toys there was nothing. The talking truck came out of the box, but no friends materialized to make it exciting. The action figure did not give him automatic power, and when he jumped off the sofa in his Batman pajamas he crashed to the floor instead of soaring around the room. Many toys point toward a future but do not deliver it.

The future, unlike the past or present, does not yet exist, is not yet inscribed into our senses, our memories, our brains. It is purely present as the horizon of possible being. Often we miss its pervasive demand upon us; we do today as we did yesterday, we move forward through habit and extend the present into the tomorrow. We assume a continuity of the present until the future brings the unexpected: an accident, a stroke of fortune, a surprise encounter with a friend from long ago, a terrorist attack. Suddenly the future, full of infinite and tenuous possibilities, opens up before us once again. Tomorrow may be completely different from today, and we have very little sense of what it might be. We might look toward that unknowing with pleasurable anticipation of a new fullness of life, or with dread of a future that brings suffering and death. Though woven into the present, the future is purely imaginary. In Heidegger's (1972) sense, past and future are modes of absence—they are beyond the horizon of the present. However, without them the present would not be. The past refuses the present, and the future withholds it, and by doing so they make the human experience of the present possible. The future—and the past—are part of the imaginary lining of the present, and they give it depth and resonance.

In the context of our reflections on toys, the imaginary, absent nature of the future points toward an important dimension: a toy promises activity so that the child can move into a future that is interesting and new. But that future is also withholding the present and makes the child reach beyond what is here right now. It is in the nature of play that the promising future is purely imaginary. It requires the child's participation and effort in making it real in the present. The child him- or herself has to take up the toy and make a particular future happen. In Heidegger's terms, the child has to move toward that future with *anticipatory resoluteness*, leaving other possible futures aside (1962). When Nicholas ran through the store, crying, "I want, I want, I want," he desired blindly but could not commit his future to a particular action. Playing requires commitment and an effort of the imagination, and a good toy allows the child to find many possible futures behind its facade. "In life it is the future that carries the creative factor in it" (Minkowski 1970, 41), because it requires imagination and action to see and realize its possibilities. The more determined a toy is, the less future is in it; it allows only the future already prestructured by adults to emerge. An undetermined toy, like the silk cloths, is an invitation to the imagination to play out the many futures waiting ahead and step resolutely into what is coming toward the child *in her or his own way*. Free play fosters creativity, and the children meet themselves in the future they have created in play.

THE LIVED PAST

The past refuses the present. It has been and is no more. But the lived past leaves traces in the present and comes to children in a number of different ways: as the narrated past in family tales, as a personal past that is sometimes marked by loss and mourned, as a traumatic past that dooms the child to repetition, as the cultural past that on the one hand has left traces in buildings and family artifacts in the child's environment and on the other is intentionally transmitted in the education process.

The Narrated Past

In Piaget's interviews the younger children could not grasp a concept of the past that did not include them. When he asked six-year-old Aud if he had preceded his father into the world, the answer was yes; when four-year old Bor was asked about the birth of his older brother, he declared: "Oh sure, I was there," and Myr could not "remember" whether her mother was born before her (1970, 204). Within their lived sense of the past the children assumed that they had always been present because, as far as their memory stretches back, they were always there to record other people's activities: "From their point of view, time, and hence the existence of older people, begins with the dawn of their own memory." Children cannot imagine nonexistence and a time when they were not there to witness family life. Piaget calls this phenomenon "temporal egocentrism" and sees it as a sign of the "incoherence of the intuitive and pre-operational idea of temporal succession" (206).

However, from a phenomenological perspective, the children's answers are not a failure of understanding time, they point to a deeper aspect of the human experience of the past. Bor is sure that he was there when his older brother was born because, in all probability, he has participated in the family narratives that tell of his brother's birth: he heard the tales and imagined how it was. He was there, as we all were there in our early childhood memories. Like him, we vividly remember scenes that were told to us in family stories. Memory is a funny thing: we are not sure if we truly are the authors of our early memories, or if they were written by others. Is it a true memory when I recollect my grandfather holding me over the fountain to catch a water spray, or do I remember it because I saw the picture in our photo album? Do I really remember how he jumped with me over ditches or took me to the local pub when I was little, or were these memories made and changed in the stories my family told? Narratives create and alter memories, particularly in young children, who participate and imagine so intensely.

For most people, direct memories of their own infancy are inaccessible. Why is that so? What Piaget regards as the cognitive failure of the child's incoherent understanding of temporal succession is a problem of narrative. The egocentric consciousness of the infant and preschooler does not organize temporal phenomena into abstract sequences. Early memory is episodic and not narrated because the infant does not yet command the web of language that can catch a memory and place it in line with others. And when they can do it, it takes time to share, tell, and listen to narratives. This does not mean that there are no early memories, because there are many enduring events that are experienced and inscribed into the body and the senses. However, they never reach the level of language and narrative and so are not shared with others. Narrative is a social, coexistential structuring of time, and it attempts to catch and preserve the past: "This happened when your brother was born, and then he had to be taken to the hospital . . . , and then, and then, and then . . ." Our early memories are cocreated by others. Bor's, Myr's, and Aud's participatory consciousness internalizes the family narratives, so that the impersonal past of the "then" becomes the personal past of the "Oh sure, I was there." In the realm of the remembered past, reality and imagination are deeply entangled.

Tamed Things and the Personal Past

A child's personal past resides in things that are *still there* (Langeveld 1960)—and if they are no longer there, a child can deeply feel the slipping away of time. When our son, Nicholas, was six years old, we moved to a new house. He had to leave his best friend, Daniel, his street, his favorite climbing tree behind. He seemed to handle the transition well, especially since he saw Daniel in kindergarten every morning. A few months later we sold our second car, a little red Toyota that we had had since Nick was a baby. A woman picked up the car one afternoon, and that night Nicholas fell apart. Before sleep, tucked in with his blanket and after bedtime story, he started to cry. My husband took him into his arms, but he turned his face away and said: "That was the car in which we picked up Winchester when he was a puppy, and you took me to my first day in kindergarten. I loved that car. *You sold my memories.*" A new wave of sobs racked his little body. For about six weeks he cried every night before sleep, mourning the loss of all the car stood for. Even now, a decade later, he remembers the name of the woman who bought the car: Penny.

A child grieves the loss of his family's car. One of my earliest memories is of the small blue Fiat my parents sold when I was three years old. One day I saw it forlornly sitting in the rain along a roadside, and I fell apart. How could they sell it? It was ours, and now no one cared for it! After that I kept looking for it whenever I was in the new car, but I never saw it again. I understood what Nicholas felt because I had experienced it as well, but he articulated it so succinctly: "You sold my memories." For the parents the car is just a thing, a commodity to be traded in when a bigger or better car is needed. But for us as children it was something else: it carried our memories.

Antoine de Saint Exupéry (2000) captures the nature of memory in the encounter between the little prince and the fox. The fox asks the little prince to tame him by approaching closer every day, at a regular hour, to waste time with him. Wasting time with something makes it intimate and important: "'The only things you learn are the things you tame,' said the fox. 'People haven't time to learn anything. They buy things ready-made in stores. But since there are no stores where you can buy friends, people no longer have friends. If you want a friend, tame me!'" (60).

When you tame someone, the fox explains, that someone becomes distinct in the web of the world. For him the wheat field, which is initially a matter of indifference, becomes a reminder of his friend's golden hair, "and I'll love the sound of the wind in the wheat" (60). It carries the memory of the beloved friend. "Here is my secret. It's quite simple: One sees clearly only with the heart. Anything essential is invisible to the eyes" (63).

Memory rests in the invisible, the absence of the present, in what refuses to be there but which also creates the opening that makes full presence possible. The small red car is surrounded by a halo of past experiences, of events, interactions, moods. The little prince's flower is special because it has been cared for and loved. Like the tip of the iceberg, the functional automobile that the parents see with their eyes appears differently when seen in the depth of the heart's vision. For the child, memory is not an intangible, mental reproduction of mnemonic traces in the brain—it belongs to the things themselves. Rilke (1950) would say that things that are truly lived with hold our humanity within them. The red car gathers a world around it, and that world threatens to slip into oblivion when the car is no longer present. The child is not grieving for a lost object, he is mourning a lost world.

With the sale of the car the tangible connection with the past had been broken, and Nicholas sensed the loss of a whole way of being that had been experienced intensely and loved but also taken for granted. In his remembrance before going to sleep, he is shaken by the realization that what is remembered is no longer accessible to the senses. As long as he could sit in the car, touch it and feel it, the old neighborhood was still present. Now it is severed from the visible world, a pure memory:

it is no longer there. Behind his grief stands the dawning awareness that in the passage of time life gets lost and the present falls into forgetting and oblivion. Memory holds what the past withholds from the present. As Minkowski describes it, all remembrance plunges into the "*mass of the forgotten*" (1970, 155) that surrounds it like a vast and infinite zone. The past must be forgotten, and memories arise from the mass of the forgotten as a recollection of isolated episodes. We become aware of the past as past when we experience the painful but inevitable loss of something loved. Once a beloved person or thing has become memory, it is on the way to be forgotten. The past falls into nothingness. The primitive intuition of the past tell us that "when we look back we see things, whatever their importance may be, climbing slowly toward the eternal silence of oblivion" (163). When the little prince has to depart, he regrets that he tamed the fox and caused him grief. But the fox accepts the tears as the price of the taming "because of the color of the wheat fields." The tears dissolve the bonds memory has to the sensible, which, for a little while, resounds with the fullness of the previous world's sensations.

After six weeks our son's grief faded, and the past once again took on the function of concentrating and gathering behind him into a single block. It was, in Minkowski's terms, "surpassed" and allowed to fall "progressively into silence" (1970, 164). The past does not lie before our eyes in a linear sequence of bygone events. It condenses and gathers behind us into the mass of the forgotten *without losing anything of its force.* Its sole purpose, Minkoswki says, is to be the foundation from which our élan vitale can surge anew and carry us toward the future.

The recalled past is always episodic. Some memories arise out of the silence, while others remain forgotten. In the mass of the forgotten, some things, as the fox knew, have mattered so deeply that, even when grieved for, they do not lose any of their force and can change the future. They are "prospective memories" in which the past has been "surpassed," and they provide the concentrated ground from which the élan vitale can stream into the future. The wheat field will remind the fox of friendship and joy, and it now deserves special attention and care and will give him a simple pleasure. It is part of the world that is good. I do not know how the little red car has shaped our son's life. Some things are too simple and too deep to talk about.

Trauma and Repetition in Play

For some children, however, the past cannot be "surpassed"—it is not allowed to fade into the eternal silence of forgetting. It keeps on clamoring for attention, while at the same time barring the way into an open and free future. Physical or sexual abuse, losing a parent, or being the victim of crime, war, or a natural disaster can produce profound trauma in children. "Psychological trauma occurs when an actual or perceived threat of danger overwhelms a person's usual coping ability" (James 1994, 9). A piece of the past does not fit itself into the tableau of the mass of the forgotten and it restructures the child's experience of present and future. Post-traumatic stress disorder is a disorder of the remembered past. The symptoms of children's post-traumatic stress disorder fall into four categories. I paraphrase from James:

1. A persistent state of fear, to which the child responds by crying, clinging, regression to an earlier developmental stage, regressive tantrums, aggressive behavior;
2. Disorders of memory, where past event intrude into awareness as flashbacks (repetitive reenactments) or disturb sleep through nightmares; children use protective dissociation to avoid overwhelming emotions, thoughts, and sensations;
3. Dysregulation of affect, where children's moods swing from severe constriction of affect to out-of-control affective storms; alexithymia, where children notice only the bodily aspects of an emotion but cannot recognize the meaning of what they feel and "cannot describe or predict [their] own affective experience" (14); intense affect often makes it impossible for children to connect language with the memory of the traumatic events;
4. Avoidance of intimacy because traumatized children cannot bear to feel vulnerable and lose control (for example, through clingy behavior, hyperactivity, avoidance of eye contact, withdrawal, oppositional behavior, disgusting personal habits).

The child is compelled to relive the past, but unlike the adult victim of trauma, children are often less verbal and more *active* in the repetition of the traumatic memory: they repeat the event in post-traumatic reenactment or post-traumatic play. The case of Gabby (Gil 1991) illustrates the power of the lived past. Gabby was a three-and-one-half-year-old girl who had been sexually molested by two adolescent boys during a babysitting episode. The previously well-adjusted child was now anxious, fearful of many situations, suffered from nightmares, and had difficulty falling asleep. She was lethargic and regressed to thumb sucking, baby talk, and wearing diapers. She shied away from contact with her father and older brother. The experience of evil restructured her life and changed her relationship to the future.

Minkowski's investigation of the remembrance of past events revealed an astounding phenomenon: we rarely remember good events in their particularity, but evil experiences stay with us in all detail. Ethical acts generate the future and, as Minkowski says, they do not stay with us as clear remembrances: "they disappear, as they came, without leaving a trace except for *the luminous ray which they constantly project before us*" (1970, 156; my emphasis). Like a guiding beacon, the good that parents do is absorbed by the silent past, but it also provides the foundation on which a child can enter the future with hope and confidence. Perhaps this is why young adults often do not remember the good in their childhoods: preeminent in the tableau of remembrance are acts that cannot fade into the dimension of the forgotten. Minkowski calls this "evil," either that which we do ourselves and then remember with remorse or that which is done to us and which can, in extreme cases, lead to trauma: "*Evil cannot disappear without leaving traces in the past*" (159; my emphasis).

Within the flow of time, the experience of evil forecloses the clear path toward the future and obstructs the child's horizon. Evil cannot be forgotten, but it can be transformed, as we see in Gabby's case. Before her work with a therapist, she seemed to be doomed to repeat the hurtful event in dream and play. It threw a shadow over the rest of her life: the luminous ray of the good in her past life had been eclipsed. This undermined her experience of being well and safe within the circle of her family. Because at her age the distinction between world-engendered and self-engendered events is very tenuous, her feeling life colored the ambient world in threatening hues. The present was contaminated by the past, and she regressed to a less capable, more infantile little girl who scanned the future with mistrust and suspicion. Regression was her attempt to reconstitute a way of being that preceded the rape, to recover a past where she had been protected by her family's presence.

For the first three months of therapy with Eliana Gil, Gabby repeated the same play scenario in every session: she placed a small figure of Garfield the cat in a corner of the sand tray, surrounded him with rows of tall fences and trees, and aligned large groups of threatening spiders, dinosaurs, bugs, lions, tigers, and soldiers right outside the fence. She noted: "they climb trees and jump fences" (Gil 1991, 151).

The forces of evil stood right behind a fence that gave too little protection. Gil commented: "The implication was clear: the boundaries were permeable and attack was inevitable. The single object in the corner could not hide, and no one was around to come to his aid" (Gil 1991, 151). It is interesting to note that her trauma play did not repeat the sexual assault; rather, it symbolized the narrowing of her world through the constant threat of attack. Her memory of the event returned not as an exact picture of the past but as a precise mood that could be displayed and enacted. A trauma returns as a mood, or "intentional feeling" as Langeveld calls it: "For in the history of our personal feeling life there are some feelings that remain always present, gruesomely present, and the tissue of personal development grows around them and forms an eternally tender lump" (1960, 46–47).

Through the steady process of play therapy, Gabby and her therapist worked hard so that the traumatic experience would not turn into a cancer of the soul. Gradually she began to trust the therapist and her play changed. Instead of compulsively repeating the threat of assault, Gabby began to vary the scene, and with it her anxiety changed. Step-by-step the fence retreated from the Garfield figure. A friendly giraffe and a protective bear joined him under an arching tree. The therapist commented: "I think that Garfield is much safer now." And Gabby replied: "Yeah, the giraffe and the bear stay with her and watch out for her" (Gil 1991, 153).

While nothing could take away the evil she experienced, that evil could, over time and through her relationship with the therapist, be allowed to join the stream of the forgotten. Her future began to open up again when she accepted the goodness and strength of companionship. By working through the consequences of evil she could reclaim her life and see again the "luminous ray" that the good projects into her future. Perhaps her path will always be somewhat rocky, and the flow of her life will have to bend around the sediments of a past evil deed, but now it "is nevertheless destined to open up into the great road of life and to free the way again toward the blossoming of the personality and toward the search for ethical action" (Minkowski 1970, 159).

The Reach of the Personal Past: Old Things and Family Narratives

The certainty that *a* past is *my* past is not an internal phenomenon. J. H. van den Berg (1961) has shown that the past is carried by things and evoked by repeated events. In cultures where there is continuity in the life-forms and the uses of artifacts between the past and present generations, the past is not experienced as different or alien. In our rapidly changing time, however, the past has difficulty reaching toward the present, and children find it only in fragments around them. The past is present in children's experience through things that belonged to a different generation but still exist. The fragments of the past, the old things that are still here, evoke powerful moods, and once we pay attention we see how the past is contained in the artifacts that accompany a child's daily life.

My own childhood was littered with things that held the past and evoked that particular mood of "long ago": pictures from my grandparents' wedding, old clothes in the attic, my mother's childhood books, and Toni and Froni, the strange celluloid wind-up dancers that were a gift from her older brother and still sit in her china cupboard. I played in the same neighborhood streets where my father had played hide-and-seek when he was a boy: I knew where he had set a doormat on fire and where his friends had had their hiding places; we both had to rescue our little brothers when they fell into the local fountain—he in 1941, I in 1968. These things and places felt old to me when I was a child because they resonated with my parents' past. But old in a deeper way was the bedroom in my German hometown's castle museum. I hurried past the other exhibits and left the adults behind so that I could be alone with that beloved room and take my time gazing at the short bed, the wooden cradle, and the small doll cradle, all made up with blue checked coverlets. I fantasized about living there: an ordinary princess in a plain room who could look out over the whole city.

The "long ago" mood was especially strong when my grandmother took me to visit her sisters. I sat on overstuffed sofas sipping my milk from delicate gilded demitasses while I looked at their strange hairdos and pointed glasses and smelled the scent of the past in their apartments. The past penetrated the present, and as a child I could sense it in smell, sight, sound, touch, and taste. But it was a strange, unfamiliar past, like the glimpse of a vaguely familiar face in the window of a train rushing by. I could not live there, but once in a while I could watch this curiously uncanny past reach me through its artifacts and appreciate this unfamiliar country that was my grandparents' time.

Many of the artifacts of the past were woven into family stories, and often stories were told because there was a place or a thing that elicited a narrative from the adults. My life as a child was surrounded by a past that came before me. I ran through the same city streets as my father, and I read the strange-smelling, cheaply made books that my mother had read on Sunday afternoons surrounded by her six brothers and sisters. I begged my grandmother, "Erzähl mir von Früher" (Tell me about the earlier time) and listened to her narratives about her childhood at the turn of the twentieth century. Over the two decades of my childhood and adolescence the family past was told in bits and pieces whenever a thing, an event, or a question stirred the collective memory.

I experienced the power of shared family narratives a few years ago, when I picked up Günter Grass's book *My Century* (2000). The book is a compilation of one hundred short stories about German popular history, one for each year of the twentieth century. I was born in Germany in 1959 and emigrated to the United States in 1980, which means that I experienced German culture directly only in the 1960s and 1970s. Reading Grass, however, I had the surprising experience that I understood and felt ownership of the first fifty years of German twentieth-century culture as well. The half century before my birth was *my century*, too, and I knew what kind of people and events Grass was talking about. On the other hand, I have no connection at all to U.S. history and American culture before the Ronald Reagan years. *Leave It to Beaver* is a foreign culture to me, and though I appreciate the beautiful walls and bridges that the Public Works Administration built in Pittsburgh parks in the 1930s, they do not speak to me of the hardship and suffering of men and women during the Great Depression.

As a child I felt that my personal history encompassed my grandparents' life. They were born in 1903, and since I knew them so well I also knew their slice of German history. When I was five years old my grandmother told me stories about the emperor's birthday party, where she and her four sisters were all dressed in altered hand-me-down-dresses and saw him ride past in a parade. I asked her over and over again to describe to me what the dresses looked like, and how her mother, sitting for nights at her sewing machine, had taken apart two of her own dresses to make four for her young daughters. The different colors of shiny bows in the four girls' hair always gave me a shiver of delight. I assumed that my grandmother, just like me, was five years old at the time. *I was there*. And the dark years of the German century were mine as well, because they lived in the stories my parents and grandparents told: the neighbor sent to prison for telling a Hitler joke (another neighbor must have turned him in); my favorite great-uncle joining the Nazi Party at the earliest opportunity, while my grandfather always maintained that Hitler would ruin us all; he hid the *Schwarzes Corps* Nazi propaganda paper under the counter of his Catholic bookstore until the Gestapo closed him down. In the family stories I was there when our roof was hit by an incendiary bomb and when 90 percent of our city was turned to rubble by British bombers a few days before the war ended. My father, fourteen at the time, saw dead bodies lying in the street. *I saw them, too.* The schools had closed in the winter of 1945 because there was no more fuel. I watched my grandmother cry because she had nothing but margarine and dry bread to pack for lunch on the first day of my father's apprenticeship as a plumber. When I was a child we never had noodles because my mother could not bear the taste: for months that had been all she had ever had in her lunchbox.

As I write these snippets of family history I feel the emotional involvement out of which these stories arose: they were chosen because they were memorable to my parents and grandparents, and they were told to us children because they showed the adults as victims and heroes in an insane time. Out of the flow of ordinary life in extraordinary times, adults choose the narratives that amuse or educate their children—and also the ones that make them look good. What they tell is the truth, but not the whole truth, as we come to find out later. Their stories had a profound effect on me: I have always felt responsible for the Nazi years and the atrocities against the Jews, not because I committed them, but *because the culture that did is so intimate to me*. The untold cultural background that I discovered as I became older creates coherence and makes sense of my episodic family stories. History fills in the picture. "Evil," as Minkowski (1970, 159) wrote, "cannot disappear without leaving traces in the past." The traces of the German past return again and again. They cannot easily go into the silence of the forgotten as long as our personal history is entwined with them. I still belong to the twentieth century. It was *my* century. It lives in my personal memories and makes them complete.

Schooling and the Cultural Past

While family narrative provides an indirect access to our cultural past, education is a direct and intentional transmission of cultural memory. It is strange to realize that the whole process of formal education is the immersion of young minds into the memories of a culture's past. Handing down past experience and knowledge to the next generation is practiced by hunter-gatherers as well as by highly technological people. We find it in oral cultures, where children learn much by indirect and participatory instruction, and we find it in literate cultures that have a more formalized system of schooling. Human culture preserves and reproduces itself through the knowledge and experience that one generation transfers to the next. Collective memory gathers in a culture and promises an easier, less threatening future. Knowledge is the cultural mass of the forgotten, which has been preserved through mnemonic devices and technological artifacts.

A large portion of our modern childhood is spent acquiring the artificial cultural memory tools of literacy and mathematical notation. After that we are immersed in our culture's past for almost two decades and have to remember and reproduce what teachers and textbooks dredge up out of the mass of the forgotten. Is it so surprising that children, in general, do not like school? How can the child's natural desire for coming things be made to linger in such a protracted past? This, I think, is the paradox of education: the future-oriented child has to engage the past-oriented knowledge of the culture. The task of true pedagogy is to bring these two sides together by understanding the child's psychology and by carefully selecting from the infinite store of cultural memory.

The task of bridging the gap between transmitting past knowledge and appealing to the child's future-oriented élan vitale requires a deep understanding of child development that goes beyond tailoring pedagogical method to cognitive stages. In the mass of the forgotten, there are some stories and skills that connect to the child's own way of being in the world at a particular age. I have seen the best example of a developmentally correct re-collection of the cultural past in Rudolf Steiner's Waldorf education. In a disciplined way, through twelve grades, Waldorf tries to gradually transmit cultural knowledge as it speaks to the child's developing physical, emotional, and cognitive capacities. In the ninth year, for example, children become critical and "wake up" out of a world they have taken for granted, and the third-grade Waldorf curriculum offers them the history of the Jewish people from Genesis and the fall from paradise through the wanderings in the desert to the founding of Mosaic law. Concurrently with this, they learn about farming and house building. Reading, writing, mathematics, and science are all integrated into the larger care for a nine-year-old child who lives in a newly fragmented world and looks for ways to survive. This kind of knowledge speaks to children because it offers them intellectual and practical ways to understand their own experience.

True education happens when the educational material is presented in such a way that children can recognize themselves and their own concerns in what they learn. Then the cultural past becomes a framework for understanding and changing the present, and knowledge can surge forward with the vigor of the child's élan vitale. Our hope for the future lies in our children's ability to take up our cultural past, make it their own, and step into what is coming with initiative and creativity.

LOOKING BACK

The path we traversed in our reflections about lived time has been cir-cuitous, but let me recapitulate some of the way stations. Guided by Piaget's research on children's understanding of time and other obser-vational material and findings from developmental psychology, we at-tempted to develop the beginning of a *genetic phenomenology* of lived time, that is, to examine the intentional network of time as it arises in infancy and early childhood. Through dialogue with philosophical thinkers, the findings of developmental research were affirmed and deepened and, in turn, the developmental material supported phenom-enological thinking on lived time.

The linear lineup of past, present, and future does not hold up under scrutiny because in experienced time, having been, being present, and coming to be do not simply lie behind, with, and before us. The past can call out of the future, the future repeats the past, the present expands or contracts. Yet within the temporal network of intentionality, present, fu-ture, and past come to children in different ways: in lived time, they ap-pear as different moods or ways of finding oneself in the world.

Young children have a clear sense of time, but it is intuitive rather than logical-operational: "It is now afternoon because I have had my nap." Temporal scripts or frames allow children to grasp the order of events and, to a certain degree, predict the future. Time is tied to action se-quences that are enacted repeatedly in particular places, and it is a func-tion of the rhythms of daily life. For the young child, time exists not as the abstract measure of clock or calendar but as rhythmic action time that encompasses a remembrance of the past, an easy flowing along with the present, and an anticipation of the future. But, as we saw, it is pos-sible to interrupt the child's immersion into the temporal network by destroying the rhythms of the present activity. In more extreme cases, the child's full growth into the future can be constricted by unresolved traumatic memories.

Children assume that the *present* time is not homogenous for all be-ings, but that each lives in its own time, which can shrink or expand de-pending on particular activities. Children—unreflective about them-selves and turned toward the world—strongly sense the flow of ambient becoming, where things move through time alongside the child's own being. To be in the present means to be cotemporal *now* and *with* oth-ers in action space. Children easily let go and forget what is no longer part of their direct experience of ambient becoming. In the world of the young there is no central time-master who assures that all are governed by the same abstract time frame.

Children assume that *the future* does not continue infinitely: when a person has reached the fullness of his or her being, time seems to stop. Parents are just old and do not get older for a long time, and if I eat more I will be older than my older brother. In children's conception of time, growth is not homogenous and time not continuous. On a more visceral level, the young are directed toward the *future* in their desire for coming things. The range of the future, the width of its horizon and the openness it provides to the child's initiative, is strongly determined by parental presence. The strength of the child's élan vitale, his or her reach toward what is coming, has its foundation in the trust and hope a healthy parental environment inspires. Freedom for the child means to be granted the opportunity of meeting oneself in a future that is created, in safety, through one's own initiative and imagination. The future is the realm of the possible, and it exists for us always as a purely imaginary dimension. In creative play, children resolutely step into the network of imaginative possibilities and create a world that is all their own.

Children assume that, in the *past*, they were always there, and that time begins with their own memories. Our past is cocreated through the narratives we share with the people in our early environments. The past condenses into the mass of the forgotten, and only some parts of it can be recalled. Memory is held in the fabric of tales that a person, a family, or a culture rescues out of the mass of the forgotten. Memory is episodic: it reappears in bits and pieces through artifacts, events, and narratives that remind us of the past. A child's grief over the loss of the family car is an indicator of the tight bond that exists between things and the past. The past is there because things from the past are still there and, in the child's mind, to lose the thing also means to lose the presence of the memory. A beloved thing on the threshold of the mass of the forgotten is mourned. Once it passes, grief eases and, like the memory of the beloved, returns only once in a while. But some traumatic events in a child's life are not allowed to recede gently into the forgotten past; they intrude into the present and obstruct the future. They return as moods that suffuse the present with suspicion and fear. Evil cannot disappear without leaving traces in the past, and we have to deal with it as it is active in the mass of the forgotten or it will warp and reshape the child's development in the future.

This is true not merely for a child's personal past but also for a culture: evil reshapes the future for generations to come. Children participate in their culture's past through family narrative and the education process. Family narratives shape children's early memories of their own lives, and it becomes impossible to separate what a person remembers firsthand from memories generated by intense, imaginative participation in other people's narratives. Even the untold or repressed family stories are part of the total fabric of a person's history. Narrative participation creates a sense of cultural belonging and allows the child's life to transcend its own generation. In the education process, the child is inserted into the officially sanctioned narrative of a culture's past. Education is the transmission of cultural memory. The problem of education is the clash between the child's future-oriented desires and the culture's need to immerse children in the past in order to preserve itself.

Lived time, as we saw, is deeply woven into all aspects of children's lives. It is obvious that each of these reflections on present, future, and past provides only fragments of a larger picture. Rereading these ideas on time, I find myself continually urged to notice what I have not said, to go deeper, to say more. Time is, to say it with Merleau-Ponty, "a network of intentionalities" (1962, 417), and as such impossible to exhaust. But this should not grieve us. Beyond the horizon lies the joy of stepping into the mystery and beginning the work again—at another time.

SEVEN

Babble in the House of Being

Pointing, Grammar, and Metaphor in Early Language Acquisition

Nameless, the beginning of the world. Naming, the mother of a million things.
Lao-Tzu, Tao Te Ching

Language lives only from silence; everything we cast to the others has germinated in this great mute land which we never leave.
Maurice Merleau-Ponty, The Visible and the Invisible

Language seeks to disappear; it seeks to die as an object.
Paul Ricoeur, "Structure, Word, Event"

NAMES

Every afternoon my grandmother's uneven steps echoed through the hospital hallway, and I knew she was coming long before she appeared in the doorway. My bed was in the middle, wedged between two others in the children's ward. I was five years old, in the hospital for a week to have my tonsils removed, and in the next bed was Klaus, who was six and had already been there for a few days. He knew the ropes and proudly showed me the bandage on his appendix incision. When I was homesick, he comforted me. We shared my food, especially the ice cream after surgery. He was always hungry. My grandmother brought treats for both of us.

One evening before sleep, Klaus and I started to list all the things we knew. We wanted to name everything we could think of, speak all the names in the world. We began by naming the beds and the curtains, the flowers and the grandmothers, the doctors and the nurses, and all the things we could see around us. Then we named the remembered things at home: brothers, dolls, beer (his parents owned an inn), streets, cars, trees, fields, clouds. It seemed to me that we spent many hours that night stringing together the beads of our words. Finally we took our list into sleep and then continued it as soon as the sun was up. After we had reached the moon and stars, however, there came a point when we caught each other naming things we had said before. I remember the startled emptiness when there were no new words, the sick sense of disappointment that we had exhausted the known world. Was it my fault for being only five, or was there an end to the saying? Could the fullness of the world be depleted in one night and half a morning?

THE QUESTION OF LANGUAGE

Four decades ago Paul Ricoeur pointed out that phenomenology could not afford to ignore the turn toward language that the social sciences and philosophy had made in the wake of de Saussures's and Hjelmslev's work on linguistics and semiology. "This detour through the science of language is not something one can choose or not choose to make: it is essential to phenomenology today if it is to survive" (1967, 14). Ricoeur pointed the way through the detour: recover and bring together the fragments of Merleau-Ponty's existential analysis of the speech act and engage in the "hand-to-hand struggle with the presuppositions of semiology" (19) in order to reconquer the fundamental capacity for meaning that has been undermined by post-structuralism. "What phenomenology must do, then, is to take up again the theory of meaning and put it to the test of semiology in order to proceed to a genuine dialectic of semiology and semantics at every level of the units of speech" (23). According to Ricoeur, linguistics challenges phenomenology in three areas: the relationship between signifier and signified (sign and thing), the status of the speaking subject, and the nature of the symbolic function.[1]

In the following pages we will revisit Merleau-Ponty's analysis of the speech act and Ricoeur's semantic analysis of language and link them with a number of phenomena in infant language acquisition. We will look at preverbal linguistic phenomena and the beginnings of the symbolic function in the first year of life. We will investigate the emergence of words and their connection to things (signifier/signified) and address the notion of speech and situated communication between parent and infant (the status of the speaking subject). Finally, we will turn to the acquisition of grammar and the practice of metaphor in the young child, providing a window into the working of the linguistic symbolic function.

THE CHILD BATHES IN LANGUAGE

In his series of lectures at the Sorbonne, Merleau-Ponty (1964a, 1994) placed the question of language at the center of his reflections on child psychology. In the child we see language *in statu nascendi*, and we can witness its unfolding over time. Critiquing the language theorists of his time, Merleau-Ponty found Kantian idealism as well as contemporary empiricism wanting. Idealism turned language into an extension of thought, which nullifies it as a phenomenon in its own right. It "is denied all philosophical meaning and becomes an exclusive technical problem" (Merleau-Ponty 1973, 3). Empiricism, on the other hand, conceived language as the mechanistic reproduction of stimuli in the brain (Merleau-Ponty 1962) and excluded the whole question of its meaningful situatedness in communication. Neither saw language as a complex *existential* event but isolated one aspect of the language phenomenon and totalized it as the essential feature of language. As a dialectical thinker, however, Merleau-Ponty did not dismiss these two positions. From idealism he retained the insight that language is woven into thought, with the caveat that this very intertwining needs to be investigated. He agreed with the empiricists that language is profoundly dependent on our human biology and that it begins with the body, but with the caveat that the body, as we experience it and as language encounters it, is not mechanistic and self-enclosed but always already woven into the meaningful structures of its environment.

The fullness of the phenomenon of human language includes bodily and intellectual elements, but it is also permeated with desire and intentionality: the child wants to speak—and the human world calls the child to do so. If the adult world fails to issue the call, the child does not acquire language. Children deprived of the symbolic forms of speech, be they verbal or signed, cannot participate in the symbolic life of their culture. It is through shared speech that language is born, and no human being learns it in isolation (Candland 1995). To do justice to the language phenomenon, we must go beyond it as a mere epistemological or biological event and recenter it as an *existential* phenomenon. In human experience language appears as *speech*—as an act of communication in the presence of other human beings. To induce the child into the human language requires a particular language, a communication partner, and something that comes to expression in words and sentences. As Merleau-Ponty (1973, 14) is fond of quoting from Delacroix: "The child bathes in language."

SPEECH AND MUSIC: SO MANY WAYS
OF SINGING THE WORLD

Human infants are amazingly attuned to the properties of human language. Even in utero fetuses are sensitive to sound, and during the last month of gestation their heart rate goes up when they recognize a recurrent sound pattern (DeCasper et al. 1994). Newborns prefer the maternal voice to that of a strange female, and they recognize the prosodic pattern of a recurrent speech pattern at birth. DeCasper and Spence (1986), as we saw in earlier chapters, had mothers read the familiar Dr. Seuss story *The Cat in the Hat* to their unborn babies during the last six weeks of pregnancy and found that immediately after birth the infants recognized the sound pattern of the poetry and picked it out over an unfamiliar poem read by their mothers: they changed their sucking rate on a wired pacifier, which in turn activated either the familiar poem or a strange one. DeCasper and Spence comment that the infants must have learned and remembered something about the acoustic cues of *The Cat in the Hat,* such as *syllabic beat, the voice-onset-time of consonants, the harmonic structure of sustained vowel sounds, and/or the temporal order of these sounds.* Not only is the mother's voice familiar but newborns can differentiate her specific speech patterns.

The implications of these findings go beyond a simple acknowledgment of fetal learning. For our study of language acquisition it means that (1) newborn human beings are equipped to recognize basic auditory patterns; and (2) they prefer to hear patterns they are familiar with. French four-day-old newborns suck more vigorously when they hear French than Russian. Russian newborns have the opposite preference (Mehler et al. 1988). The beat of the language sequence, the melody of consonants and vowels, and the temporal unfolding of the speech pattern are all elements of the music of language. *Prior to encountering language as a referential or conceptual tool, human infants are bathed in its musical substructure:* when Mehler and colleagues muffled the consonant and vowel sounds so that only the melody of French came through, the infants still preferred it; but when they distorted the melody by playing the language backward (which still preserves the vowel and consonant sounds) the babies did not prefer it anymore. Newborns know the musical pattern of their language, which is more than a random assemblage of vowel and consonant phonemes.

There are indications that some of the musical qualities of language patterns are universal. Across the globe the speech of mothers with their infants has interpretable qualities: a rise-and-fall contour for approving, a set of sharp staccato bursts for prohibiting, a rise pattern for directing attention, and smooth legato murmurs for comforting (Fernald 1989, 1991). The musical intensity of human speech transcends cultural difference and directs us to language in its presymbolic and transcultural dimension.

Kristeva (1984) would call this presymbolic dimension of language the "semiotic process" and the musical dimension of speech part of the pulsating stream of the "semiotic chora" (25), which designates the unconscious, primary process and instinct-driven semiotic foundation of symbolic language. In the following pages we will cover some of the same semiotic, presymbolic ground but without recourse to psychoanalytic concepts of ego and id, instinct and repression, mirror stage and subject, sexuality and death drive. Phenomenology aims for the same latency as psychoanalysis (Merleau-Ponty 1982/1983) but does not conceptualize what is unconscious as an internal, repressed, instinctual phenomenon. The unconscious lies *before* us:

> This unconscious is to be sought not at the bottom of ourselves, behind the back of our "consciousness," but in front of us, as articulations of our field. It is "unconscious" by the fact that it is not an *object*, but it is that through which objects are possible, it is the constellation through which our future is read—it is between them as the interval of the trees between the trees, or as their common level. It is the Urgemeinschaftung of our intentional life, the *Ineinander* of the others in us and of us in them. (Merleau-Ponty 1968, 180)

The semiotic, unconscious processes of language have their origin in the primal coexistentiality, the *Ineinander* (intermingling) of speaker and listener, self and other. Within this intersubjective field, however, infant perception and feeling are never submerged in a blooming, *unstructured* mass of impressions. There is never a "choric" Eden, not even in the womb. From the beginning infants structure what they perceive and have an ability to recognize patterned configurations (Bower 1977). Constantly the pulsating chora gives itself away into the stream of experience, gets lost and reconfigured with the transformations of infant experience.

Meltzoff and Borton (1979) found that young babies recognize the *visual* configuration of a thing even when they have only *touched* it before—the process of cross-modal perception that we discussed in chapter 4. This amazing ability of newborns to perceive a unified perceptual world also seems to apply to the speech act. Kuhl and Meltzoff (1982) discovered that fourteen-week-old infants recognize the correspondence between auditory and visually presented speech sounds. Bower (1977) reports that two-week-old babies know that their mother's face goes with her voice and that they strongly disliked the bizarre experimental situation in which a stranger appeared to be talking with their mother's voice. We know that after only a few days newborns recognize and prefer the sound pattern of the language that is spoken around them, and that by eight to twelve months they narrow down their ability to discriminate between the phonemes of all languages to just the sounds used in their mother tongue (Werker and Tees 1999). Infants at that age are also predisposed to distinguish word boundaries through the cadence of their mother tongue. By nine months (but not at six months), American babies have figured out that most words in their language are trochees: the stress pattern in English places the emphasis on the first syllable (Juszyk 1997), and the beginning of English words can be inferred from their rhythmical-musical structure. And beyond sound and their own rhythmical babbling, infants engage in rhythmical movements of limbs and jaw (Kelly et al. 2002). Rhythmically organized activity is a hallmark of the infant's bodily activity and vocalization during the first year. From these and other research findings we can conclude:

1. Infants attend to the human voice and prefer it over unstructured sounds.
2. They are actively seeking meaningful patterns in the speech they encounter.
3. They discriminate between the familiar and strange aspects of a speech encounter and find islands of consistency within its forms.
4. The melodic, presymbolic speech patterns have a motivating function and are deeply affective as well as cognitive.
5. There are cultural and transcultural structures to human language, and infants are more or less open to them depending on their developmental level.

However, the results from laboratory research give the illusion of an isolated (even if capable) infant mind performing its solitary feats of integrated perception. But infants do not experience the perceptual world without the presence of caring others. What is easily missed, but nonetheless essential to the above examples, is the communicative dimension in the exchanges of speech between adults and infants. The communicative function of language is presymbolic and prereferential. Mothers and infants communicate and understand each other even when the words exchanged have no meaning. A musical substructure of meaning pervades spoken language and suffuses it with emotional intensity. It is not surprising that the musical patterns Fernald (1989, 1991) found in the speech of mothers have to do with praise, warning, directing attention, and comforting. And when they heard the familiar prosodic sequence of *The Cat in the Hat*, DeCasper's infants had lowered heart rates because they were soothed and relaxed.

In his thinking about language, Merleau-Ponty maintained that speech was rooted in human embodiment, and that despite all later symbolic development, it stayed deeply connected to the body as the foundation of expression and speech. Current infant research affirms that the preverbal, musical substratum of language is a reality, and that we come into the world with a capacity for attending to it. The music of speech does not express the world as concept; it evokes the emotional insertion of the human being into the web of things. In Merleau-Ponty's words, "the words, vowels, and phonemes are so many ways of 'singing' the world," (1962, 187). They express the emotional essence of things rather than represent them through objective resemblance. Mothers, when they speak, know that their voice comforts their baby or can stop the toddler from putting his or her hand into the fire. The world into which the new human being comes is not a neutral place but a web of beings and things that evoke desire, pleasure, surprise as well as fear, disgust, and discomfort. Speech responds to the emotional lining of the world and harmonizes with it in its melodic cadences.

POINTING

Starting Point

Eleven-month-old Lea is carried by her father to the window. Outside a woman walks by with her big black dog. Excitedly Lea extends her arm and index finger, looks outside, says "da," and then looks back at her father's face. Her father looks outside and replies: "Yeah, that's a big doggie." In the months before Lea pointed she has learned how to share attention by following the father's line of vision when he turned his head—a phenomenon called joint attention—but until nine months of age she did not follow the trajectory of the outstretched finger. She stared at the hand and its movement, understanding *its* perceptual spectacle as the event worthy of attention. Now, as the father points to the sky and says "airplane," she does look up and find the speck of moving, humming silver in the air.

One of the milestones of the first year of life is the moment when the infant understands that a gesture refers beyond itself: at around nine months of age babies will no longer stare at the parent's pointing finger but follow its trajectory; by eleven months they point themselves and expect the parent to look at what they indicate. By twelve months more than 60 percent of all gestures consist of or involve pointing (Butterworth 2003). Pointing reorients the gaze of the other person so that a thing or event becomes the shared focus of attention. Butterworth lists three criteria for deictic pointing (I reversed the order):

1. The direction of what is being pointed at is seen as away from the pointing hand.
2. The gesture serves to single something out that the addressee comprehends to be the referent.
3. It is dialogic in that it requires an audience and is for someone else's benefit.

When the infant follows the parent's extended index finger, we witness a profoundly human transformation of the perceived world that is not found in other species. My dog will remain "glued" to my outstretched finger, completely caught up in the immediate perceptual experience of my hand; and even though some chimps will point when raised by human caretakers, they will do so mostly with their whole hand and never at each other. In the wild chimpanzees have not been observed to point intentionally (Povinelli, Bering, and Giambrone 2003). The infant's pointing stands at the cusp between preverbal and verbal expression and marks the emergent symbolic ability of the human infant. Finger pointing is closely associated with language learning, and the earlier babies start to point the more words they know by twenty months of age. There are also indications that babies begin to point in the same week they begin to understand names for things, such as *cat* and *ball* (Butterworth 1997).

When we consider pointing as a bodily phenomenon, the intimate connection between the hand and the eye becomes apparent. Butterworth (1997) argues that, from an evolutionary perspective, the postural antithesis to pointing is the pincer grip, in which the tip of the index finger and the thumb are in opposition. The pincer grip requires fine motor coordination and is the most delicate intentional human holding gesture. It guides the eye close and inward, focusing attention on the tips of the fingers and creating an event within the narrow body space of the upper torso. In pointing, on the other hand, the arm is extended away from the torso, the hand moves out of the close body space, and the index finger extends the outward move beyond the immediate activity of the human body. The deictic finger directs the eye to follow and look outward (the word *deictic* comes from the Greek and means "to show, to point out directly"). We must leave the action space of the hand, must, so to speak, "jump over" and forget the body as the spectacle and direct our attention to something that is yet invisible but already indicated by the intentional line of the other's finger. The extended finger becomes a sign.[2]

The gesture of pointing responds to a particular experiential field. The activity of the eye sweeps over the panorama of the space open in front of Lea and her father. Unlike the closeness and detail of the visual field during the pincer grip (when, for example, Lea picks up a piece of cookie and examines it closely), while pointing at the dog the child's visual panorama is large and vague, with many diverse patterns and events. Extending the reach of the human body through the pointing finger structures the perceptual field and singles out for attention one of its domains. "Look there, an airplane, and look there, a big black moving thing that we call a dog." In the shared attentive gazing, which Werner and Kaplan (1963) have named *contemplation* because it is without the desire to possess (although there are other, less contemplative and more demanding instances of pointing in infancy, too), father and daughter transcend their direct involvement with each other and direct their attention to the world: the dog and the airplane come into focus. The world before them unfolds and beckons. It marks a moment of distance, a first detachment from the primordial sharing situation of early infancy. Lea and her father try to come together in something that is not immediately obvious and at hand: it is *transcendent.*

When Lea follows the line of her father's outstretched finger, she understands that his body invites her to enter the world in a particular way. The world beyond the tip of his finger is already structured by his perception and calls her to see it in the same way. When Lea follows the invitation and looks up to the sky she conforms her own gestures to fit into the world that he has indicated. She sees what he sees within a particular bodily horizon. He delineates a field for her perception and invites her to assume the intentionality of his gesture as her own, which makes it possible for both to have a shared world. What he does with his deictic finger, she does with her eyes. Human imitation, as Merleau-Ponty (1973) has shown, is not a copying of another's gestures but a *reconformation of one's own body to reach the same intentional goal in the world.*

Through the pointing gesture, human beings reach beyond what is graspable *here and now* and direct others to the *there and then.* Franko and Butterworth (1996) showed that infant pointing is not a failed grasping for something but, from the beginning, a communicative gesture in its own right. It always has the declarative purpose "Look at that." In order to understand her father's pointing finger as a sign, Lea must trust that its intentional direction is pointing to something that is not yet here but a possible future perception. The deictic moment requires a leap of faith and a willingness to align oneself with the one who points in the hope that something more will show itself in the world. When Lea looks away *from* the hand and begins to look *with* it, she transcends the hand as a perceptual event in its own right and enters the domain of symbolic referents.

Like the outstretched finger, language is not an object (even though linguists treat it as such); it is *mediation.* Through it we move toward a shared reality. In speaking we always say something about something, and by so doing language becomes transparent and recedes into the background. "Language seeks to disappear; it seeks to die as an object" as Ricoeur (1968/1974, 85) puts it. Lea's "da," which her father understands as meaning "there," is the sonorous accompaniment to her need to call attention to something in her world. The pointing finger and the word invite her father into a shared reality. They refer to something, say something about something. And in the saying they become transparent. Like the pointing hand that must be transcended in order to understand it as a sign, Lea's referential gestures and sounds must be forgotten in the moment of use in order to be useful. The pointing finger transcends itself and by so doing it opens up a world that can be shared beyond the immediate range of the hand. The sound of the word must be forgotten in order to evoke the thing spoken about. The symbolic, mediating activity of language becomes possible in the leap beyond the hand and the voice as immediate perceptual events. The body disappears as it opens toward a particular transcendental panorama. At the same time, it signifies the world as an extension of its gestural field. Language is born in the tension between the embodied, immanent "here and now," and the symbolized, transcendent "there and then."

Da . . . Da . . . Da . . .

In the previous pages we have analyzed the phenomenon of pointing primarily from a bodily perspective, but like all existential phenomena, bodily being is always woven into the spatial, coexistential, and temporal dimensions of a child's existence. Through the application of linguistic models to children's language acquisition it has become increasingly apparent that language use is a deeply social phenomenon, and that speech always happens in a human context. Sociolinguistic theorists have placed the communicative function of language and the speech acts between children and others, particularly their mothers, into the center of their investigation (Bruner 1993; Dore 1979; Nelson 1977; Snow 1972). The pointing gesture of the eleven-month-old infant, even though directed at the world before her or him, nevertheless is also a gesture directed at her or his parent. Without the presence of the other, infants do not point at the world: Lea turns around and makes sure that her father is looking to where she points, searching for his shared attention.

Stern (1985) reports that infants begin to point at the same time they begin to communicate intentionally with their parents. This intentional communication is different from the intention to simply influence the other person, as in crying or smiling, because infants persist and modify their signaling behavior until parents understand and align their gestures with what the child is indicating. Stern interprets this new "interintentional" ability as the infant's awareness that the other has a different perspective and ability to "[attribute] an internal mental state to that person" (131). Other researchers speak of the infant as understanding "the inner psychological states of others" (which chimpanzees, along with most other animals, fail to do) (Povinelli, Bering, and Giambrone 2003, 45). However, from a nondualistic, phenomenological perspective, shared attention does not imply that Lea suddenly has magical insight into the hidden, "internal" psyche of her father. If we follow Merleau-Ponty's analysis, the psyche is not an interiorized subject in an objective body; "it is above all a relation to the world" (1964b, 116)— that is, a meaningful conduct or intentional comportment within a particular shared environment. "Thus it is in his conduct, in the manner in which the other deals with the world, that I will be able to discover his consciousness" (117). *Shared attention is not an understanding of the other's interiority but an attempt to enter a project that the other delineates in the world.*

We saw in chapter 2 how the structures of spatiality influence the structures of human embodiment and consciousness. As soon as infants become mobile and leave the narrow circle of arms and lap, their action space encompasses things that are in a varied and confusing sensory field. Lea can move now of her own accord as she reaches for things, and the world is changed from a vague place where things magically appear to a space that has fixed and shifting perceptual patterns that invite her to move through them. The parent becomes the secure base from which to explore the unknown world, but in order to establish the alignment of experiences and a shared world, infant and parent have to work: communicative gestures and words sometimes fail and have to be repeated or modified. In the infant's act of pointing and shared reference we find a first awareness of the transcendence of the world: not everything is present and at hand. Shared presence requires effort because there is only a partial overlap between the parent's and the infant's perspective on the world. Transcendence implies a gap, a rift, a "divergence"—or *écart*, as Merleau-Ponty (1968) puts it—between what is grasped and what is intended. Pointing, as Werner and Kaplan (1963) indicated, already presupposes a certain distance from the world and from the other. It tries to reestablish proximity in distance.

Language is born out of the desire to bridge the gap and overcome the divergence (*écart*), to invite the other to enter that region of the transcendent world that I delineate with my pointing finger or, later, with my words or sentences. Merleau-Ponty said of the speaking subject that it does not possess words as emblems of abstract thoughts or ideas; it has them because it intends something. This intending is of the same nature as when I move my body to that particular, intended place in the room (1968, 201). The speaker reaches toward something absent and as yet unspoken that can come into language only through the act of using speech. In symbolizing by pointing or speech we have something compelling before us that comes into being in articulation. The pointing finger is the gestural bridge between the infant's desire and intention to share the perceived world with the parent, and the experience that there is more out there that can come into being only through symbolic speech. It invites into consciousness what has not yet been grasped.

The significance of the symbolic leap becomes apparent in Helen Keller's autobiography (1905). Six-year-old Helen was deaf and blind and very limited in her means of understanding and communicating with other people. She frequently erupted into prolonged storms of rage. The day when she grasped the symbolic dimension of words was a watershed in her young life:

> We walked down the path to the well-house, attracted by the fragrance of the honeysuckle with which it was covered. Some one was drawing water and my teacher placed my hand under the spout. As the cool stream gushed over one hand she spelled into the other the word water, first slowly, then rapidly. I stood still, my whole attention fixed upon the motions of her fingers. Suddenly I felt a misty consciousness as of something forgotten—a thrill of returning thought; and somehow the mystery of language was revealed to me. I knew then that "w-a-t-e-r" meant the wonderful cool something that was flowing over my hand. That living word awakened my soul, gave it light, hope, joy, set it free! There were barriers still, it is true, but barriers that could in time be swept away. (22)

For Helen Keller, the mystery of language is deeply tied to the "thrill of returning thought." As language came to her (in the clumsily spelled letters of the word *water* on her hand), her mind opened up and thought began to unfurl. Now she could receive ideas from other people and she could express her own. Language gave a world to her that her eyes and ears could not experience but that her hands and her mind could grasp and expand.

Beyond breast and lap, communication is fraught with pitfalls and misunderstandings but also open and full of new possibilities. The transcendence and call of the world and the desire to remain one with the other are the two archetypal strands of human experience that weave together into the thread of speech. Words are born beyond the tip of the index finger but they arise in the presence of someone who can follow the child's mind into the world-region indicated.

WORDS

The Halo of Things

When Lea points, how does her father know that she means the dog? This is the problem of reference: how signifier and signified are related to each other. We can never be absolutely sure that we see what the other intended: pointing toddlers often excitedly indicate something they want from the top of the counter, and we parents have no clue what it is. We ask, picking things up: "Is it this? . . . No? . . . This?" But we can be relatively certain that when we follow the line of the finger we are in the field of perception where the important thing is happening. Something of significance is going on, and it must stand out to the person pointing. The very line and movement of the extended arm and finger indicate that only one thing or event is singled out, unlike the gesture of the sweeping arm and hand, which opens upon a whole panorama. Lea's gaze is drawn by the dog and follows its movement. It stands out in Lea's perceived world as a particular figure before a ground of other perceptions. The pointing gesture makes sense only when there is something to point at. The connection between the pointing finger, the sign, and what it points at, the signified, is not arbitrary. The perceived is structured and assumes areas of significance because the eye (and the rest of the body) *is invited by the gestures of things.* The child's personal history of desire and fear, familiarity and strangeness, encounters the gestural field of the moving black dog and it stands out in the larger field of perception. If the person walking the dog had been her mother, the child's pointing finger would in all likelihood have referred to her, rather than the dog, and the father would have said, "Oh, there is Mommy." The father understands because of his shared history with Lea. There are degrees of significance in the panorama of the world, and sometimes we miss the one intended by the other. *But the pointing finger always indicates that there is something that we ought to pay attention to, and that a particular region of the perceptual field is meaningful.*

Young children are biased learners when it comes to language. They assume, for example, that a word refers to the whole object, and not to its parts: "da" refers to the dog, not a dog ear or a tail. And if one thing has been named, an unknown thing must have a different name: when father says "doggie," "lady" does not refer to the dog and so must belong to the other walker (Pinker 1995). The finger singles out a being with a definite contour, and Lea's father supplies her with its name and puts it at the end of his sentence for emphasis. The relationship between the name and the thing is arbitrary in the sense that the father could be speaking Hindi or Swahili or French, but what is not arbitrary is the relationship of meaning between a particular and repeated sonorous pattern and what has been singled out in the perceived world in the exchange of glance, gesture, and speech between a parent and a child.

The phenomenology of the child's pointing gesture reveals two aspects of the sign that are essential: it vanishes in the act of communication, and it outlines a region of being for another. The German word *Bedeutung,* which is often translated as "reference" or "meaning," has its roots in the word *deuten,* which means "to point." *Bedeutung,* which Ricoeur translates as "pointing," refers to the event of naming in which the signified arises out of the encounter between the perceiving mind and the thing (1967). Meaning is not located in some abstract sphere but dwells in the region of being the sign points to. The meaning intention, as Husserl says, breaks the enclosed circle of the sign and reaches the reality of the thing, because language is the saying of something about something (2001). The moment of naming becomes possible when the sign as such—Lea's or her father's pointing hand—is transcended in the communicative act of calling upon the world of things.[3] The "big doggie" Lea's father names is not merely an incidental accessory to the language game between father and child. It is one of the essential constituents of speech: *it is the something about which we speak*. Yet there is not a one-to-one relationship between the signifier and the signified. As we saw before, the pointing finger and the word "da" delineate a region of being rather than a literal object. The father specifies: "Yeah, that's a big doggie," evoking other qualitative aspects of dogness. Some of them might be tinged with apprehension or fear or even appreciation of the animal's size.

Blind toddlers, even though they cannot follow the pointing finger or the parent's gaze, still acquire symbolization and language at the same rate as other toddlers, even though the word meanings they come up with "map onto a different sensory world" (Gleitman 1988, 172). I would assume that the parents of blind children have found other ways of "pointing," *evoking regions of being to be shared* with the child though touch or hearing. Because of the changed horizon and the different immediacy of perception without vision, things are present to these children less as a defined contour and more as textural variations and interpenetrating soundscapes. The divergence between the seeing parent's perceived world and the blind child's is probably greater than in other dyads, which might lead to an *increase* in verbal language to supplement the missing visible landscape. The stars can come to a blind child only through the descriptive, poetic language of other human beings.

Merleau-Ponty has shown how our perception of the world is permeated with the unperceived, the void, silence (1962): there are hidden aspects to the dog and to the child's perception of it. If Lea and her father were to stand at the window for a long time, the dog might reveal other aspects of its being, such as its greeting behavior with another dog or its predilection for a particular corner of the hedge. Like Heidegger's lectern (Safranski 1998), the dog could infinitely expand in the halo of meaning that surrounds it: it is "worlding," which means that it assembles a whole world in terms of time and space and is the visible fulcrum for a larger, invisible region of being. As such, it can give rise to further speech: more and more could be said. *Language is a function of the worlding of things.* The need for speech arises when the father searches for the specific meaning in the region of world Lea opens up with her finger. His speech is the desire to more closely approximate her world: "yeah," the father says, emphasizing the positive and satisfied recognition of Lea's intentionality. When the parent misses the child's intention, more speech is produced. "Is it this? . . . or that?" The *écart*, or divergence, between what is said and what could be said, what is understood and what more can be grasped is what drives language acquisition. Lea and her father want to speak because more can be said, and in the saying their worlds will coincide more closely.

In the *écart* of the speech act, cognition transcends the perceived and thinking begins to work in the invisible region of the plenum. The child thinks and speaks in response to the other's speaking because there is a divergence in speech between what he or she perceives and the world that the conversation partner evokes. "The other's words from a grillwork through which I see my thought" (Merleau-Ponty 1968, 224). For many years young children see their own thought through the grillwork of conversation but are not consciously aware of thinking as a thematized and particularly human activity. And yet thinking grows as spoken language holds open ever-new dimensions of what might be speakable in the future.

The phenomenology of pointing affirms Merleau-Ponty's (1962) insistent claim that we must look at the speech act in its totality if we want to understand the phenomenon of human language. It is not enough to isolate the linguistic structure of language, or the mind/brain neural substructure, or the cognitive capacities of the nine-month-old, or the attachment relation between infant and parent—we have to *return language to the existential circle.* Linguistic deep structure, physiology, cognition, and attachment are all elements of a comprehensive placement of language into the complex web of human experience. Language arises out of a particular human relatedness to the perceived world, and speech, once it is grasped by the infant, inevitably transforms the perceived world. It brings into shared presence the invisible, the unperceived, the void, the silence.

From Pointing to Speech

As a typical toddler, Lea will slowly acquire the next fifty words in the second year of her life, most accompanied by expressive gestures. In her "primitive speech acts" (Dore 1979), nouns will predominate, designating people or animals within the environment or things the child can manipulate, but there are also action and social words: *Mama*, *Papa*, *milk*, *dog*, *car*, *no*, *mine*, *please*, *give*, *bye-bye*, *up* (Owens 2001). Why do infants pick up nouns so quickly? Hirsh-Pasek and Golinkoff (1996) summarize what language researchers have found out about nouns:

1. Nouns are heavily stressed in a sentence.
2. Nouns are often used by themselves or in the last position of a sentence.
3. Nouns mostly refer to concrete, perceptual things in the child's environment rather than to abstract concepts like "truth" and "beauty."
4. Nouns have distinct morphological markers like "a" and "the" in English.
5. Nouns are often introduced to young children as objects are being manipulated (either by them or by an adult), pointed to, or gazed at.

Nouns stand out because there are, on the one hand, *musical markers* that designate their position and importance in the flow of spoken language (see points 1, 2, and 4 above). On the other hand, there are powerful *perceptual/gestural markers* that attach the noun to something that is present in the child's bodily field (see points 3 and 5 above). Music and gesture are the semiotic underpinnings of noun acquisition.

The nouns Lea knows are neither too big nor too small: she will know the words *kitty* and *cookie* but not the word *house*, because it does not become thematic in her action space. It is interesting to note that the word *diaper* is not part of the early vocabulary, probably because the toddler experiences it passively. Some words will be too general, and she overextends them. Others will be too specific, and she underextends them. *Mommy* designates only Lea's mother, not her friend Lara's, and *wauwau* can be the family dog as well as a pair of furry slippers or a bowl of coleslaw. Only gradually, with practice, will her word meaning approximate that of the people around her, and she will enter a social world where things have a speech label that is conventional, conceptual, and abstract (Owens 2001). Sometimes this process is painful, as Stern (1985) has shown: much of the global, perceptual richness of the "worlding" of things cannot be expressed in conventional language or is censored and becomes unspeakable. Psychoanalysts have long known that the entrance into the symbolic order of language is also an alienating process (Kristeva 1984; Lacan 2002).

The pivot that connects the pointing finger and the first words is that they are both gestures. Initially, the body-signifier and the word-signifier refer to a thing or event present to immediate perception, but later, when word order and grammar appear at the end of the second year, speech begins to designate a reality much less literal and at hand: "The spoken word is a gesture, and its meaning is a world" (Merleau-Ponty 1962, 184). In the above analysis it has become clear that the signifying gesture intends something in the world and outlines a region in which it can be found. It is also at the same time an invitation to the other to appropriate this gesture in his or her own way and begin to dwell in the region of being indicated. Gesture is referential and intentional in that its reach is already a meaningful structure within the world and in that it ceases to make sense when there is no complement in the world before it. To understand speech as gesture does not mean that words point at literal things or that we have a one-to-one relationship between signifier and signified. Speech as gesture is Bedeutung, "indication" or "meaning" in Ricoeur's sense, because its roots lie in the encounter between conversation partners and the things of their shared world that they reach for in the act of speaking to each other. Merleau-Ponty's concept of gesture allows us to articulate language as a phenomenon that is not primarily cognitive, nor is it mechanistic or essentially biological—properly, it is existential.

Gesture arises out of the chiasm between body and world. "The gesture which I witness outlines an intentional object" (Merleau-Ponty 1962, 185), and it reveals the other's particular way or style of being in the world. When Merleau-Ponty speaks of language as gesture, his intention is not to reduce it to a bodily phenomenon but to show its rootedness in the lived, gestural body and how it transcends and alters the perceived world. Understanding one another in the gestures of body and speech is not an operation of abstract concepts in two separate minds; it is the act of mutually assuming the world that the speaker's language delineates. Speaking intends a world, and listening allows that world to be assumed by the other.

The "worlding" of the intended event, like the halo of meaning that surrounds Lea's dog, is always present but not thematized or consciously recognized. While the larger region of an event can be indicated through the bodily gesture of pointing, its details remain undifferentiated. Speaking, on the other hand, differentiates the plenum. The multifaceted quality of the world of things can be articulated and raised to awareness, and many regions of being come into existence for the human mind only through language. Yesterday and tomorrow, subject and object, active and passive, up and down, yes and no become possible gestures for the child because language carves them out of the large, inexhaustible block of the "worlding" world.

GRAMMAR

Innate or Learned?

Nicaragua had no sign language or education for the deaf until the latter half of the twentieth century. In the early 1980s the Sandinista government created the first schools for the deaf, which focused on drilling the children in lipreading and speech. The results were dismal. But during breaks in the school day the children figured out a way to communicate with each other: they pooled their home signs and created their own pidgin sign language. Today this language is known as LSN (Lenguaje de signos nicaraguense) and is spoken by deaf adults who were ten or older when they picked it up from the other children on the playgrounds at the schools for the deaf. Like all pidgin languages, it is a compilation of gestural signs from various backgrounds and relies heavily on indirect expression and suggestion. It does not have a consistent grammar (Pinker 1995).

If the story stopped here, we could be appreciative of the children's resourcefulness and admire their tenacity in finding ways to communicate. But there is a second chapter to Nicaraguan sign language that is even more amazing than the first. Some children came into the school environment when they were four years old. LSN was in full swing among the older children in the hallways and playgrounds, and these little ones picked it up without trouble. But with them the sign language changed. While it was used haphazardly and with great idiosyncrasies among the older students, the young children standardized it and now, as young adults, they all speak the same sign language. Their signing is more fluid and compact and looks less like a pantomime. Their modification of LSN has become known as ISN (*Idioma de signos nicaraguense*), and rather than a pidgin, it seems to be a true creole language—that is, it has a fully fledged grammar. Pinker summarizes the achievements of the young Nicaraguan signers:

> ISN has spontaneously standardized itself; all the young children sign it the same way. The children have introduced many grammatical devices that were absent in LSN, and hence they rely far

less on circumlocutions. For example, an LSN (pidgin) signer might make the sign for "talk to" and then point from the position of the talker to the position of the hearer. But an ISN (creole) signer modifies the sign itself, sweeping it in one motion from a point representing the talker to a point representing the hearer. This is a common device in sign languages, formally identical to inflecting a verb for agreement in spoken languages. Thanks to such consistent grammar, ISN is very expressive. A child can watch a surrealistic cartoon and describe its plot to another child. The children use it in jokes, poems, narratives, and life histories, and it is coming to serve as the glue that holds the community together. A language has been born before our eyes. (1995, 25)

Bickerton (1981) reports a similar transformation from adult use of a pidgin language to children's invention of a grammatically sophisticated creole. Before the turn of the twentieth century, international plantation workers in Hawaii combined their different mother tongues and created a pidgin language, but their children invented Hawaiian creole. Bickerton thinks that while adults pool their words in order to communicate, the *grammar of a creole language is a product of the minds of children.* It is also reported that the children of deaf parents, who acquire sign language after their own childhood and are not fluent in it, learn the broken, ungrammatical ASL (American Sign Language) from their parents but then improve upon it and work out a grammatically very sophisticated use of ASL without explicit instruction (Pinker 1995). Again: a language is born before our eyes.

The difference between the first- and second-generation Nicaraguan sign users is significant. Not only did the younger generation of children learn word signs, they invented a grammar. The pantomimelike signs of the pidgin signers are still intimately tied to their gestural bodies and the particular situation in which they are communicating with each other: most signs directly refer to things or activities, and many signs are required to express a simple event like "I talk to you." The creole signing children, on the other hand, standardize and streamline the sign's usage, that is, they extract it from the immediate context of the "wild" gesture. This frees them to inflect the sign itself by standardizing the *grammatical gesture* (the prepositions "from . . . to") in the sweep of the sign itself between speaker and listener. The child's mind seems to want to (1) standardize particular signs; and (2) find the most efficient grammatical forms for communicating complex experiences and ideas. This facility for grasping and applying grammatical structures to speech or sign seems to have its critical period before the age of ten. Adolescent and adult signers seem to have missed a window of opportunity for acquiring the elegance and fluency of a full spoken or signed language if they are not exposed to it in early childhood.

Pinker and other linguists argue that these examples point toward an innate grammatical ability in children. From the broken speech of their elders, these children abstract universal grammatical rules and apply them to their language. These rules must preexist in the child's mind. Other, more ordinary examples also seem to point toward a genetic predisposition for grammar. By the time children are three or four years old, they use the grammar of their mother tongue with great facility, and they do this without instruction: no one teaches toddlers the correct grammatical forms. Some of the mistakes children make also point to an underlying grasp of grammatical inflection: they say, "I helded the kitty" and apply the past tense inflection "ed" to irregular verbs, which they cannot have learned from adults.

The current debate over the nature of language has its pivot in how we understand grammar. Beginning with Chomsky's groundbreaking work (1965), "nativist" linguists have claimed that infants are born with some abstract concepts about the structure of language, and that part of their biological makeup includes a language acquisition device (LAD) that becomes activated during the process of early development. The LAD allows the infant to understand and apply the principles of universal grammar, and language, like the ability to walk, unfolds automatically with minimal input from the environment (Pinker 1995). In his famous debate with B. F. Skinner, Chomsky (1959) argued that the poverty of stimulus in infants' language exposure leads to the conclusion that children must know general principles of syntax that they could not have acquired from input, and so must be built into the human mind. We are genetically preprogrammed to apply universal grammar. Grammar, according to Chomsky, is a matter of pure form, independent of meaning or human understanding, and it can be studied without taking them into account. Nativists do not like to speak about language *learning* because the most important element of language acquisition is not a factor of cognition: words might be learned, but the grammar program unfolds automatically once it is activated. Pinker goes so far as to compare the human ability to use language to the spider's ability to spin a web: it is an instinct that is hardwired into the brain.

Gleitman (1988, 160) summarizes the three main arguments in the research community that favor innateness of language: (1) across linguistic communities language acquisition proceeds in uniform ways despite great variations in input provided to individuals (children in poor language environments acquire grammar as well as children in enriched environments); (2) what children learn is not simply related to what they are exposed to (their use of grammar is generative); (3) "the child acquires many linguistic generalizations that experience could not have made available"(they say things they have never heard before).

The Chomskyan, innatist perspective has been widely criticized on technical and philosophical grounds. Tomasello (2000) argues that the findings of contemporary language research show that young children do not apply abstract grammatical structures in their generative language use but imitate linguistic structures and items from adult speech. "When applied across the board, the finding is that children's language development is gradual and piecemeal in the extreme, with individual items and structures being learned on a one-on-one basis, and generalizations and abstractions coming only some time later" (9). Lakoff and Johnson point out that the Cartesian assumptions underlying Chomsky's linguistic theory are inconsistent with the findings of second-generation linguists' empirical research on mind and language.[4] This research shows that syntax is structured

> not independently of meaning, but so as to express meaning
> not independently of communication, but in accordance with
>   communicative strategies
> not independently of culture, but often in accord with the deepest
>   aspects of culture
> not independently of the body, but arising from aspects of the
>   sensori-motor system (1999, 479)

Many psycholinguists understand language acquisition as an interactive event that is embedded in the child's physical and social environment (Bloom 1993; Bruner 1983; Nelson 1977; Slobin 1988; Snow 1972). The structures of syntax and other grammatical forms are a reflection of the child's ability to process experience. "Interactionists" study the "language acquisition support system" (LAD) (Bruner 1993): some focus on the dialogal situation between infants and caregivers, others look at the social-cultural production of language, and a third group focuses on the importance of gesture and the body in articulating a cognitive linguistics. A number of researchers (Iverson et al. 1999; Kelly et al. 2002; McNeill 2002), especially linguists from a neuroscience background, have made a very strong case for the gestural underpinnings of language acquisition, which means that language is not a purely mental matter. The combination of speech and nonverbal gesture seems to help young children "break into" an understanding of more complex forms of language (Kelly et al. 2002). Hirsh-Pasek and Golinkoff (1996) call interactionists the "outside-in" theorists to distinguish them from the nativist "inside-out" theorists, who believe that the essential structures of grammar are inborn.

The two positions—language is innate vs. language is learned—reach back deeply into Western thinking. In the biblical tradition, language is a gift from God to all humankind (which we messed up when we built the tower of Babel); Augustine, on the other hand, wrote in his *Confessions* that he learned language by imitating his mother. Since the Chomsky-Skinner debate, scholars feel called to man the barricades on one side or the other: language is either innate, or it is learned. A careful look at the appearance of grammatical forms in early language acquisition might help us think through the nature of grammar more clearly. Perhaps we should suspend our assumption that we know what a grammatical *rule* is and look at it afresh.

Lived Grammar: Word Order

In *Gulliver's Travels* (Swift 1962), the protagonist visits the Grand Academy of Lagado and observes the professors at work on their inventions. In the School of Languages some professors attempt to shorten discourse by condensing polysyllables and dropping verbs and participles "because in reality all things imaginable are but nouns" (183). Others, who share the same assumption, want to eradicate spoken language altogether, so that people can preserve their lung capacity and live longer. In order to communicate, they carry all manner of things around and silently lift them up as the objects of their discourse: "I have often beheld two of those sages almost sinking under the weight of their packs, like peddlers among us; who, when they meet in the streets would lay down their loads, open their sacks and hold conversation for an hour together; then put up their implements, help each other to resume their burthens, and take their leave" (184).

Swift's wonderful satire shows the absurdity of reducing language to nouns that have only one clearly delineated referent. The linguists of Lagado have eradicated grammar from their language, and in consequence they can only pantomime and refer to what is immediately present, staggering under the weight of their packs. Words allow us to leave present things behind, and grammar connects words into a web of signif-icances that transcends the single referent. Grammar becomes a further extension of the symbolic world opened up by words. Words can appeal to something that is absent, but grammar structures the perceived and symbolic worlds of experience. For the human mind grammar holds the possibility of structuring spatiality (prepositions), temporality (tense), self and otherness (pronouns), and it encodes basic actions (subject, predicate, object) that appear in the world.

Word order is one of the earliest grammatical forms that infants understand. Even before toddlers put two words together they can com-prehend a sentence by its syntax, that is, the sequence of subject, pred-icate, object. Sixteen- to nineteen-month-old babies, when asked, can point to the video screen where "Big Bird is tickling Cookie Monster" and avoid the one where Big Bird is tickled himself (Hirsh-Pasek and Golinkoff 1996). Hirsh-Pasek and Golinkoff found that children in the one-word stage, who do not produce sentences, are nevertheless sen-sitive to the order of both nouns around a verb and comprehend the importance of word placement in another's speech. The infants under-stand that the subject is the one doing something, and it comes first in an English sentence, and the object comes later, after the verb. Infants at seventeen months of age grasp the order of subject, predicate, object: they have syntax.

Let us push this a bit deeper. What happens when infants, placed in front of two video screens, are exposed to Hirsh-Pasek and Golinkoff's (1996) imperative speech act: "See Big Bird tickle Cookie Monster"? Big Bird is the subject engaged in an action (the predicate "tickle"), which he does to the object (Cookie Monster). If we look at Big Bird and Cookie Monster as discrete things, there is not much difference be-tween them: they are both large puppets moving about on the video screen. One is yellow; the other is blue. In terms of their worlding, they both belong in the same environment of the *Sesame Street* TV show. However, as soon as they are placed in a syntactic relationship and word order is assigned to them, they undergo a significant change: one be-comes the active agent, the other the passive sufferer. Big Bird initiates the action: it is the intentionality of the sentence-subject that deter-mines the flow of the event. The linear nature of human language, which is implied in the notion of word order, means that some things will be named first and others follow. Language itself has a basic tem-poral structure that imparts significance to some words over others. The words *Big Bird*, *tickle*, and *Cookie Monster* interact with each other through their word order. They, to use a phrase from Paul Ricoeur, undergo "semantic contamination" (1985, 66): they infect each other with meaning. It matters which one comes first. Words are polysemous, that is, they have a shifting significance when they enter the web of a sentence. They no longer refer to things as discrete entities, they refer to the action space between them. *Syntax opens up a space where the sign is no longer a direct referent but a contaminated element in a semantic web.*

The call to "See Big Bird tickle Cookie Monster" *restructures the child's experiential field:* it is an appeal by a conversation partner to refocus attention on Big Bird, the active agent. Without the languaged appeal both screens probably hold the same interest for the child. After the call all infants turn to the video where Big Bird is the agent. If we take our earlier analysis of pointing into account, we can see a parallel between the deictic finger and word order: the "actor first" rule delineates a region of being that the infant is called to attend to *together* with the speaker: for why would the speaker not pay attention to the active agent that she or he points out to the child (unless the speaker is a disembodied voice in an infant research laboratory!)? *In situated discourse, the motivating function of word order is to establish joint attention* (on Big Bird in this case), and once infant and speaker turn in the same direction, more aspects of the situation disclose themselves. Once joint attention is established, both conversation partners can talk about what they see and why it is important. More language bubbles to the surface.

The finding that infants recognize word order supports our earlier insight that certain structures and activities of things stand out to the perceiving infants and claim their attention. Moreover, syntax, which is one of the key elements of grammar, is not an arbitrary assignment of word order but is tied to the experienced world. We saw above how "nouns" come to be within the larger syntactic framework of the musical and gestural dimensions of speech. Grammar, as the case grammarians have shown, is connected in meaningful ways to basic semantic concepts that represent events and relationships that can be found in all environments (Owens 2001, 50). Language researchers like Bloom (1993) and Greenfield and Smith (1976) hypothesized that the underlying semantic basis of language develops prior to syntax. Word order is tied to the basic agent/activity structure of the infant's experienced world. But instead of arguing which comes first, language or experience, we should note that human language and human experience are coexistential and form a chiasmic figure. The basic metaphors of language are rooted in the body (Lakoff and Johnson 1999), but body and perception are irrevocably shaped by the exercise of human language.

Lived Grammar: Morphemes

When our daughter, Lea, was thirty-two months old, she understood and used the word "no" very well, but she could not negate a whole sentence. She would say, "Me want cereal" and shake her head vigorously. Here gesture supplied the grammatical marker for negation. "I do not want cereal" is a very complex grammatical structure, which has the reflexive personal pronoun "I" in the first place and the confusing composite verb "do want" as the predicate. At this time she also struggled with the pronoun "I," saying sentences like "Me eat breakfast" and then correcting herself: "I eat breakfast." At thirty-eight months she would know but confuse the correct grammatical markers for *to be:* "Me am going outside—I are going outside." These self-corrections of a young child speak to the intuitive sense the child has for a misused grammatical form. She has grasped that in the English language the present continuous is formed with a version of *to be* (am, is, are), which changes according to who (I, she, we) is speaking. Lea was creatively experimenting with grammatical forms and at the same time listening to her own language. Her early uses of morphemes (prefixes and suffixes that are grammatical markers that modify verbs and nouns) were not copies of adult phrases but linguistic motifs that she played through like a jazz musician who improvises on a particular musical theme.

Besides syntax, there are other very early grammatical markers in infant language: possession ("Lea doggie"), location ("doggie out"), negation ("no doggie"), disappearance ("all gone doggie"), and reappearance ("nuther doggie"). Of the early morphemes, the present progressive expresses temporal duration ("I walk*ing*") and is the first and most frequently used verb ending of English-speaking toddlers. It is followed by grammatical forms expressing containment ("*in* basket"), support ("*on* floor"), number ("*two* ball*s*"), prior occurrence ("it *broke*"), and possession ("Lea*'s* ball") (Cole and Cole 2001; Owens 2001).

Most adults are somewhat grammar phobic because we have come to think of grammar as a painful subject of our earlier foreign-language studies. Do you remember how excruciating it was to memorize Latin declensions or the French definite articles that gave every noun a gender? I can testify to the madness of English grammar: try to remember how to make the conditional past participle tense and what it is called! "I would have been going" ("if you had not stopped me") already has five grammatical morphemes in it. Pity the young German child who has to figure this one out on an exam. The point is: most of us use the complex grammar of our native tongues all the time and we do not even think about it. Neither do our infants.

The miracle of grammar lies in the economy and flexibility it gives to words. The sentence "Lea sees the dog" is a straightforward subject-predicate-object construction. We think of Lea as she looks out the window and sees the dog. Let us add a few morphemes: "Lea sees the dog*s*," and now the big black dog is joined by one or more others. "Lea *saw* the dog": now we refer to something that is no longer present, that has happened in the past; we could also add some morphemes to make the future tense: "Lea *will be seeing* the dog." Other complications are possible: "Lea *her* dog," or "*Does* Lea see the dog?" or "The dog *is seen* by Lea." You get my drift: our four little words can expand tremendously through the addition of grammatical markers. Each morpheme changes the sentence radically: it adds a whole new dimension of meaning. The four words metamorphose through number, tense, possession, question, and passive voice. And these are only a few of the possibilities we could have explored. The power of speech lies in the infinite use of finite means (Ricoeur 1985).

The scene at Lea's window will change over the next three years. First, as we have seen, she is carried by her father to the window, points at the dog, and utters, "da." At two she runs to the window and yells excitedly: "Daddy, doggie shoe," because the dog has stolen her father's shoe from the front porch. At three she will call her father: "Daddy, come quickly! A dog has taked your shoe. What's he doing with it?" Her grammar at four is fully functioning, and she can understand and express very complicated events in her sentences. With new grammatical forms, the world opens up in particular ways. Or vice versa: new experiences call for greater grammatical flexibility. Grammar is not merely a linguistic form that is memorized—it marks new aspects of the child's world. When toddlers are able to move toward what they desire, the possessive word "mine" suddenly acquires deep significance. When the experiential horizon widens and things and people appear and disappear, "all gone" and "nuther" and "no doggie" appeal to the dialectic between visible and invisible. Two cookies are more than one, and mothers frequently talk to their toddlers about the future: "Do you want to go to the park?" We find the other elements of the existential circle—

coexistentiality, embodiment, spatiality, and temporality—reflected in the early grammatical forms. Language is an existential event, and there is a parallel between children's ability to structure the complexity of their perceived world and the complexity of their language. *Grammar is learned not by memorizing what adults say but by experiencing the need to inhabit the shared linguistic world of other human beings.*

What grammar adds to words is the extension of their meaning. Morphemes push language beyond word order (syntax)—which is still tied to the spatiotemporal unfolding of sound through the body—and we enter the phenomenon of inflection, where a syllable that is meaningless in itself evokes and brings to mind a previously hidden dimension of the word's meaning. *Morphemes focus words in particular ways.* The past tense, for example, refers not to anything present anymore but to an absence. The linguists of Gulliver's Grand Academy of Lagado could not have spoken about the past because there is no noun for it. They sacrificed all the morphemes of their language and impoverished it to save their breath. The past exists only because we have grammatical morphemes that call forth the bygone temporal dimension into our discourse. We can recollect and narrate the past because we have the ability to capture it in the web of significances that grammar weaves. The past comes into being because it is speakable. The thing or event that we cannot see or hear anymore becomes memory because it has been preserved in narrative. Time, as Ricoeur discovered, becomes human only through narrative (1984). It becomes real when it is captured in the web of grammatical signifiers and the sequence of syntax in the exchange of speech. The web of grammatical signification, however, does not kill its prey or pin it down. The speaking of the past is always surrounded by the voices of silence and the void of what is yet to be said.

Merleau-Ponty recognized that the differentiations of the verbal chain, the grammatical markers, make meaning possible. But meaning is not on the word or phrase "like the butter on the bread" (1968, 155). Nor is it a second layer of internal, psychic representation spread out over the sound. It is not in the mind of the speaker, nor is it "out there" to be simply picked up. Once the child enters the symbolic order of human speech, meaning lives in language, and language opens invisible dimensions of the plenum and brings them into presence between conversation partners. The small porcelain cups in the china cupboard (a purely sensory event) become the pivots for a narrative about the past: they were given to Mom by her grandmother's five sisters when she was a little girl. Once talked about, some of the meanings that surround them come out of dormancy, and a person's individual past appears to be woven into ancestral and cultural time. When the child has heard her mother's stories about the cups, they are never again a purely sensory event. The moods of the past cling to them, and sometimes you can catch the scent of a different era still lingering when you open the cupboard door. Language can "catch a meaning in its own mesh," and it does so "without exception each time it is conquering, active, creative language, each time something is, in the strong sense, said" (Merleau-Ponty 1968, 153). Meaning lives and amplifies itself through language. And it changes the child's perception of the world: "the whole landscape is overrun with words as with an invasion, it is henceforth but a variant of speech before our eyes."

METAPHOR

Word meaning, as we saw above, does not present a fixed relationship between a literal object and its name; rather, it evokes the halo of meaning that surrounds a perceived thing. Ricoeur (1985) assigns the term *polysemy* to "the phenomenon of language by which words have more than one signification or meaning" (61), but it is on the level of discourse that polysemy achieves its true function. In speech the polysemous word can appear in more than one context with different meanings, so that the word "doggie" applies to the black animal outside as well as to Lea's stuffed animal or a picture in a book. When Lea is in her third year, her finger play can assume the gesture of a walking dog, or she might pet the sofa pillow and say, "There, there, doggie, it's okay" when she is upset. It is within the sentence that words reach for aspects of the void of meaning, and their polysemy interacts with other words and creates new meaning. On the level of the sentence, in the purview of grammar, language becomes truly creative: once three-year-olds have mastered the basic forms of language, they continually produce new sentences and speak new things. That is the power of grammar: it is an open system that allows for the use of language in addressing other people and speaking about the world.

Ricoeur stressed that there are some discourses that try to restrict polysemy, while others cultivate and enhance it. Univocal discourse—discourse that tolerates only one meaning—attempts to hide the semantic richness of words by establishing an identical frame of reference for all the words of the sentence (Ricoeur 1968/1974). This is the discourse of mathematics and science, which strives for exactness and tries to eliminate ambiguity. Poetic discourse, on the other hand, plays with the polysemy of words and even enhances it through its sonorous form: rhyme and meter create a further level of relationship between the words and produce a "semantic contamination between significations" while "they are charmed by each other" (Ricoeur 1985, 66). For Ricoeur, this semantic contamination is the foundation of metaphor because, even on the level of the sonorous form, it displaces and transports the literal meaning of a word.

The importance of the semantic contamination of everyday language becomes obvious when we look at a child's use of metaphor (and here I include the simile within the category of metaphor). Piaget and his three-year-old daughter, Jacqueline, took a walk by the lake and saw some small waves push little ridges of sand forward and backward onto the beach. Jacqueline exclaimed: *It's like a little girl's hair being combed* (1962, 227). In a metaphor two opposing terms are brought together and begin to interact. The sandy ridges and the girl's hair are and are not alike: there is a tension between the *is* and the *is not* of the metaphor/simile. On the literal level it is absurd to say that the sand is the same as hair. But on the metaphorical/poetic level we begin to see the sand in a different way when we see it as the hair of a little girl. The semantic collision between sand and hair creates a new dimension of meaning, and here we find the properly creative capacity of language to create a surplus of meaning and to be ever new. Jacqueline sees the waves combing the beach, and she also knows what it feels like when a little girl's hair is combed. Does the sand feel the fingers of the lake? Does it hurt? Is it pleasurable? Does the lake care as much as the mother who combs Jacqueline's hair? The child's metaphorical activity allows her to understand and appropriate further meanings by feeling her way into the *is* of the unknown: "It is like . . ." The semantic collision illuminates aspects of being that are hidden in the void. It projects a horizon of being that potentially can come into spoken discourse in the future. Jacqueline knows something more about the waves, and this insight resonates in her words even though she might never articulate it any further.

Lakoff and Johnson (1980) have shown that metaphorical thinking like Jacqueline's is the foundation of all human conceptual thinking. Jacqueline recognizes the similarities between one world of experience and another. She uses her imagination to understand and articulate the structures of her experienced world. "Imagination, in one of its many aspects, involves seeing one kind of thing in terms of another kind of thing—what we have called metaphorical thought. Metaphor is thus *imaginative rationality.* Since the categories of our everyday thought are largely metaphorical and our everyday reasoning involves metaphorical entailments and inferences, ordinary rationality is therefore imaginative by its very nature" (193).

Metaphorical thought organizes the child's experience into categories of similar events. The child's imaginative rationality sees correspondences in the world, some of which Western adults (like Piaget) would call magical. According to Lakoff and Johnson (1980), we adults should not scoff at the child's exuberant and playful metaphor: our scientific or cultural concepts, through which we explain the world and organize reality, are also metaphors. We might not recognize their rootedness in lived experience because they have metamorphosed and become abstracted over time, but they have their origin in the child's imaginative experience of consistent islands of meaning in the flood of daily events: "human thought processes are largely metaphorical" (6). Metaphor is not merely a linguistic trope; it is a fundamental activity of the human mind. We find it in the young, and it designates the fulcrum where the sensory and the symbolic worlds entwine.

It has been argued that children's understanding of metaphorical figures of speech develops only during late childhood and early adolescence, but observation and controlled studies have shown that even very young children produce metaphorical expressions, which is followed a bit later by comprehension and only in late childhood by the ability to explain the rationale of a metaphor (Vosniadou, Ortony, and Reynolds 1988; Winner, Rosenstiel, and Gerdern 1988). Billow (1988) found in his research that preschool children between the ages of two years, seven months and six years do make consistent and intentional use of metaphorical language. However, his study revealed a *decreasing* occurrence of spontaneous metaphor with advancing age. *The younger the children, the more metaphorical the activity!* This indicates that metaphor is one of the very basic and elementary functions of language.

In terms of developmental appearance and psychological function, metaphor is deeply woven into the processes of symbol formation in language and play. Billow observed a child of three years and five months taking a little rubber animal and gliding it around the observer's back, saying, "It's going for a walk in the forest and" (as it reached the observer's hair) "it's going to eat some grass" (1988, 319). The back is the forest, the hair is the grass: two related metaphors. The surplus of meaning appears when the semantic contamination between back/forest and hair/grass unfolds. Here we witness the birth of play, which follows the invitation of the void: explore the is/is not, find out what happens when the little animal walks up the back into the unknown forest. New ideas are generated when the hair becomes grass, and a story unfolds. Metaphorical activity is the driving force of the imagination, and it assumes a place of prominence in the young playing child. It brings together what the child already knows with what is yet unknown. Imagination here "is not the producing of images in the sense of sensorial residues, but the projecting of a horizon of being capable of changing the horizon of our own existence" (Ricoeur 1985, 68). Human development in the first years of life is suffused with this imaginative impulse: the child must continually change the horizon of his or her existence in order to grow.

In the process of language acquisition, the metaphorical impulse preserves the polysemy of words that is the perfect linguistic accompaniment to the worlding of things. By keeping language free and open and by preserving the essential silence of what is not said, the metaphorical impulse guides the child's curiosity into new regions of experience. By stretching its language and by living in it, thinking can be free and open, and reach for things that have not been thought before. Words have the power to evoke the unsaid without speaking it, to make present what is not in the senses. Grammar provides the dynamic, transformational template that brings the polysemy of words to interaction and thus produces a surplus of meaning. This surplus of meaning directs the child's mind beyond the present and opens up the dimension of symbolic referents that make cultural discourse possible.[5]

EIGHT

The Invention of Childhood

Historical and Cultural Changes in Selfhood and Literacy

From the City Chronicle of Cologne, AD 1213:

In this year occurred an outstanding thing and one much to be marveled at, for it is unheard of throughout the ages. About the time of Easter and Pentecost, without anyone having preached or called for it and prompted by I know not what spirit, many thousands of boys, ranging in age from six years to full maturity, left the plows or carts which they were driving, the flocks which they were pasturing, and anything else which they were doing. This they did despite the wishes of their parents, relatives, and friends who sought to make them draw back. Suddenly one ran after the other to take the cross. Thus by groups of twenty, or fifty, or a hundred, they put up banners and began to journey to Jerusalem. They were asked by many people on whose advice or at whose urging they had set out upon this path. They were asked especially since only a few years ago many kings, a great many dukes, and innumerable people in powerful companies had gone there and had returned with the business unfinished. The present groups, moreover, were still of tender years and were neither strong nor powerful enough to do anything. Everyone, therefore, accounted them foolish and imprudent for trying to do this. They briefly replied that they were equal to the Divine will in this matter and that, whatever God might wish to do with them, they would accept it willingly and with a humble spirit. They thus made some little progress on their journey. Some were turned back at Metz, others at Piacenza, and others even at Rome. Still others got to Marseille, but whether they crossed to the

Holy Land or what their end was is uncertain. One thing is sure: that of the many thousands who rose up, only very few returned.[1]

CHILDREN ON THE MOVE

In AD 1212, between the fourth and fifth crusades, twenty-five thousand German children left their homes to follow a charismatic youth from a little town near Cologne. They marched for a thousand kilometers across the Alps to the Mediterranean coast in Italy, where they awaited the prophesied parting of the sea in order to walk all the way to the Holy Land. Inspired by St. Francis of Assisi and wearing an emblem of his cross on their clothes, they wanted to convert the "infidels" and free Jerusalem with innocence and peace. Needless to say, the miracle did not happen, and most of the children were never seen or heard from again. It is said that many were sold into slavery or died on the long way home. A similar story is told about thirty thousand French children who started their peaceful "crusade" but were summarily sent back home by the king's troops (Munro 1914).

This obscure moment in the history of childhood should give us pause. We are startled by the difference between then and now: how could more than one hundred thousand adults let their children, some as young as six years old, wander off into the unknown? It is impossible to imagine that this could happen in France or Germany or the United States today. What was the relationship between medieval adults and children, so that children felt free and confident enough to leave their villages and towns to go on a thousand-mile crusade and the adults let them do it?

In this last chapter we will look at the historical evolution of the concept of childhood: a changing adult world has necessitated the existence of a separate ontological state of human being, which we call childhood. Although, of course, there have been young human beings since the beginning of human societies, childhood, as I will show, became necessary as a cultural and psychological phenomenon only in the late Middle Ages.

Children's lives are woven into the structures of adult existence. Their bodies, their spaces, their time, their relationships with others, and their language are fundamentally determined by the adult culture they are born into, and they change along with it. On a larger historical scale, we can see specific ideas and practices that permeate a historical period and shape the world that adults set up for children—and the philosophical or pedagogical concepts that rule childhood institutions. A phenomenological exploration of child existence, like all good phenomenology, has to be aware of the historical assumptions and the sedimented matrix of meaning that surrounds its phenomena, and move beyond them by means of a historical-critical process that Husserl (1970) calls *epoche* and Merleau-Ponty (1962) calls *reflection*. A historical awareness of changes in child existence allows us to see the contemporary child more clearly and grasp the complex web of significances that shape childhood today. And even though the journey of fifty thousand medieval children is a mere blip in the unfolding of recorded Western history, in the *psychological history of childhood* it marks a significant turning point.

During the century before the children's crusade, theology and philosophy had built the foundations for a new understanding of the person. What we mean today when we casually speak of "the self" is one of the great discoveries of the late Middle Ages. "For earlier medievals, *person* denotes office, function, role variously derived from the word's origin in the Latin *persona*, a mask. For us it means the essential individual, conceived as having a unique personality, physique, and psyche" (Illich 1996, 25). This new understanding of the individual and this new feeling and search for an independent, interior self was reflected in new forms of friendship and marriage, reading and reflection, satire and confession. Pilgrimages to other parts of the known world were frequent, and people left their homes and loosened their family ties to go on strenuous and prolonged spiritual quests. They sloughed off their *personas*, their masks, and followed their personal destinies. The metaphor of *peregrinatio*, pilgrimage or journey, pervades the twelfth century. From the massive, clamorous response to Bernard of Clairvaux's call to the crusades to Hugh St. Victor's quiet, scholarly "peregrination" through the holy texts, we find the people of the high Middle Ages on the move. Illich points out that the metaphor of peregrinatio is appropriate for a new sense of self that wants to come into its own:

> With the spirit of self-definition estrangement acquires a new positive meaning. Hugh's call away from the "sweetness of one's native soil" and to a journey of self-discovery is but one instance of the new ethos. Bernard of Clairvaux preaches the crusades which are another way of expressing the same invitation: they address people at all levels of the feudal hierarchy to leave the common mind-set of the neighborhood, within which identity comes from the way others have named and treated me, and to discover their selves in the loneliness of the long road. At Bernard's beckoning tens of

thousands leave their village community and discover that they can survive on their own without the bonds which had sustained them and constrained them within the predetermined feudal *ordo*. As pilgrims and crusaders, as traveling masons and mill mechanics, as beggars and relic thieves, as minstrels and wandering scholars they take to the road by the end of the 12th century. (23)

And the children heard the call as well. But while the adult crusader survived his time as the heroic protagonist of many a romantic tale (for example, Robin Hood, Ivanhoe, and Richard the Lionheart), the figures of the child crusaders, even in their own time, evoked pity, derision, and ridicule. Why the difference? The phenomenon of the children's crusade highlights the failure of the child when confronted with the project of adult subjectivity. The adult pilgrimage required intellectual and material resources that the children on their own lacked. When the children broke their family ties and went off on their own, they also lost the material and social support of their families. Many accounts of the children's crusade speak of the folly of children leaving without food or money for the journey. Within medieval society Nikolaus and Stephen, the young German and French prophets, and the children who followed them had been woven into the social fabric of family and class, but their crusade exiled them from the customs and support of their known world. Nikolaus's father was held accountable for helping to lure away other parents' children—and hanged for this crime in retribution for the damage his family had done to other families. The individual family members were subsumed under the umbrella of family ties: their identity came from the way others had named and treated them.

Adult pilgrims planned their pilgrimages, making sure that the social fabric at home was maintained during their absence and could be resumed upon their return. The children, obviously against the wishes of their parents, impulsively followed an idealistic calling to their doom (a motif that is also taken up in the Pied Piper story), taking to the road without money or provisions, lured by the dreams of a visionary. Adults returned from their peregrinations—either in person or through reports of their demise from other crusaders or pilgrims. Most of the children were never heard from. Their exile meant that they were lost to their communities and that the journey did not lead to local fame and spiritual enrichment, but to failure and death.

The story of the children's crusade was the first modern portrayal of the emancipation of childhood from adult ties—and its failure. Its weight for the Western psyche lies in the insight that exile from home and community in order to live out the new ethos of self-discovery may be appropriate for adults, but it fails where children are concerned. The children's crusade highlighted the beginning of a dividing line between adults and children that grew ever greater with time. By the seventeenth century the division between adulthood and childhood had become a wide gulf that separated the mature from the immature. It prefigured the world of the modern self and highlighted the status of the child as a child—that is, as a human being who is yet incapable of adult action.

The children's crusade adds a different facet to the debate of the historians of childhood about the status of childhood in the Middle Ages (Aries 1962; Hanawalt 1993; Orme 2001; Shahar 1990; Shorter 1977; Stone 1977). The peregrinatio, according to Illich (1996), was a loosening of the communal bond that had sustained and constrained people within the customary political and personal order. Within the communal bonds, the medieval child could assume a place that was scarcely distinguished from the adult (Aries 1962; Mook 1977). Children past infancy worked, played, celebrated religious festivals, and witnessed birth and death just as adults did. The "monovalency" and continuity of the medieval lived world—the stability and continuity of customs and values over time—assured that adult life was present and visible to the children and that they could slip into it without any particular training or effort (van den Berg 1961). Medieval parents loved and cared for their children as much as we do (Hanawalt 1993; Shahar 1990), but they were not sentimental about childhood. Sentimentality is a mark of distance, a feeling of having lost something that is therefore precious. Medieval childhood was not precious because the adults had not yet lost it. As Barbara Tuchman (1978) points out, medieval behavior was characterized by the childishness of all age groups, which meant that, for the majority of people, there was not much difference between adults and children. They shared the same physical and symbolic world.

"The child is only childlike in comparison to what is not childlike" (van den Berg 1961, 32), and when adults become unchildlike the true nature of childhood appears. Children become children when adults become more "adult." A change in our understanding of adulthood brings with it a change in childhood. As long as the adults existed in the same visible and understandable lived world as the children, the difference between them did not matter. The difference was more one of size and economic status than a psychological reality. With the peregrinatios of the twelfth century, however, the adult risked the solidity of the home community and moved into an ever-changing world of new experiences and ideas. The children, on the other hand, could not follow on their own. In this new adult world they could not take care of their bodies, distinguish friend from foe, fact from folly. Away from "the sweetness of one's native soil" and without explicit adult guidance, the children lost their way. Childhood appeared on the horizon of Western consciousness. It now designated a class of human beings who failed to master the adult project of the search for the individual self.

Within the framework of the discussion in the earlier chapters, the children's crusade highlights how historical changes alter the coexistential structure of children's lives. Because of developmental dependency the child is intimately tied to adult care. The social/communal organization of adult existence—whether tribal or individual—has a profound effect on how the early human years are experienced and conceptualized.

THE INTERIOR SELF

In AD 1216 the Lateran Council instituted the churchwide practice of confession, demanding from each person yearly scrutiny of their personal conscience and individual accountability for their sins. Prior to the practice of confession, sin and penance were public events, and atonement for transgression was a communal as well as a personal experience. Local communities dealt swiftly with violations that threatened their social fabric. The loss of honor, which was always bestowed by one's fellow human beings, was often experienced as worse than the loss of life. The unwritten code of honor was upheld by the community rather than by the law. If you were a northern French wife beater, for example, you would "get rough music": the neighbors would cover you with mud and push you around the village in a wheelbarrow, accompanied by teasing doggerel and the clanging of pots and pans (Illich 1982). Justice was for all to see and participate in, and the children learned by example.

Confession changed the relationship between the individual and the community. It required the penitent to withdraw from the community, search his or her individual soul, make a secret report to a clergyman, and receive penance and absolution by performing a mostly private act. Illich points out that the institution of confession was the expression of a profound shift in Western consciousness. It forced the church to write down the laws of conduct in order to give guidelines to its flock for their yearly confession. Compulsory confession was "the first and by far the most effective step toward the acceptance of the written law" (1982,

153). It required a new, educated kind of clergy who were versed in hearing confession and teaching and judging their flock. With compulsory confession the church also made its first and most effective step toward the acceptance of universal education. Psychologically, confession creates self-reflection and interiority:

> The new confessional order relocated penance from the outer to an inner space; it compelled each "soul" to create this new space within itself, and to create it according to the architectural rules laid down in church law. Unlike public penance, done *once* over a period of years for a life's outstanding crime, confession meant a yearly accounting of secret transgressions against laws formulated by a catholic, that is, universal institution, Mother Church. Confession creates an "internal forum." Once a year, the sinner opens the intimate chamber of his soul to a public, church appointed judge who, in absolute secrecy, listens to the culprit's self-diagnosis. (154–55)

The psychological effects of confession, compulsory for every person within the domain of the Catholic Church, were staggering. The Lateran Council instituted the creation of an *interior space*, an unshared, invisible, private dimension of life. It forced the faithful to reflect upon themselves and to articulate what they saw there in solitude and without the community. The diagnosis of morality and transgression was no longer the community's; it belonged to the individual self and its institutional, clerical judge. A few hundred years later the Reformation resisted the process of confession, but not out of a desire to reverse the interiorization and privatization of the self. Just the opposite: the impulse of the Reformation deepened the isolation of the penitent by removing even the connection with the "church appointed judge." Confession was now heard only by an invisible, interior God, and faith was a matter not of visible ritual gestures but of the "inner man," the inner self, "an absolutely inner quality" (van den Berg 1961, 229).

The kind of interiority required for confession is alien to the child's mind. As we saw before, young children are egocentric, participatory, and animistic in their experience of the world. Child consciousness, until well into middle childhood, does not distinguish between self and world very clearly, and the reflective distance necessary for scrutinizing and surveying one's life, as is required by confession, does not come to the child naturally. Awareness of one's self and self-reflection are processes that comes to fruition only in later childhood and adolescence. The interiority and conscious self-reflection instituted by the Lateran

Council is almost impossible for children to achieve: children are not interiorized creatures. *Adults from the Renaissance on have walked through an interior landscape, and their children cannot follow them there.* Reflective distance from the world, self-reflection, and interiority must be inculcated into the young through a process of adult guidance over many years. We call this process "education." We shall explore this subject further at the end of this chapter.

The "architectural rules laid down in church law," according to which the ground floor of the interiorized self is laid out, are marked, like all laws, by the recognition of violation and transgression. The feeling that accompanied earlier medieval transgressions was the fear of the loss of one's standing in the esteem of other people. The feeling cultivated by the secrecy of confession was a new sense of shame. Shame requires secrets. Secret feelings, deeds, and desires have to be hidden away from the world "in the intimate chamber of [the] soul," as Illich words it, and then disclosed in a secret penitential ritual. Earlier medieval culture knew little shame and there was little privacy surrounding such "sins" as fornication and debauchery (Elias 1978).

Postman (1994) points out that the cultivation of shame is one of the hallmarks of the shift away from the communal, medieval culture and is a turning point in the history of childhood. One of the main differences between adults and children is that adults keep certain facts of life secret from their children, particularly facts that have to do with sexuality.

One might say that one of the main differences between an adult and a child is that the adult knows about certain facets of life—its mysteries, its contradictions, its violence, its tragedies—that are not considered suitable for children to know: that are, indeed, shameful to reveal to them indiscriminately. In the modern world, as children move toward adulthood, we reveal these secrets to them in what we believe to be a psychologically assimilable way. But such an idea is possible only in a culture in which there is a sharp distinction between the adult world and the child's world, and where there are institutions that express that difference. The medieval world made no such distinction and had no such institutions (Postman 1994, 15).

The late Middle Ages invented such an institution in the same years that witnessed the few stragglers return from the failed children's crusade. Confession was the first in a series of institutionalized acts that drew a demarcation line between adults and children.

The children who set out on the children's crusade were little medieval adults whose parents let them go, albeit reluctantly, because there was not much difference between adults and children. The children who did not return from the children's crusade were modern children: they needed to be protected from the dangers, cruelties, and obscenities of the adult world.

BOOKISHNESS

On the visible level, the ability to live without the sustaining and constraining bonds of community marked the new adult. On a more invisible level, the peregrinatio was also a journey of the spirit, a leaving behind of familiar forms of thinking and religious feeling. The new Western self that was announced in the twelfth century was trying to achieve an inner distance and a new consciousness of itself apart from its familiar social and ideological context. Illich (1996) shows how a whole new relationship of distance between the human mind and the written text was created through the work of the twelfth-century monk Hugh St. Victor. One of the strangest outcomes of Hugh's work was a new practice of reading: before the twelfth century reading was always done aloud. If you entered a monastic scriptorium or library you would have heard the monks mumble the words they read, and the scribes would copy a text by dictating it aloud to their own hands. Hugh changed all that. The monastic generation that followed him *instituted the practice of reading silently.*

To us it seems unfathomable that medieval people could only read aloud. Illich (1996) mentions that even though antiquity knew the practice of silent reading, it was considered a feat: Augustine was puzzled when his teacher Ambrose occasionally would read a book without moving his lips. The advent of silent reading changed the nature of the written word. Medieval texts were recordings of oral narrations, and the reader would slowly reconstitute and reproduce the sounds from the symbols on the page. Reading was profoundly *auditory:* sequenced in time, expressive, meditative, immediate, shared. Silence made the act of reading almost exclusively *visual.* It allowed the reader to read much faster and only for her- or himself. Visual, silent reading led readers to distance themselves from the immediacy of the script, to scan the written word, to treat it not as a narrative to be repeated but as a text to be manipulated: "From the teller of a story the author mutates into the creator of a text" (Illich 1996, 105).

It is no surprise that following Hugh St. Victor a new technology of text production took over. In the twelfth century the Western world invented page layout, chapter division, the consistent numbering of chapter and verse, indices, tables of contents, introductions, library inventories and concordances. Illich points out that this change in the technology of textuality fostered a change in the way reality was conceived. It created a new kind of reader, "one who wants to acquire in a few years of study a new kind of acquaintance with a larger number of authors than a meditating monk could have perused in a lifetime" (1996, 96). The new kind of reader and writer looked at the page and experienced the exteriorization of a *cogitatio*, a thought structure, a thought outline of reasons. The new relationship between text and mind, the ability to conceive of the written word as an abstract and inaudible record of thought, was the foundation for the print culture that began with the fifteenth-century invention of the printing press. Outwardly this change manifested itself in a shift from the monastic practice of meditative, auditory contemplation of manuscripts to the production of knowledge in the lecture halls of Europe's bookish universities. Hugh St. Victor and his monastic colleagues laid the seeds for an attitude that began to flourish and permeate cultural life after the Renaissance introduced the printing press. Postman (1994, 27) writes:

> But with the printed book another tradition began: the isolated reader and his private eye. Orality became muted, and the reader and his response became separated from a social context. The reader retired within his own mind, and from the sixteenth century to the present what most readers have required of others is their absence, or, if not that, their silence. *In reading, both the writer and reader enter into a conspiracy of sorts against social presence and consciousness. Reading is, in a phrase, an asocial act* (my emphasis).

Literacy had its beginnings not in the dissemination of printed material after Gutenberg but in the profound psychological shift of the twelfth century, which began to see the written word as a record of an individual's thought processes and turned intellectual activity into an asocial act.

With the shift from audible to visual text came more subtle changes in the way reality was experienced. The shift from oral to literate culture psychologically decentered the person from the middle of a full sense-world to its periphery, and this brought with it a new understanding of the universe: "Only after print and the extensive experience with maps that print implemented would human beings, when they thought about the cosmos or the universe or 'world,' think primarily of something laid out before their eyes, as in a modern printed atlas, a vast surface or assemblage of surfaces (vision presents surfaces) ready to be 'explored'" (Ong 1982, 73).

Child culture, prior to reading instruction, was a profoundly oral culture in Ong's sense. Schooling initiated the shift from oral to literate childhood culture. Psychologically, this shift in the medium of knowledge transmission from listening to reading restructured the child's world (Egan 1988). Reading removes the "concrete operational" children from the communal, conversational, and tactile experiential sphere of learning and initiates them into the domain of invisible images, abstract ideas, and solitary activity. Moreover, as Ong points out, literacy brings with it a shift in *cosmology*—the very way the child orders the universe. Like the monks at St. Victor, the preliterate child experiences the immediate power of the spoken word within a given context. For oral child culture, the cosmos is an ongoing event with the child's experience at its center. Preoperational children find themselves at the umbilicus mundi, the navel of the world. And this world is a profoundly social world. Literacy not only removes the child from the center but also destroys the social fabric. Reading is an asocial act. The child has to be induced, over many years, into the asocial presence (or social absence?) of other readers. Learning to read gradually destroys animism, participation, and egocentrism and places the child at the periphery of a world centered on and constructed by adults. Literacy leads to the production of thought structures above the level of lived experience and profoundly changes the use and meaning of language.

THE PORTRAIT: LOYAL REMEMBRANCE

The art of the portrait came into its own between the end of the Middle Ages and the seventeenth century and testifies to a changing understanding of the person as an individual. In the late fifteenth century, concurrent with the appearance of adult portraits, we also find children immortalized on canvas. Earlier paintings of notable people, like kings or prelates, were depictions of idealized or stock characters, and the actual appearance of the subject was less important than the representation of the political and social institutions within which they wanted to be seen. The Renaissance, however, discovered the human face, and the growing belief in the autonomy and dignity of the individual found its appropriate symbolic form in the art of the portrait (Schneider 1994). In the earliest fifteenth-century paintings of van Eyck, we discover the need to represent a face *as it is* and the artist's desire to attest to the painting's authenticity as a likeness of the sitter. In the portrait of Tymotheus from 1432 (which is one of the first Western portraits on record), van Eyck tells us very clearly what a portrait is for: carved into the withered stone parapet below "Tymotheos" is the inscription *Leal Souvenir*, which means "loyal remembrance," and it carries the exact date of its production, October 10, 1432. Van Eyck goes so far as to show the blemishes of the skin and the veins throbbing in the temples of his subject. The need for this loyal remembrance of what something looks like is a desire to capture a moment in time and eternalize it through the portrait: time is fleeting and destructive. People have probably always known this, but the powerful and intense appearance of the portrait in Western history in the fifteenth century expresses a new awareness of the historicity of the person. It testifies to a growing interest in the individual apart from his or her social role and a desire to preserve, through art, the uniqueness of an individual personality so that some of it survives the passage of time.

Aside from religious art, we do not find individual children depicted until the late fifteenth century. In earlier medieval iconography, the only difference between adults and children was size. Children looked like miniature adults, a trend that was retained in some quarters until the seventeenth century. "The child . . . ," says Aries (1962, 38), "was not missing from the middle ages, at least from the 13th century on, but there was never a portrait of him, the portrait of a real child, as he was at a certain moment of his life." The desire for "loyal remembrance" did not encompass childhood, either one's own or that of one's offspring.

The Renaissance discovered the face of the child, and a striking example of the complexity of this discovery is Caroto's painting *Boy with a Drawing* from around 1530. Looking over his shoulder, addressing us with his gaze, a red-haired boy smiles broadly and proudly holds up a sketch of the human figure, which is in all likelihood his self-portrait. The roughness of the child's drawing contrasts sharply with the sophistication of the artist's ability in capturing the child's features, and before us opens the gulf between a child's and an adult's perception and skill.

In Caroto's painting we see depicted (for the first time in Western art) a conscious awareness of developmental differences between adults and children. Schneider (1994) points out that Renaissance artists were attempting to establish norms for the perfectly beautiful human figure, and in the process they began to understand much about the deviations from this norm. The interest in the child figure and the child's drawing arose in this context, and "it may have gone hand in hand with a new interest in specifically childlike patterns of perception as such, including their manner of portraying reality in drawings, since the child was no longer merely viewed as a small adult" (144). Children are the deviation

Figure 3. Giovanni Francesco Caroto, *Boy with a Drawing*, 1530. Oil on wood, 37 × 29 cm. Museo di Castelvecchio, Verona, Italy. Courtesy of Scala/ Art Resources, NY.

from the norm: they differ from adults in bodily proportions, style of thinking, level of education, and skill in making a living.

But Caroto also shows us the boy's joy and enthusiasm and his simple and straightforward emotional life, which directly appeals to our heart. In this painting, unlike most of the adult portraits of the time, there is nobody hidden behind the facade. Unlike the adult, the child has no interiority, no hidden demons, nothing that needs to be veiled. In its simplicity, this five-hundred-year-old child's drawing is indistinguishable from the drawings of twenty-first-century children. The child's participatory and expressive relationship to his or her world has not changed. Yet adulthood, since the Renaissance, has altered drastically, and in its wake the child is pulled along into the deep waters of Western subjectivity and a cosmology increasingly complex and shaped by scientific knowledge.

Childhood in the Middle Ages was fragile, and too many children died in infancy. Aries thinks that because of high mortality rates, "nobody thought, as we ordinarily think today, that every child already contained a man's personality" (1962, 39). The consequence was a certain callousness and indifference with respect to the death of children. It is the more surprising that despite the high infant mortality rate, which continued until the eighteenth century, we find child portraits like Caroto's emerging at the beginning of the sixteenth century, attesting to a paradigm shift in the understanding of human existence: it "*marked a very important moment in the history of feelings*" (40). In the eyes of adults children suddenly acquired individual souls, and the care for a child's memory extended beyond this life. Dead children were now portrayed among the living family members, as we can see, for example, in Holbein's painting *The Virgin and Child with the Family of Burgomaster Meyer* from 1528. We know that of the six people clustering around the Virgin three had died in 1526, namely, Meyer's first wife and his two young sons. The dead children are portrayed at the age of their death. At the same time, we find a new religious interest and attitude toward children that is best expressed in *De disciplinis* (1531), the work of the pedagogue Juan Luis Vives (1492–1540). "According to Vives, children were born with a spiritual ability to withstand the base materialism of instinctual avarice; this spiritual predisposition was the 'germ of all art and science'" (Schneider 1994, 147). Not only did children acquire a soul but its purity and innocence were held up to adults as an example of a true spiritual life.

Ghirlandaio's *Portrait of an Old Man with a Child* is another example of the new feeling for children. It is perhaps the earliest painting of a nonreligious and individual representation of a child. In the double portrait we see a young, golden-haired boy leaning into the embrace of an old man, probably his grandfather, and gazing lovingly into the man's eyes. The child seems riveted to the old man's face, but for other rea-

Figure 4. Domenico Ghirlandaio, *Portrait of an Old Man with a Child*, 1488. Tempera on wood, 62 × 46 cm. Musée du Louvre, Paris. Courtesy of Réunion des Musées Nationaux/Art Resources, NY.

sons than our own as viewers: we stare at the old man's nose because it is disfigured by a skin disease. (Ghirlandaio made a number of sketches of this disease in his notebooks in order to get it just right.) The boy looks past the deformed nose and truly sees the kindness and graciousness of the other, which is shown in the tender touch of his outstretched hand upon the chest of the old man. Ghirlandaio seems to play with us, the adult viewers, and holds up the mirror of a child's innocence: you, adult, get caught up in the appearance of things, but the child sees right through them. The play of light on the two faces is also illuminating: the child looks as if he is lit from within and shines in his own *lumen*, while the old man is clearly lit by a light source from above.

This portrait, with its focus on the expressiveness of the human face, shows the depth of feeling between an old man and a child, and it precedes the painting of Leonardo's Mona Lisa by a quarter century. Even though there are a few marks of social status discernible in the rich clothes of the subjects, the man's disfiguration and the sparseness of the interior transcend rank and class and lead us deeper into a contemplation of the relationship between an old man and a child. We definitely witness two individuals captured in an intimate, personal moment. The painter thought that this was important enough to preserve for posterity!

Underlying the pious interest in the innocence of children, however, lies a deeper feeling. In order to see the innocence of children, the adults themselves must have begun to feel less than innocent. Childhood appears because adulthood has changed. The child enters Western art because in it the adults begin to see something that they have lost, something they once were but are no longer. "The causes of the change in the child's nature must lie in the changes of the nature of maturity," van den Berg says (1961, 32), and he identifies the changes as a growing increase in the discontinuity, pluriformity, and multivalency of the adult world. "That is exactly what being a child means—to be defenseless against this multivalency and to shrink back from it."

After discovering the child, Western culture invented the family to protect the "young plant" against the vagaries of adult maturity. Jean-Jacques Rousseau, three centuries after Ghirlandaio, expresses this sentiment perfectly. In his book *Emile*, he admonishes mothers: "It is to you that I address myself, tender and foresighted mother, who are capable of keeping the nascent shrub away from the highway and securing it from the impact of human opinions! Cultivate and water the young plant before it dies. Its fruits will one day be your delights. Form an enclosure around your child's soul at an early date. Someone else can draw its circumference, but you alone must build the fence" (1762/1979, 37–38).

The adult world is no longer a world safe for children, and adult life has become so complex and difficult that it takes children almost two decades to catch up with their elders. The thirteenth century laughed about the failed attempts of children to be adults; the Renaissance looked at the child developmentally for the first time and appreciated the child's difference and innocence; the seventeenth century developed pervasive schooling and the nuclear family; and the eighteenth century finally called for the complete separation between children and adults because the adult world was seen as too corrupting in its influence on the young. In the portraits of the eighteenth century the child becomes cute, innocent, and helpless, as we see in Fragonard's portrait of a little boy.

The change in the complexity and multivalency of adulthood, which made childhood a necessary Western concept, can be seen in the adult portraits of the sixteenth century. The Renaissance portrait captures the autonomy and dignity of the individual, and we find many portraits of successful burghers, scientists, and politicians who seem to revel in the new openness of the Renaissance world. But some of these portraits show the disturbances that come with a reflective interiority. The emphasis on the feeling life of individuals and their peculiar idiosyncrasies became prevalent in the portraits of the sixteenth century.

The individuals in Dürer's 1499 portrait *Oswolt Krel: Merchant of Lindau*, and the subject of the 1526 picture *Hieronymus Holzschuher* stare at the viewer with piercing eyes. We feel looked at by persons with much going on behind the facade. As the Mona Lisa's smile covers the depth of her emotional life, Dürer exposes the new inner world and its more disturbing currents. While Holzschuher's choler seems ready to break through, Krel's portrait shows a more disturbed, abnormal personality. Krel is the first "psychological" study of a human face, attesting to the new interiority that is realized in the Renaissance.

A few years later Leonardo articulated this new psychological function of the portrait succinctly: he demanded that the portrait show "the movement of the spirit," and it "should not restrict itself to the imitation of external reality, but should contrive to translate mental activity into visual effect" (as quoted in Schneider 1994, 56). Demons no longer menaced the soul from the outside, but they took on a new habitat in the psyche. Popular opinion in sixteenth-century moralizing literature, however, soon demanded that this open display of the inner world cease, and that the sitter's psyche be concealed and veiled (Schneider 1994).

Figure 5. Jean-Honoré Fragonard, *A Boy as Pierrot*, 1776–80. Oil on canvas, 60 × 50 cm. The Wallace Collection, London. Courtesy of the trustees of The Wallace Collection, London.

After the individual self had been discovered, it seems to have been too painful to look at for too long.

With the Renaissance, a new world came into being, opening up the social and intellectual life of the monovalent and continuous medieval world. The Renaissance person was born into a time rife with the infinite possibilities of mathematics, astronomy, alchemy, natural history,

Figure 6. Albrecht Dürer, *Oswolt Krel: Merchant of Lindau*, 1499. Oil on lime panel, 49.6 × 39 cm. Alte Pinakothek, Munich. Courtesy of Fotoarchiv Marburg/Art Resources, NY.

Figure 7. Albrecht Dürer, *Hieronymus Holzschuher*, 1526. Oil on limewood, 51 × 37 cm. Gemäldegalerie, Staatliche Museen zu Berlin, Berlin, Germany. Courtesy of Bildarchiv Preussischer Kulturbesitz/Art Resources, NY.

Figure 8. Moretto da Brescia, *Count Sciarra Martinengo Cesaresco*, or *Portrait of a Young Man*, c. 1542. Oil on canvas, 114 × 94 cm. National Gallery, London. Courtesy of the National Gallery, London.

anatomy, philosophy, politics, literature, art, religion, travel, and commerce. "Alas, I desire too much" is the motto on Moretto DaBrescia's c. 1542 *Portrait of a Young Man*, which shows a young, wealthy, melancholic Renaissance man sadly gazing at us with a faraway look.

Melancholy is a response, as Burton wrote in *The Anatomy of Melancholy*, to too much exposure to books "and to the confusing contradictory opinions and theories expressed in them" (as quoted in Schneider 1994, 71). The source of melancholy lies in a consciousness that recognizes too much of the world and the infinity of possibilities, and which is forced to reflect upon itself within an all too complex and uncertain culture. In the original version of the *Portrait of a Young Man* the count was leaning not on two pillows but on a stack of books! Melancholy is obviously the "pathology of choice" for the fashionable Renaissance intellectual. Accompanying the intellectual excitement of the age of discovery is a distinct undertone of confusion, sadness, and what Petrarch called *acedia:* "In the whole wide world I find nothing that can make me content; wherever I turn I only see thistles and thorns" (as quoted in von Gleichen-Russwurm 1929, 17).

Petrarch's and Moretto's adult melancholia forms a striking contrast to the straightforward innocence of Caroto's and Ghirlandaio's children. While adult consciousness becomes self-reflective and aware of itself, child consciousness remains turned toward the world and unreflective of itself. Adult interiority presupposes that consciousness dwells in and on things *other* than the world of experience and the enchantment of the senses. The mind engaged in literacy lives in a complex symbolic world that is accessible only through print. What we call "interiority" is an illusion: we do not have an inner chamber in our bodies in which the self dwells (not even the pineal gland, as Descartes claimed). What we do have is an invisible symbolic activity that is cultivated by the self's annexation of the world of ideas from books and its elaboration through discourse with one's contemporaries. The self is cultivated through the rituals of bookishness. What we call interiority is actually the mind engaged in a symbolic activity that transcends the senses and the immediate experience of the world.

The interiorized self is created though the process of education. The function of education is not merely to transmit writing technology to the next generation but to reproduce the symbolic world- and self-structures that sustain the contemporary mind. Education and literacy lead to the acquisition of the symbolic, invisible superstructure of Western knowledge and the models of selfhood it presents through philosophy, literature, art, and the dissemination of scientific concepts.

LITERACY AND EDUCATION

The invention of the printing press by Johannes Gutenberg in 1452–54 revolutionized the dissemination of knowledge. The new reading skill acquired by the monks of the twelfth century found its perfect application through the new medium of print. Books became widely available, and readers acquired the ability to read them silently and quickly. With the dissemination of printed material the ability to read acquired a new urgency. Medieval education, even at the university level, was primarily an oral affair, where students could study for many years without being able to read, but they had to be able to memorize and recite text read to them (Aries 1962). The printed book changed all that: a schoolmaster's signboard by Hans Holbein the Younger from 1516 appeals to burghers and craftsmen, ladies and virgins, boys and girls to learn how to read and write so that they can understand and sign business transactions in their own name. From an occupation of the few, reading and writing became a necessity for the masses, and the written word superseded oral agreements and memorized accounts in business and law. Within fifty years after Gutenberg's first printing of the Bible, more than eight million books had been produced, and by 1480 there were presses in 110 towns in six different countries (Postman 1994).

Print creates a new symbolic universe in which human thinking and action are reshaped. From the oral, immediate, social horizon the reader turns to a textual, invisible, asocial horizon. Print does not require merely the ability to read, it leads to the practice of *being educated*, which means to be conversant with a conceptual world of information and thought that is transmitted through books. Books become a storehouse for memories of all sorts—records of legal transactions, historical events, philosophical argument, poetry, scientific inventions and ideas, religious texts and commentaries, maps and calendars. Book content is the currency that is transferred in the conversations of literate people and determines the intellectual and moral climate. "More than any other device, the printed book released people from the domination of the immediate and the local. . . . print made a greater impression than the actual events. . . . To exist was to exist in print: the rest of the world tended gradually to become more shadowy. Learning became book learning" (Lewis Mumford 1934, as quoted in Postman 1994, 28). Thoughts had always been powerful, but it was difficult to disseminate them on foot. The printed text, on the other hand, can speak in many places at once and multiply the echoes of powerful words and sentiments. Without print the Reformation would not have been possible because Luther's voice would have been local, and because the idea that everyone could read the Bible and see for themselves would have been unheard of. It took Luther completely by surprise when his theses, which were meant for a small academic circle, were reproduced a thousandfold and spread like wildfire among people who were barely literate!

Books do not merely contain information, they structure the way we think about reality. Literacy makes it possible to erect a conceptual scaffold above our everyday experience, which then is disseminated and transmitted through the authority of media and education. This makes it believable and compelling, even if it contradicts our senses. The immediate and local experience has been sacrificed to the symbolic dimension of texts. Ideas in books allow us to approach the immediate with ideas that we did not generate ourselves. For example: the chance appearance of Ptolemy's book *Geographia* in the group around Brunelleschi in fifteenth-century Florence led to study and conversations about optics, and Brunelleschi invented linear perspective drawing through application of those optical principles to the church next door. Without the book it is unlikely we would have linear perspective, and without print there would not have been a Copernican revolution. The inventions and permutations of technology require a literate community.

It should be apparent by now that literacy is not simply the acquisition of the alphabet—it is the tool with which the architecture of interiority, which the Catholic Church had sketched out with the practice of confession, is built and elaborated. "The self is a cloth we have been weaving over centuries in confessions, journals, diaries, memories, and in its most literate incarnation, the autobiography to tailor the dress in which we see our first person singular" (Illich and Sanders 1988, 73). Writing allowed the means to write about oneself and reflect upon one's experiences and ideas. Montaigne, born in 1533, invented the personal essay, which was printed and spread for anyone to read. Montaigne's commentaries and opinions on everything from child rearing to philosophy express and elaborate a newly discovered individual and textual voice. Writing became a tool for self-reflection and self-creation. "Print," as Postman remarks, "created a psychological environment within which the claims of individuality became irresistible. This is not to say that individualism was created by the printing press, only that individualism became the normal and acceptable psychological condition" (1994, 27).

Postman argues that the invention of print and the symbolic world it produced led to the cultural appearance of childhood. Those who could read and were educated were altered by literacy. Children were left behind when "Literate Man" was invented: "From print onward, adulthood had to be earned. It became a symbolic, not a biological achievement. From print onward, the young would have to *become* adults, and they would have to do it by learning to read, by entering the world of typography. And in order to accomplish that they would require education" (1994, 36).

Most educated, literate adults today are completely unaware how profoundly literacy has altered and shaped the very structure of their lives and how much time they spend engaging a fictional world of ideas. Children do not participate in this world until they become literate and are educated, which means that they only gradually absorb the symbolic universe the Western mind has created. Unlike biological adulthood, which comes with puberty, symbolic adulthood requires education and has to be culturally reproduced in children.

CONCLUSION

In this chapter we examined the historical changes in adulthood that have led to our contemporary view of childhood. Childhood appeared on the horizon of Western consciousness when adulthood embraced individualism and literacy. Individualism lessened the importance of communal living, as we saw in the medieval peregrinatios, which in turn made it difficult for children to live the same lives and engage in the same ideas and cultural practices as adults. The individual adult self has been elaborated over the past eight hundred years through various methods of self-reflection: the institutionalized form of confession; the literary forms of autobiography, personal essay, and diary; and the artistic form of the portrait. With literacy adults acquired a second-order reality, a symbolic, textual order removed from the immediate engagement with the sensuous world, which for most Western adults is more real than the natural world. What we call the interiority of the self is actually the adults' continual immersion and exchange of ideas in the literate, textual symbolic order. Children have to be induced into this order through the process of acquiring literacy, which in turn restructures their relationship with the social and sensuous world and produces educated, interiorized adult selves over the course of the long process of schooling.

Since the thirteenth century children's lives and the cultural practices of child rearing have changed significantly, and we can see these changes in light of the existential themes that we discussed in earlier chapters. Children did well as communal beings when woven into *coexistential* forms of care, but they did not fare so well when they were required to

Figure 9. Jan van Scorel, *The Schoolboy*, 1531. Oil on panel, 4.6 × 35 cm. Museum Boijmans Van Beuningen, Rotterdam, Netherlands. Courtesy of the Museum Boijmans Van Beuningen, Rotterdam, Netherlands.

be independent, individualized selves. Their syncretic, *participatory consciousness* has trouble understanding and assuming the rituals of interiority, which require a repression of children's natural tendency to attend to the *bodily*, sensuous world around them. The "inner space" or "interior architecture"—instituted first through confession and later through textuality—contradicts children's sense of experienced, *lived space*. The traditional, direct oral forms of instruction have given way to the second-order, abstract symbolism of literacy and textuality, which permeate and carry the cultural discourse of adults. *Language* changes its relation to body, space, time, and other people when the child has to move beyond the social and bodily speech of oral discourse into the isolated, purely mental world of literacy. Living in texts requires the metamorphosis of the active, *lived body* into a sleeplike appendage of the mind. *Lived time* is no longer tied to perceived events but to the turning of a page, or a clock on the schoolroom wall.

In Jan van Scorel's painting *The Schoolboy* from 1531 a twelve-year-old boy gazes at us in half profile, serious, confident, quill poised above a piece of paper. "This young burgher with his red beret has such a fresh, vivacious expression on his face, such a lively desire to learn in his manner, that he seems already a fully developed, confident individual" (Schneider 1994, 147). The boy stands at the cusp between childhood and adulthood, personally as well as culturally.

Personally, he is undergoing the personality formation that comes with literacy: he must restrain his body in a sterile environment for long periods on end, he must listen to his teachers and shape his thoughts according to their whim, he absorbs and converses about the mental topography that they present to him, and he is acquiring the kind of intellect necessary for a good reader: "a vigorous sense of individuality, the capacity to think logically and sequentially, the capacity to distance oneself from symbols, the capacity to manipulate high orders of abstraction, the capacity to defer gratification" (Postman 1994, 47).

Culturally, this Renaissance boy finds that the threshold that leads from childhood to adulthood is not too high. He is not yet infantilized, not yet placed behind his mother's fence to protect him from the corrupt adult world. That will happen to his offspring a number of generations later in the eighteenth century. His world is only just being permeated by the books and the knowledge that drive some of his more mature contemporaries to melancholy. He stands at the threshold to an adulthood that will become ever more complex and multivalent, and a childhood that expands over two decades or more before it achieves the symbolic adulthood of the literate person.

NOTES

CHAPTER ONE

1. Bachelard continues: "From my viewpoint, from the phenomenologist's viewpoint, the conscious metaphysics that starts from the moment when the being is 'cast into the world' is a secondary metaphysics. It passes over the preliminaries, when being is well-being, when the human being is deposited in a being-well, in the well-being originally associated with being."

2. "Being body means being I, and being body means being you. But being body means also: to have a world and to be in the world and to be a body for others. Being body means to be in the world, but also to be *with* the world, to reach, see, and serve with and toward things" (Langeveld 1968, 130).

CHAPTER TWO

1. "My personal existence must be the resumption of a pre-personal tradition. There is, therefore, another subject beneath me, for whom a world exists before I am here, and who marks out my place in it. This captive or natural spirit is my body, not that momentary body which is the instrument of my personal choices and which fastens on this or that world, but the system of anonymous 'functions' which draw every particular focus into a general project. Nor does this blind adherence to the world, this prejudice in favor of being, occur only at the beginning of my life. It endows every subsequent perception of space with its meaning and it is resumed at every instant. Space and perception generally represent, at the core of the subject, the fact of his birth, the perpetual contribution of his bodily being, a communication with the world more ancient than thought. That is why they saturate consciousness and are impenetrable to reflection" (Merleau-Ponty 1962, 254).

2. Perhaps people find swimming so pleasurable because it allows for the touch of the water all over the skin. Temple Grandin, an autistic animal-behavior researcher, developed a pressure chute that is effective in calming cattle and that also seems to work with autistic people. The pressure chute applies even pressure all over the person's body, and Grandin found it very helpful in relieving anxiety (Saks 1996). I wonder if it works because it reassembles the

patchy and varied perceptions of the skin into a sensory whole: the world is no longer fragmented but comes to the patient as a unified field of experience.

3. It is interesting to note that young children often sleep with their arms outstretched and their hands resting above their heads. I always thought that this was a sign of full abandonment to sleep because the child felt completely safe. In middle childhood the sleep gesture changes and the arms are held in and under the covers, as if the child is more separate now and has to hold in the protective space by him- or herself.

4. The limbs are probably the first region of the body to come to awareness because they are the most immersed in action space. I discover my will when my limbs move into and change the world—and are changed by it. Adult punishment techniques often focus on restraining movement of feet and hands: the limbs are the body's organs of willing, which have transgressed the adult-set boundaries and need to be controlled. Erikson (1968, 114) saw the achievement of the second year as the walking toddler's struggle for autonomy and experience of him- or herself as a willing being: "I am what I can will freely." The "I can body" in its action space becomes the matrix for the child's sense of agency and identity.

5. "But the morbid world does not only spread around the individual, surrounding him on all sides. A much more intimate contact seems to be established between the two, a contact so intimate that the boundaries are almost obliterated. The morbid world penetrates the individual and robs him of everything intimate and personal, so that he becomes dissolved in the mysterious environment which envelops him and becomes one with it. And it is this diminution of the intimacy, of the personal character of the ego, which our patient's complaints seem to express—complaints related to the deprivation of his freedom, the smiles imposed upon him, the drawings executed against his will, the 'directive' character of the voices, and to the impression that everything he reads, everything he writes, everything he does and thinks is repeated outside or accompanied by conversation" (Minkowski 1970, 426).

6. "The mythical phenomenon is not a representation, but a genuine presence. . . . Every 'apparition' [*Erscheinung*] is in this case an incarnation, and each entity is defined not so much in terms of 'properties' as of physiognomic characteristics. So much is validly meant when we talk about infantile and primitive animism: not that the child and the primitive man perceive objects, which they try, as Comte says, to explain by intentions or forms of consciousness—consciousness, like the object, belongs to positing thought—but things are taken for the incarnation of what they express, and because their human significance is compressed into them and presents itself literally as what they mean. Since mythical consciousness has not yet arrived at the notion of a thing or of objective truth, how can it undertake a critical examination of that which it thinks it experiences; where can it find a fixed point at which to stop and become aware of itself as pure consciousness, and perceive, beyond its phantasms, the real world?" (Merleau-Ponty 1962, 290).

7. *Plenum* comes from the Latin word *plenus*, which means "full." The German noun for fullness is *Fülle*, which is Husserl's term for the infinite qualities of the natural world that are under assault in the modern sciences. *Plenum* (*Fülle*) refers to the complex sensory qualities that are given to our perception as a total form. Color, sound, warmth, heaviness, spatial organization, and temporal duration in their intersecting qualities are part of the plenum. Husserl insists that their qualitative web is destroyed when we dissect the plenum and assign its qualities as "sensory data" to specific sense organs: visual stimuli to the eye, sound waves to the ear, and so on. In the world of experience the plenum is not chaotic but already ordered (Husserl 1970). Merleau-Ponty's understanding of the invisible that permeates the visible also addresses the transcendence of space that holds itself in reserve (Sallis 1973). I especially like Minkowski's idea of the "fullness of life," which is found in the richness and variety of spatial experiences and is part of the "organopsychic solidarity" we have with the world (1970, 406).

8. In his childhood, the poet Rilke had a passionate hatred for dolls. The doll concealed the alien face of the plenum, the unperson (Simms 2004). He describes how on certain afternoons the doll would cease to respond to the child's desire to play, boredom set in, and behind it stood a threatening emptiness that began to permeate the solid floor, the walls, the chair, the rocking horse, and the doll (Rilke 1966, 3:537–38; my translation):

> When nothing was lying around to captivate and change our train of thoughts, when that idle creature continued to stupidly and heavily spread itself like a peasant Danae who did not know anything else but the infinite golden rain of our feelings: I wish I could remember whether we started up in anger and told that monster that our patience was at an end? Whether we did not face her, trembling with rage, and wanted to know, post for post, what she was doing with all our warmth and what had become of all this wealth?—Then she was silent, not because of arrogance, but silence was her continuous excuse because she was made of a good-for-nothing, completely irresponsible stuff—was silent and did not even think to be proud of it, although it provided her with great importance in a world where fate and even God himself have become famous for facing us with silence. At a time where everybody made an effort to give us quick and soothing answers, the doll was the first who made us suffer this immense silence that later on would often breathe at us out of space whenever we stepped on the limits of our existence. Facing her as she stared at us we experienced for the first time (or am I wrong?) that certain hollowness in our feeling, this pause of the heart in which one would perish if the whole, soft, far-reaching nature would not carry us like a lifeless thing across the abyss. Are we not strange creatures that we obey and let ourselves be instructed to invest our first tender inclinations where they must remain unsatisfied?

9. Merleau-Ponty refers here to Minkowski's discussion of "dark space," which we discussed earlier in the context of primal spatial experience: "It seems much more material to me, much more 'filled' than light space, which, as we

have seen, fades away, so to speak, before the materiality of the objects which are in it. Precisely because of this it does not spread out before me but touches me directly, envelops me, embraces me, even penetrates me, completely, passes through me, so that one could almost say that while the ego is permeable by darkness, it is not permeable by light. The ego does not affirm itself in relation to darkness but becomes confused with it, becomes one with it" (1970, 429).

10. All quotations from Langeveld 1960 are my own translations.

CHAPTER THREE

1. "A vision which perceives all things as belonging to the same plane is a vision which transforms the depth of the world. Depth as a matter of levels becomes depth as a matter of spatial distance from the viewer. Horizontal depth replaces vertical depth and things, or beings, which either belong to different levels of existence or are marked by different levels of value, like angels or demons, will progressively lose their place in the homogenous space of the world opened up by linear perspective vision" (Romanyshyn 1989, 43).

2. "People have long spoken of infantile 'animism'; but the expression seems improper to the extent that it invokes an interpretation in which the child would confer a signification on the qualitative givens which is distinct from them, would construct souls to explain things. The truth is that there are no things, only physiognomies" (Merleau-Ponty 1963/1983, 168).

3. Jean Piaget became Merleau-Ponty's successor to the chair for pedagogy and child psychology at the Sorbonne in 1952. The discussion about the nature of child consciousness between Merleau-Ponty (1964a, 1994) and Piaget (1971) highlights a deep rift between the two thinkers with respect to the status of child rationality and more generally the relationship between human consciousness and the perceived world. While Piaget articulates an anthropology based on Cartesian dualisms and a scientific view of the world, Merleau-Ponty challenges the very separation of consciousness and world and the predominance of scientific rationality. Piaget's understanding of human development as the phasic appearance of the epistemic subject (Piaget 1971) contrasts sharply with Merleau-Ponty's project to investigate the relationship between consciousness and the body subject. Piaget was clear about the intent of his research: he wanted to establish a *genetic epistemology* and show the evolution of logical thinking in human development. Merleau-Ponty, on the other hand, laid the foundations for a *genetic ontology* of human existence that allows us to study how the structures of child perception and consciousness develop into adult forms. The child's knowledge processes (*episteme*) are only one small sector in the larger field of being (*ons*). Merleau-Ponty's main critique of Piaget is that he "does not try to understand the child's conceptions but merely attempts to translate them into his adult system" (Merleau-Ponty 1994, 180; my translation). The difference between adult and child, the "different equilibrium" that children have in the way they relate to the world around them, can be celebrated and explored.

4. Piaget himself is aware of the awkwardness of the term *egocentrism* and suggests the alternative *solipsism* for the complete identification of the child with the world: "*he is the world*" (Piaget 1929/1951, 152). The younger the child, the more complete her or his solipsism. He also introduces the psychoanalytic term *narcissism* for the same phenomenon but qualifies it by insisting that the infant "can make no distinction between a self that commands and a not-self that obeys." In his reflections on egocentrism, we find Piaget leaping into the unarticulated world of the infant and imagining what it must be like. Let me quote this passage, for here we see Piaget at his most poetic:

> If we admit this assimilation of the world to the self and the self to the world, participation and magical causality become intelligible. On one hand, the movement of the body itself must be confused with any sort of external movement, and on the other, desires, pleasures and pains must be situated, not in the self, but in the absolute, in a world which, from the adult point of view, we should describe as common to all, but which from the infant's point of view is the only possible world. It follows when the infant sees his limbs move at his own will, he must feel that he is commanding the world. Thus on seeing a baby joyfully watching the movements of his feet, one has the impression of the joy felt by a god in directing from a distance the movements of the stars. Inversely, when the baby takes delight in movements situated in the outside world, such as the movement of the ribbons of its cradle, he must feel an immediate bond between these movements and his delight in them. In short, for a mind that cannot distinguish, or does so but dimly, the self from the external world, everything participates in the nature of and can influence everything else. To put it another way, participation results from a lack of differentiation between the consciousness of the action of the self on the self and the consciousness of the action of the self on things (152–53).

CHAPTER FOUR

1. The word *house* is not part of the early vocabulary of infants, unlike *ball*, *shoe*, *doggie*, and the like. (Owens 2001) Early nouns designate things children act upon (for example, they do not say the word *diaper*, even though the word is frequently used in their environment). *House* is too large and too primary to become a word because it provides the background mood for all other actions.

2. See Freud 1953–74: *Creative Writers and Day-Dreaming* (1908), vol. 9; *Formulations on the Two Principles of Mental Functioning* (1911), vol. 12; *Civilization and Its Discontents* (1930), vol. 21.

3. From his interviews with children in early and middle childhood, Piaget drew conclusions that are also valid for infant consciousness. If preschoolers are participatory and animistic, infants are even more so. Since we can only observe and not ask infants what their world is like, Piaget imagined the infant world by applying his other findings to it. The infant's participatory consciousness experiences no distinction between perceiver and perceived, body and world. The "world is assimilated into the self and the self into the world." Awareness of self

as it acts upon things and awareness of things as they act upon the self are slow to emerge, and some participatory structures remain present until children reach early adolescence (Piaget 1929/1951). In the relationship between child and thing the structures of the self and the structures of the thing-world are gradually distinguished and elaborated. It takes preschoolers a long time before they understand which things are alive and which are inanimate because for them the fullness of their perception tells them that everything has intentionality and hence is alive.

4. "I see, my dear Theaetetus, that Theodorus had a true insight into your nature when he said that you were a philosopher, for wonder is the feeling of a philosopher, and philosophy begins in wonder" (Plato *Theaetetus* 155d).

CHAPTER SIX

1. "In 1928, Albert Einstein posed a seemingly simple question to Piaget: In what order do children acquire the concepts of time and velocity? Einstein's question was prompted by an issue within physics. In Newtonian theory, time is a basic quality and velocity is defined in terms of it (velocity = distance/time). Within relativity theory, in contrast, time and velocity are defined in terms of each other, with neither concept more basic. Einstein wanted to know, whether understanding of either or both concepts was present from birth or if children understood one before the other. Almost 20 years later, Piaget published a two-volume, 500-page reply to Einstein's question. The gist of Piaget's answer was that mastery of all three concepts emerged simultaneously during the concrete operations period" (Siegler 1998, 39–40).

2. I want to weigh in only briefly on the debate surrounding the validity of the universality of operational thinking for all adults in all cultures. Over the years, many studies in Piagetian conservation tasks have shown a significant performance gap between children in cultures with or without schooling. In 1972, after reviewing the evidence available, Pierre Dasen wrote: "It can no loner be assumed that adults of all societies reach the concrete operational stage" (31). Jahoda (1980) challenged these findings by pointing out that a society could not survive if its members did not understand causal relations, could not think through the implications of their actions, or were unable to adopt another person's point of view. "No society could function at the pre-operational stage, and to suggest that a majority of any people are at that level is nonsense almost by definition" (116). If we define operational abilities through abstract, school-induced tasks, we miss the complexity of a people's understanding of causality, perspective taking, and conservation as they function *within the fabric of their world*. As Eliade (1954) has shown, indigenous cultures have a profound and complex understanding of time, but it differs from Western concepts. The phenomenological investigations of lived time reveal temporality to be more fundamental, but also more complex, than a Newtonian or Einsteinian defini-

tion of time. Investigating the complex web of lived time might give us better understanding of time as it permeates the thinking of indigenous peoples, who might have taken up and cultivated a different current in the broad river of becoming.

3. Ivan Illich (1982) warned that one of the great pitfalls of the Western cultural project is the reduction of the *human being* to *homo economicus*. When being is identified as economics, we replace the great philosophical question of being with a materialistic search for ever-better means of production. The metaphor of economics limits the scope of what it means to be human.

4. Young children are not the only people who intuitively believe that all parts of a thing participate in the same movement through time. "Think about this situation: when a race car travels around an oval track, do both its doors move at the same speed? Most adults believe that they do, but in fact they do not. The door toward the outside of the track is covering a greater distance in the same time, and therefore is moving faster" (Siegler 1998, 228). Researchers label this the *single-object/single-motion intuition*, which persists long beyond childhood and is a clear indicator that the perceptual, intuitive grasp of spatiotemporal phenomena is present and active in adults and not erased by the process of formal operational development.

5. Around 500 BC Heraclitus wrote the following: "Everything flows and nothing abides; everything gives way and nothing stays fixed. You cannot step twice into the same river, for other waters and yet others go ever flowing on. Time is a child, moving counters in a game; the royal power is a child's" (cited in Wheelwright 1966, 71). To Heraclitus transience is basic, and the present is primary. Those things that exist now do not abide. They slip into the past and nonexistence, devoured by time, as all experience attests. A generation or so later we have a classic statement of the opposing view by Parmenides: "There remains, then, but one word by which to express the [true] road: Is. And on this road there are many signs that What Is has no beginning and never will be destroyed: it is whole, still, and without end. It neither was nor will be, it simply is—now, altogether, one, continuous" (cited in Wheelwright 1966, 97). To Parmenides permanence is basic. No thing ever truly comes to be or, slipping into the past, ceases to be. Past, present, and future are distinctions not marked in the static Is. Time and becoming are at best secondary, at worst illusory, as our understanding of the world confirms (Savitt 2002).

6. Choice, even for adults, is a difficult process, and in Western culture it is surrounded by much ideological baggage. We like freedom of choice. But do we? Let us look at an example. Recall standing before the bread aisle in your local supermarket: before you are seventy-five varieties and brands of bread. How do you choose which bread to buy? Maybe you like only whole wheat bread, so you scan the shelf and look for all the sections of whole wheat bread. Maybe you are lactose intolerant, and so you start reading the labels, and it takes you a while to find the ones without milk products in them. By now you have

spent probably ten minutes in the bread aisle, and ahead of you are the margarines, the jellies, the cereals, the canned goods, the detergents, the dog foods, and so on. Admit it: we hate to choose, for next time you go to the store you do not choose; you get the bread you liked last time, the jelly you liked, the margarine that had no whey in it, and so on. In the outdoor markets of Italian towns the grocers choose for you: they select the best fruit, the best bread, the best wine and recommend it. You do not have to agonize before a shelf where everything seems equal but is terribly complex below the surface. Choice gives us the illusion of freedom, but in actuality it is a burden that must be carried into freedom. There are choices that are good and necessary, and we willingly accept the burden that comes with the work of research necessary for making a wise choice. But do we want to burden our children with choices that do not mean anything? Choices with a confusing, open future where there are no guideposts for making anything but an arbitrary decision? It is not enough to let them choose one cookie or the other; we have to teach them that choice means consideration of alternatives and that a choice has weight and changes the future. Choosing is not just a privilege, it is also the obligation to work on making a good choice. Therefore, the choices children have should be limited, carefully chosen, cultivated to have significance, and be age appropriate.

7. One Christmas morning my friend Susan had set up the toys for her children around the Christmas tree. She knew that Adam, her three-year-old, would particularly love the big new playhouse, which was still in its box and too big to wrap. As Adam came running down the stairs, he took one look at the life-sized picture of a boy on the box and yelled: "Oh Mom, Santa gave me a *boy* for Christmas! I always wanted to have my own boy to play with!" After that, the playhouse was somewhat of a disappointment.

CHAPTER SEVEN

1. Ricoeur's introduction of the *semantics* of the sentence, (that is, his analysis of the sentence as speech act), his focus on the process of communication, and his reflections on the transformative function of symbolism are a philosophical roadmap for the encounter between phenomenology and linguistics. Ricoeur's work on metaphor is the bridge between linguistics and the phenomenology of existential speech (1976, 1985). A further expansion of the project that Ricoeur outlines (which goes beyond the scope of this chapter) is to follow Merleau-Ponty into his forays beyond structuralism in *The Visible and the Invisible* and think of language as an ontological, chiasmic event. But here as well we have mostly provocative fragments. But who knows: maybe fragments, like metaphors, can spur thinking to leap into the silence of what has not yet been thought and said.

2. Povinelli, Bering, and Giambrone (2003) argue that chimpanzees can be trained to associate the pointing finger with a food source, but that apes do not

understand second-order intentional states, that is, the psychological states and intentions of the pointing person. While human two-year-olds invariably follow the line of the researcher's outstretched finger to find a reward, no matter where the researcher is situated in the room, the chimpanzees almost always choose the location that is in close proximity to the pointer's outstretched hand, even if it is not the one pointed at. Povinelli and his colleagues conclude (echoing the language of other researchers in cognitive psychology) that "humans do come to appreciate pointing as a means of connecting to the inner psychological states of others" (45), while "chimpanzees may know very little (if anything at all) about attention as a psychological state. Indeed . . . we have obtained evidence that they appear to understand little about any psychological states at all" (49). De Waal, on the other hand, argues that even though chimpanzees might not point with their outstretched fingers, they will communicate to their caretakers by pointing, beckoning, panting, and calling to get them to look for a treat that was hidden outside the cage the night before. "The result was communication about a past event, present in the ape's memory, to people who knew nothing about it and were unable to give her any clues" (2005, 39).

3. Ricoeur comments: "This pointing holds together the significant and the significate only because it goes beyond the significate towards the thing. It is the pointing towards the thing which, because of its movement of transcendence, insures the internal unity of the sign. The Husserlian notion of meaning is not, then, an additional 'factor' which phenomenology would add to linguistics: it is a matter of going back to the problem of the unity of the sign on the basis of where it points" (1967, 21).

4. Lakoff and Johnson (1999) summarize Chomsky's Cartesianism in the following way (and, by the way, Chomsky is very outspoken about his Cartesian philosophy, naming his 1966 book *Cartesian Linguistics*): "As a Cartesian, Chomsky believes there is a single universal human nature, that the mind is separate from and independent of the body, and that what makes us distinctively human is our mental capacities, not our bodies" (478). "Reason, which makes us human beings, is for Descartes language-like. Language takes on for Chomsky the role of reason in Descartes' philosophy; that is, language becomes the essence that defines what it is to be human. Language is mathematical in nature, and since mathematics is a matter of pure form, language, for Chomsky, is purely formal. Language is also universal and innate, an autonomous capacity of mind, independent of any connection to things in the external world. Language must also have an essence, something that makes language what it is and inheres in all language. That essence is called 'universal grammar'; it is mathematical in character and a matter of pure form. Language does not arise from anything bodily. It can be studied adequately through introspective methods. Studying the brain and body can give us no additional insight into language" (470).

5. Luria (1981, 35) summarizes the power that language gives to human children: "The enormous advantage is that their world doubles. In the absence

of words, humans would have to deal only with those things which they could perceive and manipulate directly. With the help of language, they can deal with things which they have not perceived even indirectly and with things which were part of the experience of earlier generations. Thus the word adds another dimension to the world of humans . . . animals have only one world, the world of objects and situations which can be perceived by the senses. Humans have a double world."

CHAPTER EIGHT

1. "Chronica Regiae Coloniensis Continuatio Prima, s.a. 1213, MGH SS XXIV 17–18," in Brundage 1962.

WORKS CITED

AAP. 2006. Policy statement: The changing concept of sudden infant death syndrome: Diagnostic coding shifts, controversies regarding the sleeping environment, and new variables to consider in reducing risk. *Pediatrics* 116 (5): 1245–56.

Abram. 1996. *The spell of the sensuous.* New York: Vintage.

Ainsworth, M. D., M. C. Blehar, E. Waters, and S. Wall. 1978. *Patterns of attachment: A psychological study of the strange situation.* Hillsdale, NJ: Erlbaum.

Aries, P. 1962. *Centuries of childhood: A social history of family life.* Trans. R. Baldick. New York: Knopf.

Ayers, A. J. 1979. *Sensory integration and the child.* Los Angeles: Western Psychological Services.

Bachelard, G. 1983. *Water and dreams: An essay on the imagination of matter.* Dallas: Pegasus Foundation.

———. 1994. *The poetics of space.* Boston: Beacon.

Benswanger, E. G. 1979. A contribution to the phenomenology of lived space in early childhood. In *Duquesne studies in phenomenological psychology,* vol. 3, ed. A. Giorgi, R. Knowles, and D. Smith. Pittsburgh: Duquesne University Press.

Bickerton, D. 1981. *Roots of language.* Ann Arbor, MI: Karoma.

Billow, R. M. 1988. Observing spontaneous metaphor in children. In *Child Language: A reader,* ed. M. B. Franklin and S. S. Barten. New York: Oxford University Press.

Bleichfeld, B., and B. Moely. 1984. Psychophysiological response to an infant cry: Comparison of groups of women in different phases of the maternal cycle. *Developmental Psychology* 20:1082–91.

Bloom, L. 1993. *The transition from infancy to language: Acquiring the power of expression.* Cambridge: Cambridge University Press.

Blum, D. 2002. *Love at Goon Park: Harry Harlow and the science of affection.* New York: Berkeley.

Boss, M. 1979. *Existential foundations of medicine and psychology.* New York: Jason Aronson.

Bower, T. G. R. 1977. *The perceptual world of the child.* Cambridge: Harvard University Press.

Bowlby, J. 1969. *Attachment*. New York: Basic.

Bronson, G. W. 1997. The growth of visual capacity: Evidence from infant scanning patterns. *Advances in Infancy Research* 11:109–41.

Brundage, J., ed. 1962. *The crusades: A documentary history*, Milwaukee: Marquette University Press.

Bruner, J. S. 1983. *Child's talk*. New York: W. W. Norton.

———. 1993. From communicating to talking. In *Readings on the development of children*, ed. M. Gauvain and M. Cole. New York: W. H. Freeman.

Bruner, J. S., et al., eds. 1976. *Play—Its role in development and evolution*. New York: Basic.

Buckley, P., ed. 1986. *Essential papers in object relations*. New York and London: New York University Press.

Burman, E. 1994. *Deconstructing developmental psychology*. London and New York: Routledge.

Burnham, M. M., B. L. Goodlin-Jones, E. E. Gaylor, and T. F. Anders. 2002. Use of sleep aids during the first year of life. *Pediatrics* 109 (4): 594–601.

Butterworth, G. 1997. Starting point. *Natural History* 106 (May): 14–16.

———. 2003. Pointing is the royal road to language for babies. In *Pointing: Where language, culture, and cognition meet*, ed. S. Kita. Mahwah, NJ, and London: Erlbaum.

Buytendijk, F. J. J. 1933. *Wesen und Sinn des Spiels*. Berlin: Karl Wolff.

Campos, J. J., D. I. Anderson, M. A. Barbu-Roth, E. Hubbard, M. J. Hertenstein, and D. Witherington. 2000. Travel broadens the mind. *Infancy* 1 (2): 149–219.

Candland, D. K. 1995. *Feral children and clever animals: Reflections on human nature*. New York: Oxford University Press.

Canella, G. S. 1997. *Deconstructing early childhood education: Social justice and revolution*. New York: Peter Lang.

———. 1999. The scientific discourse of education: Predetermining the lives of others—Foucault, education, and children. *Contemporary Issues in Early Childhood* 1 (1): 36–43.

Carnap, R. 1963. Carnap's intellectual biography. In *The philosophy of Rudolf Carnap*, ed. P. A. Schilpp. La Salle, IL: Open Court.

Carson, R. 1956. *The sense of wonder*. New York: Harper & Row.

Cataldi, S. L. 1993. *Emotion, depth, and flesh: Reflections on Merleau-Ponty's philosophy of embodiment*. Albany: State University of New York Press.

Cavoukian, R., and S. Olfman, eds. 2006. *Child honoring*. Westport, CT: Praeger.

Chawla, L. 2003. Special place—What is that? Significant and secret spaces in the lives of children in a Johannesburg squatter camp. In *Secret spaces of childhood*, ed. E. Goodenough. Ann Arbor: University of Michigan Press.

Chomsky, N. 1959. Review of *Verbal behavior*, by B. F. Skinner. *Language* 35:26–58.

———. 1965. *Aspects of the theory of syntax*. Cambridge, MA: MIT Press.

Cole, M., and S. Cole. 2001. *The development of children*. New York: Worth.

Cole, M., S. Cole, and C. Lightfoot. 2005. *The development of children*. New York: Worth.

Dasen, P. R. 1972. Cross-cultural Piagetian research: A summary. *Journal of Cross-Cultural Psychology* 3:29–39.

DeCasper, A. J., J. P. Lecanuet, R. Maugais, C. Granier-Deferre, and M. C. Busnel. 1994. Fetal reactions to recurrent maternal speech. *Infant Behavior and Development* 17:159–64.

DeCasper, A. J., and M. J. Spence. 1986. Prenatal maternal speech influences newborns' perception of speech sounds. *Infant Behavior and Development* 3:133–50.

Dennis, W. 1973. *Children of the creche*. New York: Appleton-Century-Crofts.

de Saint Exupéry, A. 2000. *The little prince*. Trans. R. Howard. New York: Harcourt.

De Waal, F. 2005. *Our inner ape*. New York: Riverhead.

Dillard, A. 1987. *An American childhood*. New York: Harper Perennial.

Dore, J. 1979. Conversational acts and the acquisition of language. In *Developmental pragmatics*, ed. E. O. B. B. Schieffelin. New York: Academic.

Doria, C., and H. Lenowitz, eds. 1976. *Origins: Creation texts from the ancient Mediterranean*. Garden City, NY: Anchor.

Edgerton, S. Y. J. 1976. *The Renaissance rediscovery of linear perspective*. New York: Harper & Row.

Egan, K. 1988. *The educated mind: How cognitive tools shape our understanding*. Chicago: University of Chicago Press.

Eisenstein, E. 1979. *The printing press as an agent of change: Communications and cultural transformations in early-modern Europe*. New York: Cambridge University Press.

Eliade, M. 1954. *The myth of the eternal return*. Trans. W. R. Trask. New York: Pantheon.

———. 1959. *The sacred and the profane*. New York: Harcourt, Brace & World.

Elias, N. 1978. *The civilizing process: The history of manners*. New York: Urizen.

Elkind, D. 1987/2000. *Miseducation*. New York: Knopf.

Erikson, E. 1968. *Identity: Youth and crisis*. New York: W. W. Norton.

Erikson, E. H. 1950/1963. *Childhood and society*. New York: W. W. Norton.

Fernald, A. 1989. Intonation and communicative intent in mothers' speech to infants: Is the melody the message? *Development* 60:1497–1510.

———. 1991. Prosody in speech to children: Prelinguistic and linguistic functions. In *Annals of child development*, vol. 8, ed. R. Vasta. London: Kingley.

Fraiberg, S. 1959. *The magic years*. New York: Charles Scribner & Sons.

Franko, F., and G. Butterworth. 1996. Pointing and social awareness: Declaring and requesting in the second year of life. *Journal of Child Language* 23 (2): 307–36.

Freud, S. 1924/1953. *A general introduction to psychoanalysis.* Trans. J. Riviere. New York: Pocket.

———. 1953–74. *The standard edition of the complete works of Sigmund Freud.* 24 vols. Ed. James Strachey. London: Hogart and the Institute of Psychoanalysis.

———. 1989. *The Freud reader.* New York and London: W. W. Norton.

Gadamer, H. G. 1984. The hermeneutics of suspicion. *Man and World* 17:313–23.

———. 1996. *Truth and method.* Trans. J. Weinsheimer and D. G. Marshall. New York: Continuum.

Gil, E. 1991. *The healing power of play.* New York: Touchstone.

Gleitman, L. 1988. Biological disposition to learn language. In *Child language: A reader,* ed. M. B. Franklin and S. S. Barten. New York: Oxford University Press.

Goodenough, E. N. 2003a. Peering into childhood's secret spaces. *Chronicle of Higher Education* 49 (43): 13–14.

———, ed. 2003b. *Secret spaces of childhood.* Ann Arbor: University of Michigan Press.

Grass, G. 2000. *My century.* New York: Harcourt.

Greenfield, P. M., and J. H. Smith. 1976. *The structure of communication in early language development.* New York: Academic.

Greenspan, S. I., and B. L. Benderly. 1997. *The growth of the mind and the endangered origins of intelligence.* New York: Addison-Wesley.

Hanawalt, B. A. 1993. *Growing up in medieval London: The experience of childhood in history.* New York: Oxford University Press.

Harlow, H. F., and C. M. Harlow, eds. 1986. *Learning to love: The selected papers of H. F. Harlow.* New York: Praeger.

Healey, J. 1999. *Endangered minds: Why children don't think and what we can do about it.* New York: Simon & Schuster.

Heidegger, M. 1962. *Being and time.* San Francisco: Harper & Row.

———. 1971. *Poetry, language, thought.* Trans. A. Hofstadter. New York: Harper Colophon.

———. 1972. Time and being. Trans. J. Stambaugh. In *On time and being.* New York: Harper & Row.

Held, K. 2002. The origin of Europe with the Greek discovery of the world. *Epoché* 7 (1): 81–105.

Hirsh-Pasek, K., and R. M. Golinkoff. 1996. *The origins of grammar: Evidence from early language comprehension.* Cambridge, MA, and London: MIT Press.

Hobara, M. 2003. Prevalence of transitional objects in young children in Tokyo and New York. *Infant Mental Health Journal* 24 (2): 174–91.

Husserl, E. 1970. *The crisis of the European sciences and transcendental phenomenology.* Trans. D. Carr. Evanston, IL: Northwestern University Press.

———. 2001. *Logical investigations.* Vol. 1. Trans. D. M. J. N. Findlay. London: Routledge.

Illich, I. 1982. *Gender.* Berkeley: Heyday.

———. 1996. *In the vineyard of the text: A commentary to Hugh's Didascalicon.* Chicago: University of Chicago Press.

Illich, I., and B. Sanders. 1988. *ABC: The alphabetization of the popular mind.* San Francisco: North Point.

Irigaray, L. 1985. *This sex which is not one.* Trans. C. Porter. Ithaca, NY: Cornell University Press.

Iverson, J. M., O. Capirci, E. Lombardi, and M. C. Caselli. 1999. Gesturing in mother-child interactions. *Cognitive Development* 14:57–75.

Jager, B. 1999. Eating as a natural event and as intersubjective phenomenon: Towards a phenomenology of eating. *Journal of Phenomenological Psychology* 30:11–116.

Jahoda, G. 1980. Theoretical and systematic approaches in cross-cultural psychology. In *Handbook of cross-cultural psychology*, vol. 1, ed. H. C. Triandis and F. Lambert. Boston: Allyn & Bacon.

James, A., C. Jenks, and A. Prout. 1998. *Theorizing childhood.* Cambridge: Polity.

James, B. 1994. *Handbook for treatment of attachment-trauma problems in children.* New York: Lexington.

Johnson, A. 1995. Constructing the child in psychology: The child as primitive in Hall and Piaget. *Journal of Phenomenological Psychology* 26 (2): 35–57.

Jung, C. G. 1961. *Memories, dreams, reflections.* Trans. R. C. Winston. New York: Vintage.

Juszyk, P. W. 1997. *The discovery of spoken language.* Cambridge, MA: MIT Press.

Karen, R. 1994. *Becoming attached: First relationships and how they shape our capacity to love.* New York: Oxford University Press.

Keller, H. 1905. *The story of my life.* New York: Doubleday, Page.

Kelly, S. D., et al. 2002. Putting language back in the body: Speech and gesture on three time frames. *Developmental Neuropsychology* 22 (1): 323–49.

Kristeva, J. 1984. *Revolution in poetic language.* Trans. M. Waller. New York: Columbia University Press.

Kuhl, P. K., and A. N. Meltzoff. 1982. The bimodal perception of speech in infancy. *Science* 218:1138–44.

Lacan, J. 2002. *Ecrits: A selection.* Trans. B. Fink. New York: W. W. Norton.

Lakoff, G., and M. Johnson. 1980. *Metaphors we live by.* Chicago: University of Chicago Press.

———. 1999. *Philosophy in the flesh.* New York: Basic.

Langeveld, M. J. 1960. *Die Schule als Weg des Kindes.* Braunschweig: Georg Westermann Verlag.

———. 1968. *Studien zur Anthropologie des Kindes.* Tübingen: Max Niemeyer Verlag.

———. 1983a. The secret place in the life of the child. *Phenomenology and Pedagogy* 1 (2): 181–91.

———. 1983b. The stillness of the secret place. *Phenomenology and Pedagogy* 1 (1): 11–17.

———. 1984. How does the child experience the world of things? *Phenomenology and Pedagogy* 2 (3): 215–22.

Lecanuet, J. P., C. Graniere-Deferre, A.-Y. Jacquet, and A. J. DeCasper. 2000. Fetal discrimination of low pitched musical notes. *Developmental Psychobiology* 36 (1): 29–39.

Levinas, E. 1969. *Totality and infinity.* Pittsburgh: Duquesne University Press.

Levine, R. 1997. *A geography of time.* New York: Basic.

Lévy-Bruhl, L. 1966. *Primitive mentality.* New York: Beacon.

Lingis, A. 1983. *Excesses: Eros and culture.* Albany: State University of New York Press.

Lippitz, W. 1997. Differente Weltansichten: über die Wahrnehmung der Welt durch Kinder und Erwachsene. Eine Problemskizze. In *Biologieunterricht und Lebenswirklichkeit,* ed. H. Bayrhuber. Kiel: Institut für die Pädagogik in den Naturwissenschaften.

Luria, A. R. 1981. *Language and cognition.* New York: Wiley.

Maratos, O. 1998. Neonatal, early, and later imitation: Same order phenomena? In *The development of sensory, motor, and cognitive capacities in early infancy: From perception to cognition,* ed. F. Simion and G. Butterworth. Hove, UK: Psychology Press/Erlbaum.

McNeill, D. 2002. Gesture and language dialectic. *Acta Linguistica Hafniensia,* June 28, 1–25.

Mehler, J., P. W. Juszyk, G. Lambertz, N. Halsted, J. Bertoncini, and C. Amiel-Tison. 1988. A precursor of language acquisition in young infants. *Cognition* 29:143–78.

Meltzoff, A. N., and W. Borton. 1979. Intermodal matching by neonates. *Nature* 282:403–4.

Meltzoff, A. N., and K. M. Moore. 1998. Object representation, identity, and the paradox of early permanence: Steps towards a new framework. *Infant Behavior and Development* 21:201–35.

Merleau-Ponty, M. 1962. *Phenomenology of perception.* Trans. C. Smith. London: Routledge & Kegan Paul.

———. 1963/1983. *The structure of behavior.* Trans. Alden L. Fisher. Pittsburgh: Duquesne University Press.

———. 1964a. Maurice Merleau-Ponty à la Sorbonne. *Bulletin de psychologie* 17 (236): 107–336.

————. 1964b. *The primacy of perception.* Evanston, IL: Northwestern University Press.

————. 1968. *The visible and the invisible.* Trans. Alphonso Lingis. Evanston, IL: Northwestern University Press.

————. 1973. *Consciousness and the acquisition of language.* Trans. H. Silverman. Evanston, IL: Northwestern University Press.

————. 1982/1983. Phenomenology and psychoanalysis: Preface to Hesnard's *L'oevre de Freud. Review of Existential Psychology and Psychiatry* 18 (1–3): 67–72.

————. 1994. *Keime der Vernunft: Vorlesungen an der Sorbonne.* Trans. A. Kapust. Munich: Wilhelm Fink Verlag.

Meyer-Drawe, K. 1986. Zähmung eines wilden Denkens? Piaget und Merleau-Ponty zur Entwicklung von Rationalitaet. In *Leibhaftige Vernunft: Spuren von Merleau-Ponty's Denken,* ed. A. Metraux and B. Waldenfels. Munich: Wilhelm Fink Verlag.

Minkowski, E. 1970. *Lived time: Phenomenological and psychopathological studies.* Evanston, IL: Northwestern University Press.

Mook, B. 1977. *The Dutch family in the 17th and 18th centuries.* Ottawa: University of Ottawa Press.

Morelli, G. A., B. Rogoff, D. Oppenheim, and D. Goldsmith. 1993. Cultural variations in infants' sleeping arrangements: Questions of independence. *Developmental Psychology* 28:604–13.

Munro, D. C. 1914. The children's crusade. *American Historical Review* 19 (3): 516–24.

Nelson, K. 1977. The syntagmatic-paradigmatic shift revisted: A review of research and theory. *Psychological Bulletin* 84:93–116.

————. 1981. Social cognition in a script framework. In *Social cognitive development,* ed. J. H. Flavell and L. Ross. Cambridge: Cambridge University Press.

Ong, W. J. 1982. *Orality and literacy: The technologizing of the word.* London and New York: Routledge.

Orme, N. 2001. *Medieval children.* New Haven, CT, and London: Yale University Press.

Owens, R. E. 2001. *Language development.* Boston: Allyn & Bacon.

Panofsky, E. 1991. *Perspective as symbolic form.* Trans. C. S. Wood. New York: Zone.

Piaget, J. 1929/1951. *The child's conception of the world.* Trans. J. Tomlison and A. Tomlinson. Savage, MD: Littlefield Adams.

————. 1930. *The child's conception of physical causality.* Trans. Marjorie Gabain. New York: Harcourt Brace.

————. 1954. *The construction of reality in the child.* Trans. Margaret Cook. New York: Ballantine.

————. 1962. *Play, dreams, and imitation in childhood.* Trans. C. Gattegno and F. M. Hodgson. New York: W. W. Norton.

———. 1970. *The child's conception of time.* Trans. A. J. Pomerans. New York: Basic.

———. 1971. *Insights and illusion of philosophy.* Trans. W. Mays. New York: World.

Piaget, J., and B. Inhelder. 1956. *The child's conception of space.* Trans. F. J. Langdon and J. L. Lunzer. London: Routledge, Kegan & Paul.

Pinker, S. 1995. *The language instinct.* New York: Harper Collins.

Popkewitz, T., and M. Brennan. 1997. Restructuring of social and political theory in education: Foucault and a social epistemology of school practices. *Educational Theory* 47 (3): 287–313.

Postman, N. 1994. *The disappearance of childhood.* New York: Vintage.

Povinelli, D. J., J. M. Bering, and S. Giambrone. 2003. Chimpanzee's "pointing": Another error of the argument by analogy. In *Pointing,* ed. S. Kita. Mahwah, NJ, and London: Erlbaum.

Ricoeur, P. 1967. New developments in phenomenology in France: The phenomenology of language. *Social Research* 34:1–30.

———. 1968/1974. Strucure, word, event. In *The conflict of interpretation,* ed. Don Ihde. Evanston, IL: Northwestern University Press.

———. 1970. *Freud and philosophy.* Trans. D. Savage. New Haven, CT: Yale University Press.

———. 1976. *Interpretation theory.* Fort Worth: Texas Christian University Press.

———. 1981. *Hermeneutics and the human sciences.* Trans. John B. Thompson. London: Cambridge University Press.

———. 1984. *Time and narrative.* Trans. K. McLaughlin and D. Pellauer. Chicago: University of Chicago Press.

———. 1985. The power of speech: Science and poetry. *Philosophy Today* (Spring): 59–70.

Rilke, R. M. 1950. *Briefe.* Wiesbaden: Insel Verlag.

———. 1966. *Werke.* 3 vols. Frankfurt: Insel Verlag.

———. 1999. *The essential Rilke.* Trans. Galway Kinnell and Hannah Liebmann. Hopewell, NJ: Ecco.

Romanyshyn, R. D. 1989. *Technology as symptom and dream.* London: Routledge.

Rousseau, J.-J. 1762/1979. *Emile.* Trans. Allan Bloom. New York: Basic.

Safranski, R. 1998. *Martin Heidegger: Between good and evil.* Cambridge, MA: Harvard University Press.

Saks, O. 1996. *An anthropologist on Mars.* New York: Vintage.

Sallis, J. 1973. *Phenomenology and the return to beginnings.* Pittsburgh: Duquesne University Press.

Savitt, S. 2002. Being and becoming in modern physics. In *The Stanford encyclopedia of philosophy* (Spring 2002 ed.), ed. E. N. Zalta. http://plato.stanford .edu/archives/spr2002/entries/spacetime-bebecome.

Schneider, N. 1994. *The art of the portrait.* Cologne: Benedikt Taschen Verlag.

Seligman, M. E. P. 1991. *Helplessness: On depression, development, and death.* 2nd ed. New York: W. H. Freeman.

Shahar, S. 1990. *Childhood in the middle ages.* Trans. C. Galai. London and New York: Routledge.

Shorter, E. 1977. *The making of the modern family.* New York: Basic.

Siegler, R. S. 1998. *Children's thinking.* 3rd ed. Upper Saddle River, NJ: Prentice Hall.

Simms, E. M. 1999. The countryside of childhood: Reflections on a hermeneutic-phenomenological approach to developmental psychology. *Humanistic Psychologist* 27 (2): 301–27.

———. 2004. Uncanny dolls: Images of death in Rilke and Freud. In *The psychology of death in fantasy and history*, ed. J. S. Piven. Westport, CT, and London: Praeger.

Slobin, D. I. 1988. From the Garden of Eden to the Tower of Babel. In *The development of language and language researchers: Essays in honor of Roger Brown*, ed. F. Kessel. Hillsdale, NJ: Erlbaum.

Snow, C. E. 1972. Mother's speech to children learning language. *Child Development* 43:549–65.

Spitz, R. 1947. *Grief: A peril in infancy.* Documentary.

Steingraber, S. 2001. *Having faith: An ecologist's journey to motherhood.* Cambridge, MA: Perseus.

Stern, D. N. 1985. *The interpersonal world of the infant: A view from psychoanalysis and developmental psychology.* New York: Basic.

Stone, L. 1977. *The family, sex, and marriage in England, 1500–1800.* London: Perennial.

Straus, E. 1956. *Vom Sinn der Sinne.* Berlin: Springer.

———. 1966/1980. *Phenomenological psychology.* New York: Garland.

Swift, J. 1962. *Gulliver's travels and other writings.* New York: Bantam.

Tomasello, M. 2000. Acquiring syntax is not what you think. In *Speech and language impairments in children*, ed. D. V. M. Bishop and L. B. Leonard. London and New York: Psychology.

Tuan, Y.-F. 1977. *Space and place: The perspective of experience.* Minneapolis: University of Minnesota Press.

Tuchman, B. W. 1978. *A distant mirror.* New York: Knopf.

van den Berg, J. H. 1961. *The changing nature of man.* New York: W. W. Norton.

———. 1972. *A different existence.* Pittsburgh: Duquesne University.

van Manen, M. 1999. The pathic nature of inquiry and nursing. In *Nursing and the experience of illness: Phenomenology in practice*, ed. I. Madjar and J. A. Walton. London: Routledge.

von Gleichen-Russwurm, A. 1929. *Kultur und Geist der Renaissance.* Vol. 9. Hamburg: Hoffmann & Campe.

Vosniadou, S., A. Ortony, and R. E. Reynolds. 1988. Sources of difficulty in the young child's understanding of metaphorical language. In *Child language: A reader*, ed. M. B. Franklin and S. S. Barten. New York: Oxford University Press.

Wallon, H. 1954. *Les origines du charactère chez l'enfant: Les préludes du sentiment de personnalité*. Paris: Presses Universitaires de France.

Werker, J. F., and R. C. Tees. 1999. Influences on infant speech processing: Towards a new synthesis. *Annual Review of Psychology* 50:509–35.

Werner, H., and B. Kaplan. 1963. *Symbol formation: An organismic developmental approach to language and the expression of thought*. New York: John Wiley & Sons.

Wheelwright, P., ed. 1966. *The Presocratics*. New York: Odyssey.

Winner, E., A. K. Rosenstiel, and H. Gerdern. 1988. The development of metaphoric understanding. In *Child language: A reader*, ed. M. B. Franklin and S. S. Barten. New York: Oxford University Press.

Winnicot, D. W. 1971. *Playing and reality*. London and New York: Travistock.

———. 2002. *Winnicot on the child*. Cambridge, MA: Perseus.

Woodson, R. H., and E. da Costa. 1989. Features of infant social interaction in three cultures in Malaysia. In *Child development in cultural context*, ed. J. Valsiner. Toronto: Hogrefe & Huber.

INDEX